Maths Progress
Depth Book

Series editors: Dr Naomi Norman and Katherine Pate
Authors: Julian Gilbey and Peter Hall

1

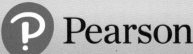

Pearson

Published by Pearson Education Limited, 80 Strand, London, WC2R 0RL.

www.pearsonschoolsandfecolleges.co.uk

Text © Pearson Education Limited 2019
Project managed and edited by Just Content Ltd
Typeset by PDQ Digital Media Solutions Ltd
Original illustrations © Pearson Education Limited 2019
Cover illustration by Robert Samuel Hanson

The rights of Nick Asker, Jack Barraclough, Sharon Bolger, Gwenllian Burns, Greg Byrd, Lynn Byrd, Andrew Edmondson, Julian Gilbey, Peter Hall, Catherine Murphy, Naomi Norman and Katherine Pate to be identified as authors of this work have been asserted by them in accordance with the Copyright, Designs and Patents Act 1988.

First published 2019

22 21 20 19
10 9 8 7 6 5 4 3 2 1

British Library Cataloguing in Publication Data
A catalogue record for this book is available from the British Library.

ISBN 978 1 292 28002 8

Printed in Italy by L.E.G.O S.p.A

Note from the publisher
Pearson has robust editorial processes, including answer and fact checks, to ensure the accuracy of the content in this publication, and every effort is made to ensure this publication is free of errors. We are, however, only human, and occasionally errors do occur. Pearson is not liable for any misunderstandings that arise as a result of errors in this publication, but it is our priority to ensure that the content is accurate. If you spot an error, please do contact us at resourcescorrections@pearson.com so we can make sure it is corrected.

Contents

Maths Progress Second Edition

Confidence at the heart

Maths Progress Second Edition is built around a unique pedagogy that has been created by leading mathematics educational researchers and Key Stage 3 teachers in the UK. The result is an innovative structure, based around 10 key principles designed to nurture confidence and raise achievement.

Pedagogy – our 10 key principles

- Fluency
- Problem-solving
- Reflection
- Mathematical Reasoning
- Progression
- Linking
- Multiplicative Reasoning
- Modelling
- Concrete - Pictorial - Abstract (CPA)
- Relevance

This edition of Maths Progress has been updated based on feedback from thousands of teachers and students.

The Core Curriculum

Textbooks with tried-and-tested differentiation

Core Textbooks *For your whole cohort*

Based on a single, well-paced curriculum with built-in differentiation, fluency, problem-solving and reasoning so you can use them with your whole class. They follow the unique unit structure that's been shown to boost confidence and support every student's progress.

Support Books
Strengthening skills and knowledge

Provide extra scaffolding and support on key concepts for each lesson in the Core Textbook, giving students the mathematical foundations they need to progress with confidence.

Depth Books
Extending skills and knowledge

Deepen students' understanding of key concepts, and build problem-solving skills for each lesson in the Core Textbook so students can explore key concepts to their fullest.

Welcome to Maths Progress Second Edition Depth Books!

Building confidence with depth of understanding

Pearson's unique unit structure in the Core Textbooks has been shown to build confidence. The Depth Books take elements of this structure and help students continue to grow in confidence.

Master

1 In the **Master** section of the Depth books, students can deepen their understanding of the key concepts introduced in the Core Textbooks through rich tasks involving problem-solving and reasoning.

Extend

2 Students who have developed fluency and a solid understanding of key concepts throughout the Depth unit can **extend** their learning.

Master
Deepen understanding of key mathematical concepts.

Unit opener
Lesson opener outlines lesson objectives.

A wealth of problem-solving questions encouraging students to:
- think in different ways
- translate contextual information
- make choices about the best method or strategy (e.g. work backwards, draw a diagram).

Investigation

Rich, problem-solving tasks to encourage deep thinking and exploring mathematical concepts at students' own pace.

Hints
Guide students to help build problem-solving strategies throughout the course.

Reasoning questions allow students to:
- practice constructing multiple chains of reasoning
- interpret and explain results
- understand how and why to apply certain mathematical processes.

Reflect

Metacognitive questions that relate to the key concepts drawn out in each lesson, encouraging students to examine their thinking and understanding.

Extend
Students can take their understanding even further by applying what they have learned in different situations, and linking topics together.

This Depth Book is designed to give the right level of additional problem-solving content to help strengthen students' understanding of key concepts. It can be used as further stretch for students who are comfortable with the work in the Core Textbook Unit.
Students who would benefit from additional scaffolding for key concepts can use the Support Book.

Progress with confidence!

This innovative Key Stage 3 Mathematics course builds on the first edition KS3 Maths Progress (2014) course, drawing on input from thousands of teachers and students, and a 2-year study into the effectiveness of the course. All of this has come together with the latest cutting-edge approaches to shape Maths Progress Second Edition.

Take a look at the other parts of the series

*Active*Learn Service

The *Active*Learn service enhances the course by bringing together your planning, teaching and assessment tools, as well as giving students access to additional resources to support their learning. Use the interactive Scheme of Work, linked to all the teacher and student resources, to create a personalised learning experience both in and outside the classroom.

What's in ActiveLearn for Maths Progress?

- ✓ **Front-of-class student books** with links to PowerPoints, videos, animations and homework activities
- ✓ **96 new KS3 assessments and online markbooks,** including end-of-unit, end-of-term and end-of-year tests
- ✓ **Over 500 editable and printable homework worksheets** linked to each lesson and differentiated for Support, Core and Depth
- ✓ **Online, auto-marked homework activities**
- ✓ **Interactive Scheme of Work** makes re-ordering the course easy by bringing everything together into one curriculum for all students with links to Core, Support and Depth resources, and teacher guidance
- ✓ **Student access to videos, homework and online textbooks**

ActiveLearn Progress & Assess

The Progress & Assess service is part of the full ActiveLearn service, or can be bought as a separate subscription. It includes assessments that have been designed to ensure all students have the opportunity to show what they have learned through:

- a 2-tier assessment model
- approximately 60% common questions from Core in each tier
- separate calculator and non-calculator sections
- online markbooks for tracking and reporting
- mapped to indicative 9–1 grades

New *Assessment Builder*

Create your own classroom assessments from the bank of Maths Progress assessment questions by selecting questions on the skills and topics you have covered. Map the results of your custom assessments to indicative 9–1 grades using the custom online markbooks. *Assessment Builder* is available to purchase as an add-on to *Active*Learn Service or Progress & Assess subscriptions.

Purposeful Practice Books

Over 3,750 questions using minimal variation that:

- ☑ build in small steps to consolidate knowledge and boost confidence
- ☑ focus on strengthening skills and strategies, such as problem-solving
- ☑ help every student put their learning into practice in different ways
- ☑ give students a strong preparation for progressing to GCSE study.

1 Analysing and displaying data

1.1 Mode, median and range

- Find the mode, median and range for a set of data

1 Four sports teams collect their results during a competition. This is the number of points that each team receives in their five games:

Team A:	3	7	7	8	19
Team B:	8	8	10	11	14
Team C:	1	2	2	4	4
Team D:	15	16	16	18	19

  a Which team has the highest median score?
  b Which team has the highest range of scores?

2 These are the annual salaries of the five employees at a small company:

    £17 000　　　£20 000　　　£21 000　　　£21 500　　　£49 000

  a What is the median salary?
  b What is the range of salaries?
  c R Does the median or the range better describe the salaries at this company? Why?

3 P-S The data shows Alice's internet speed at 6 pm for the last six days.
   The last piece of data is missing.

    180 Mb/s　　　215 Mb/s　　　150 Mb/s　　　135 Mb/s　　　160 Mb/s　　　_____

   The median is 155 Mb/s.
   What could the missing value be?

4 Here are the weights of toddlers in four different playgroups.

Group 1:	10.5 kg	14.3 kg	12 kg	11.6 kg	13.2 kg	13.8 kg	11.2 kg	
Group 2:	13 kg	11.9 kg	10.8 kg	11.7 kg	12.1 kg	13.6 kg	13 kg	12.8 kg
Group 3:	11.3 kg	14.8 kg	11 kg	13.2 kg	10.3 kg	12.4 kg	12.4 kg	10.9 kg	13 kg
Group 4:	12.3 kg	11.8 kg	10.8 kg	13.1 kg	12.6 kg	14 kg	13.2 kg	

  a Work out the median weight for each group.
  b In each group, how many toddlers weigh less than the median weight?
  c In each group, what fraction of toddlers weigh less than the median weight?

5 R Ten chocolate bars are accurately weighed. Each bar has '100 g' on the wrapper.
  The range of weights is 1.3 g. What does this tell us about the median weight?

6 **R** For each of these statements, decide whether the statement is **always true**, **sometimes true** or **never true**.

If the statement is **always true** or **never true**, explain how you know this.

If the statement is **sometimes true**, give an example where it is true and an example where it is not true.

a The median of a set of data is exactly half-way between the smallest and largest values.

b The mode of a set of data is approximately in the middle of the data.

c The median of a set of data is approximately in the middle of the data.

d The median of a set of data is between the smallest and largest values.

e Half of the range is approximately in the middle of the data.

f The mode of a set of data is one of the data values.

g The median of a set of data is one of the data values.

h The range of a set of data is one of the data values.

7 **P-S** A set of data contains four values. The mode is 5, the range is 3 and the median is 5. The smallest value in the data set is 4. Write the numbers in the data set.

8 **P-S** A car park has 12 parking spaces. The data shows the number of cars in the car park at eight different times. One value is missing.

  2   9   1   8   3   1   7   ?

Find the possibilities for the missing value, given that

a the mode is 1   **b** the median is 4   **c** the range is 10.

d **R** Why is there only one possible missing value that gives a range of 10?

9 **P-S / R** Sam says, 'I asked 10 people to choose a whole number between 1 and 10. The median of the answers was 4.6.' Show that Sam must be wrong.

10 **P-S / R** A set of data contains five values. The smallest value is 0 and the range is 10.

a What is the smallest possible median?   **b** What is the largest possible median?

c How would your answers change if there were

  i six values   **ii** seven values   **iii** ten values   **iv** twenty values?

11 **P-S / R** A set of data contains five values. The mode and the median are both 10.

a What is the smallest possible range?   **b** What is the largest possible range?

c How would your answers change if there were

  i six values   **ii** seven values   **iii** ten values   **iv** twenty values?

12 **P-S** Write a set of data with

a five values and a median of 7.5   **b** four values and a median of 7.5.

Reflect

13 What was the same and what was different about your method for answering parts **a** and **b** of Q12?

1.2 Displaying data

- Find information from tables and diagrams
- Display data using tally charts, tables, bar charts and bar-line charts

1 A student draws this pictogram. It shows the number of people in the class who like cats, dogs or rabbits.

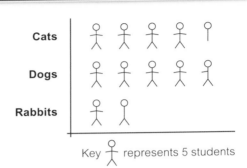

Key represents 5 students

   a Draw a frequency table to show this data.

   b What is wrong with the pictogram?

   c Draw a better pictogram to illustrate the data.

2 The bar chart shows 30 students' favourite school subjects.

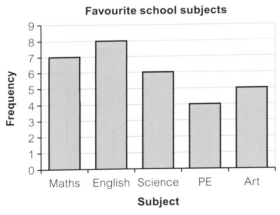

Draw a pictogram to show the same data.

3 Year 7 students were asked: 'Why do you like Saturdays?' The tally chart shows their responses.

Reason	Tally
no school	卌 卌 I
stay up late	卌
play lots of games	卌 III
other	卌 II

   a Draw a bar-line chart using the data from the tally chart.

   b Which is the modal reason?

   c R Why isn't it possible to give a median for this data?

4   The data shows the number of robins seen in 20 different students' gardens during one
    winter afternoon.

2	0	3	0	2	1	1	2	4	2
1	0	0	3	2	2	2	1	3	0

    Sasha wants to write an article about this for the Year 7 newsletter.
    Make a diagram or chart to show this information for Sasha to use with her article.

5   R   George counts the number of spots on 15 ladybirds:
    12, 13, 13, 11, 14, 13, 16, 17, 13, 15, 13, 14, 13, 13, 12
    a Copy and complete this frequency table.

Number of spots	Tally	Frequency
11		
12		

    b Draw either a bar chart or a bar-line chart for this data.
    c What is the modal number of spots?
    d R   Justine says that the median number of spots is 14. George says it is 13.
       Who is correct, and what did the other person do wrong?

6   The bar chart shows the number
    of hours (rounded to the nearest
    hour) that some students use social
    media each day.
    a What is the modal number of
       hours that these students use
       social media each day?
    b There are 13 students who
       use social media for 4 hours
       each day. How many students
       use social media for 2 hours
       each day?

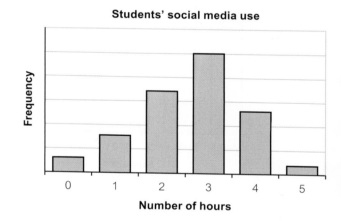

Students' social media use

Reflect

7   In Q4 and Q5, which type of chart did you choose to draw? Explain why.
    What are the advantages of each type?

1.3 Grouping data

- Interpret simple charts for grouped data
- Find the modal class for grouped data

1 **P-S** This bar chart shows the number of marks each student in a class achieved on a test.

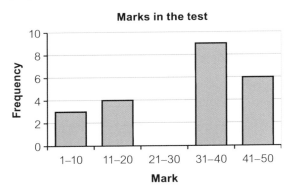

The bar for the 21–30 class has been left out.

The modal class is 31–40 marks.

a Is it possible to work out how many students there are in total?

b If yes, how many are there? If not, what is the smallest possible total number of students, and what is the largest possible total number of students?

2 **R** Malik collects data about the length of time that students in his class sleep at night. He uses spreadsheet software to draw a bar chart of his results.

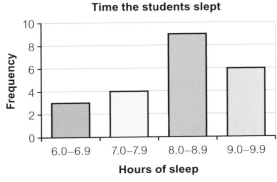

What is wrong with this bar chart? Draw a better bar chart for this data.

3 The frequency table shows the weights of students in a Year 7 class.

a What is the modal class?

b **P-S / R** Shailee finds the median weight of the students in the class and says that it is 34 kg. Can Shailee be correct? Why, or why not?

Weight (kg)	Frequency
25–29	4
30–34	11
35–39	10
40–45	5

4 Malena counts the pages in some of her son's picture books:

10	10	7	12	8	6	10	8	8
6	6	7	12	10	8	6	10	14

a What is the modal number of pages?

b Copy and complete this grouped frequency table for the data.

c What is the modal class?

d R Is the mode or the modal class a better representation of the data? Why?

Number of pages	Frequency
6–7	
8–9	
10–11	
12–13	
14–15	

5 P-S / R The students in Class 7H count the number of butterflies they see during a certain weekend. This grouped frequency table shows the results.

a What is the modal class?

Number of butterflies	Number of students
0–9	7
10–19	3
20–29	5
30–39	8
40–49	2

b The students then decide to group their data into smaller classes, like this.

Hashid said, 'The modal class will now be either 30–34 or 35–39.' Must Hashid be right? If so, explain why; if not, explain which other classes might be the modal class.

Number of butterflies	Number of students
0–4	
5–9	
...	...
40–44	
45–49	

c How useful is the modal class, given that it depends on how the data is grouped?

Investigation

6 The data shows the times, in minutes, that some students spent vigorously exercising in a day.

90, 15, 10, 0, 5, 0, 10, 20, 25, 50, 0, 0, 15, 8, 50, 45, 20, 30, 17, 10, 30, 70, 45, 25, 20

a i Make a frequency table for the data. Use 5 equal class intervals.

ii Draw a bar chart for the data.

b Repeat part a. This time use 10 equal class intervals.

c Which diagram do you think shows the data best? Explain your answer.

d Explain your choice of intervals in parts a and b.

Reflect

7 Look back at the investigation. When do you think it is sensible to use grouped data? What do you need to think about, to decide how many groups there should be?

1.4 Averages and comparing data

- Calculate the mean of a set of data
- Compare sets of data using their ranges and averages

1 **R** Here are the finishing times, in minutes, of all the runners in a cross-country race:

17, 20, 18, 24, 16, 20, 21, 18, 21, 100

a Work out the mean, median and mode.

b Which average best describes the runners' times?

c Which value in the data doesn't 'fit' with the rest of the data set?
Which average – the mean, median or mode – is affected most by this anomaly?

> **Key point** An **anomaly** is a value that does not follow the same trend as the rest of the data set.

2 **P-S / R** A set of data contains five values. The smallest value is 0 and the range is 10.

a What is the smallest possible mean?

b What is the largest possible mean?

c How would your answers change if there were

   i six values   **ii** seven values?

d Write a rule for any number of values.

3 **P-S / R** A set of data contains five positive whole numbers.
The mode and the median are both 10.

a What is the smallest possible mean?

b How would your answers change if there were

   i six values   **ii** seven values?

c Write a rule for any number of values.

4 A rowing crew has eight rowers and one cox. The cox steers the boat.

a Here are the weights of the rowers in the 2013 Oxford rowing crew:

89.8 kg, 87.1 kg, 96.2 kg, 88.9 kg, 100.2 kg, 92.5 kg, 93.9 kg, 109.8 kg

   i What was their median weight?

   ii Work out the range.

   iii Calculate their mean weight.

b The table shows the mean, median and range of the weights of the 2013 Cambridge rowers.

Mean	Median	Range
92.0 kg	91.9 kg	19.0 kg

Compare the weights of the rowers in the two crews using

   i the mean   **ii** the median   **iii** the range.

c The Oxford cox weighed 52.6 kg.

   i Work out the median of all nine members of the Oxford crew.

   ii How has the median changed?

5 R A TV company tested two new types of remote control, A and B, on a group of viewers. The number of wrong button presses made by each viewer was recorded during a test week. The table shows a summary of the information.

	Mean number of wrong presses	Range
Type A	23	9
Type B	15	12

Which design would you recommend, and why?

Investigation

6 **a** Work out the mean of these numbers: 2, 2, 2, 6, 8.
  b Add 1 to each of the numbers and work out their mean again.
   How has the mean changed?
  c Multiply each of the numbers in part **a** by 3. Work out the mean. How has it changed?
  d i What do you think will happen to the mean if you divide each of the numbers in part **a** by 2?
   ii Try it and see if your prediction is correct.

7 Work out the mean of the numbers in part **a**, then use your answer to part **a** to work out the mean of the numbers in part **b**, and so on. Think about what you discovered in the Investigation as you do this.
  a 2, 2, 5, 6, 7, 8
  b 0.2, 0.2, 0.5, 0.6, 0.7, 0.8
  c 0.2, 0.2, 0.5, 0.6, 0.7, 0.8, 0.5
  d 3.2, 3.2, 3.5, 3.6, 3.7, 3.8, 3.5
  e 320, 320, 350, 360, 370, 380, 350
  f 319, 319, 349, 359, 369, 379, 349

Reflect

8 You often see the word 'average' in headlines:
   Average screen size of TVs grows again
   The changing face of the average American

> **Hint** It may help you to write definitions in your own words.

Think about what you know about the mean, median and mode to describe averages. Are any of these types of averages appropriate for each of these headlines?

1.5 Line graphs and more bar charts

- Understand and draw line graphs
- Understand and draw dual and compound bar charts

1 The table shows the daily maximum wind speed in knots in the Hebrides in one week.

Day	Mon	Tue	Wed	Thu	Fri	Sat	Sun
Wind speed (knots)	31	33	41	41	42	57	60

a Copy the axes.
  Draw a line graph for this data.

b R Callum says this is a good model for predicting the wind speed for the next few months.
  Explain why he is wrong.

Q1 hint The ⧩ shows that some values have been left off the axis.

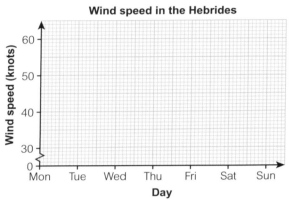

2 Kay counts the number of sparrows, robins and pigeons she sees in her garden over a week. The comparative bar chart shows her results.

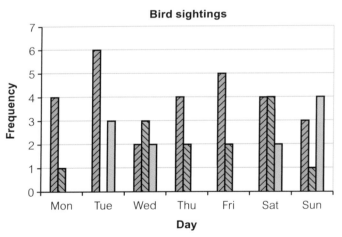

Q2 hint A dual bar chart shows two sets of data. When there are more than two sets of data, we call it a **comparative bar chart**.

Key
- Sparrows
- Robins
- Pigeons

a On which day does Kay see the greatest number of birds?
b Which type of bird does Kay see the most of?
c Some days only have two bars. What does this mean?

3 **P-S / R** This compound bar chart shows the percentages of vowels and consonants in some poems.

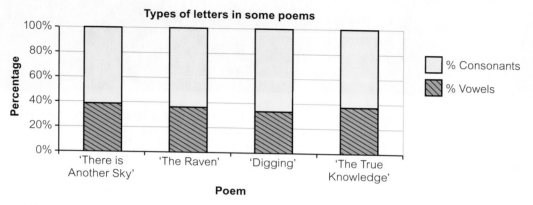

a Which poem has the greatest percentage of consonants?

b Which poem has the greatest percentage of vowels?

c Why do all of the bars have the same total height?

4 **P-S / R** The table shows data about how 30 students in a Year 2 class and 30 students in a Year 10 class travel to school.

	Car	Walk	Bicycle	Train	Bus
Year 2	12	9	4	0	5
Year 10	4	5	6	6	9

a Draw a dual bar chart for the data.

b Which type of travel shows the greatest difference between Year 2 and Year 10 students?

c What reasons could you suggest for the differences between these two year groups?

5 **P-S** The midday and midnight temperatures are recorded at a weather station. The table shows the temperatures for one week.

	Sun	Mon	Tue	Wed	Thu	Fri	Sat
Midday (°C)	16	14	15	14	18	17	18
Midnight (°C)	7	7	8	8	11	11	10

Draw a dual bar chart to show this data.

6 Here is some information about the eye colour of students in Anne's class. Copy and complete the table, and draw a compound bar chart for this data.

	Brown	Blue	Other	Total
Boys		6	4	18
Girls		3	0	13

Reflect

7 For Q4, Tim drew these axes for his bar chart.

a How many bars will he have for each year group?

b What mistake has Tim made?

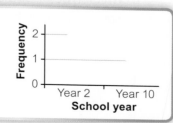

1 Extend

1 R Shaya surveys people in a shopping
   centre to find out what they have come
   to buy. She records her results using a
   tally chart.

   a Why is a tally chart useful for
      this purpose?

   b Why is Shaya's approach to tallying not
      very helpful? Explain what is problematic
      about each row.

Reason	Tally
clothes	ɪɪɪ ɪɪɪ ɪɪ
food	ɪɪɪɪɪɪɪɪ
cosmetics	ɪɪɪ ɪɪɪ ɪ
toys and games	ɪɪɪ ɪɪɪ
other	ɪɪɪ ɪɪ

2 A group of students are asked about their favourite type of fiction book.
   This compound bar chart shows the results.

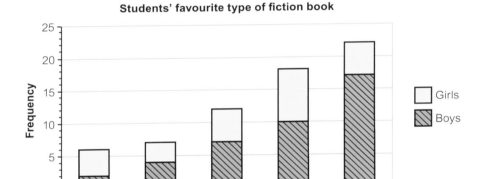

Students' favourite type of fiction book

   a Which type of fiction book is the mode for the boys?
   b Which type of fiction book is the mode for the girls?
   c Based on this data, is humour more popular among boys or girls?
   d R Make a chart or diagram which presents this data in a better way, and explain your reasons.

3 P-S / R James writes the values in a set of data.
   His pen breaks and spills ink over his work.
   James knows that the range is 6, the mode is 8, the median is 5.5 and that there are six
   values in the data set, all of which are whole numbers.
   How many possible sets of data are there?

4 P-S / R The mean of five numbers is 10. Three of the numbers are 6, 9 and 10.
   a What is the largest possible range of the numbers, and what is the smallest possible range?
   b What is the largest possible median of the numbers, and what is the smallest possible median?

5 R A mathematician once said, 'Most people have more than the average number of legs.'
   What did they mean by this?

6 P-S

    a Write a set of data that contains nine values and that has the median, mode and range all equal.

    b R What is the smallest possible set of data with this property?

Q6 hint The 'smallest possible set of data' means the set of data with the smallest possible number of values in it.

7 a P-S Find a set of data which

        - consists of integers   - has a median of 4.5
        - has two modes   - has a range of 8.

    Now find two other sets of data that also have the same properties.

    b R What is the smallest possible set of data which has these properties?

Investigation

8 a Is it possible for a set of data to have mean < median < mode?

    b Is it possible for a set of data to have median < mean < mode?

    c What other possible orders could the mean, median and mode lie in, assuming that they are all different?

    d Is it possible for two of the mean, median and mode to be equal and the other one to be different? For example, mean = median < mode or mean = median > mode? What about mean = mode > median, and so on?

Investigation

9 a The 'median side length' of a rectangle is the median of the lengths of the four sides of the rectangle. The perimeter of a rectangle is 30 cm. What are the possible median side lengths of the rectangle?

    b What would your answer be if the perimeter of the rectangle were 40 cm? What can you say about the median side length of a rectangle with any perimeter?

    c This time, the area of the rectangle is fixed at 30 cm^2, and the side lengths are all whole numbers of centimetres. What are the possible median side lengths of the rectangle?

    d What would your answer be if the area of the rectangle were 36 cm^2? What is the smallest possible median, and what is the largest possible median? What can you say about the median side length of a rectangle with any area?

Investigation

10 a What is the smallest possible median of the angles of a triangle? And what is the largest possible? Give reasons for your answers.

    b What is the smallest possible mean of the angles of a triangle? And what is the largest possible? Give reasons for your answers.

Reflect

11 Write down three things you have learned in this unit that you did not know before. Compare your list with a classmate's list.

2 Number skills

Master   Extend p29

2.1 Mental maths

- Use the priority of operations, including brackets
- Use multiplication facts up to 10 × 10 and the laws of arithmetic to do mental multiplication and division
- Multiply by multiples of 10, 100 and 1000

1 R Multiply 218 by 1000.
  a What is the value of the digit 8 after the multiplication?
  b Copy and complete: 'The digit 1 starts as a ten and finishes as a ten _____.'
  c Write a sentence about what happens to the digit 2 after multiplication.

2 Work out
  a 1 × 2 + 3   **b** 1 + 2 × 3   **c** 2 + 3 × 1   **d** 2 × 3 + 1

3 P-S Copy and complete each of these calculations in five different ways.
  a □ × □ = 24 000   **b** □ × □ = 100 000

4 P-S Copy these calculations. Fill in the missing operations.
  a 12 □ 8 □ 3 □ 2 = 26   **b** 8 □ 6 □ 4 □ 2 = 10

5 P-S Katya has 28 friends on social media.
  Sam has three times as many friends on social media as Katya.
  Alice has four times as many friends on social media as Sam.
  How many friends does Alice have on social media?

6 P-S A library has two sizes of books, tall books and short books. Each shelf can fit 80 tall books or 50 short books. The shelving can be arranged in two ways: five shelves of short books or three shelves of tall books.
  What is the difference between the numbers of books for the two arrangements?

7 P-S
  a Do any of these calculations give an answer of 9?
    A 3 × 4 + 6 ÷ 2   **B** 4 + 3 × 2 − 1   **C** 4 + 4 ÷ 2 + 3
  b Write another calculation including four different numbers and three different operations that gives an answer of 9.

8 P-S / R John's bicycle cost £110. Alison's bicycle cost four times as much as John's. Sam's bicycle cost £75 less than Alison's. What is the cost of Sam's bicycle?

9 Order these calculations from smallest answer to largest answer.

   A $3 \times 4 + 5 \times 6$ **B** $3 + 4 \times 5 + 6$ **C** $3 \times 4 \times 5 + 6$ **D** $(3 + 4) \times 5 + 6$

10 **P-S** Ali's number is 70 times bigger than Dan's number.
   Ali's number includes the digit 6.
   Dan's number is a single-digit odd number.
   What are Ali's and Dan's numbers?

11 In a band there are:
        4 musicians who are all aged 21
        2 singers who are both aged 18.
   What is the mean age of the band members?

12 **R** Replace the ⊙ symbol with +, − or × to make these calculations correct.
   a $8 \times 7 \odot 6 + 5 \times 4 = 70$
   b $8 \times 7 \odot 6 + 5 \times 4 =$ an even number between 80 and 90
   c $8 \times 7 \odot 6 + 5 \times 4 =$ a number larger than 350

13 **P-S** $5 + 3 \times 10 - 4 \div 2$
   Put sets of brackets in different places in the calculation to find as many answers
   as possible.

14 **R** Some people believe we ought to take 10 000 steps a day.
   Is this more or less than ten million steps in two years?

15 **R** Work out where to place the brackets to make these calculations correct.
   a $1 + 2 \times 3 + 4 \times 5 = 29$ **b** $1 + 2 \times 3 + 4 \times 5 = 71$ **c** $1 + 2 \times 3 + 4 \times 5 = 105$

16 **R** Work out where to place the digits 2, 3, 4 and 5 in this calculation to make
   a the largest possible answer   **b** the smallest possible answer.
   $(\square + \square) \times (\square + \square)$

17 **P-S / R** Uzma works out 270×8 like this:
   $27 \times 10 \times 8 = 27 \times 8 \times 10$
                 $= (20 \times 8 + 7 \times 8) \times 10$
   a Copy and complete Uzma's working.
   b Why does Uzma use brackets in the second line of her working?

18 **R** Work out where to put brackets to make this calculation correct.
   $1 + 2 \times 3 + 4 \times 5 + 6 + 7 = 81$

   > **Q18 hint** You need
   > two pairs of brackets.

19 Luke writes a 3-digit number. Mia writes the same number, and then puts four zeros on the
   end. What multiplication would Luke need to do to his number to produce Mia's number?

Reflect

20 We use the decimal system for our numbers. This is a system based on the number 10.
   Describe ways that you think place value and arithmetic are based on the number 10.

2.2 Addition and subtraction

- Make an estimate to check an answer
- Use inverse operations
- Use a written method to add and subtract whole numbers of any size
- Round whole numbers to the nearest 10 000, 100 000 and 1 000 000

1 **a** Attendance at UK football matches is carefully recorded.
These are average attendance figures over a season.
Round each to the nearest 10 000.

Manchester United 74 976   Arsenal 59 323   Liverpool 53 049

b These figures are the total attendance across a whole season.
Round them to the nearest 100 000.

Watford 384 388   Stoke City 556 317   Reading 184 398

c Some internet videos have been liked by over ten million people.
Round each of these figures to the nearest million.

Luis Fonsi 'Despacito' 32 700 000   Ed Sheeran 'Shape of You' 19 460 000
PSY 'Gangnam Style' 15 630 000

2 Using the data from Q1 part **a**, on average, how many more people attended
Manchester United matches than Liverpool matches?

3 Katie thinks of a number. She subtracts 27 and gets the answer 95.
What number is she thinking of?

4 What number do you need to add to 85 to reach 286?

5 **P-S** Complete these calculations by filling in the missing digits.

a		**b**		**c**	
	☐ 5 ☐		2 ☐ 5		☐ 2 9
+	2 2 3	+	5 6 ☐	−	3 ☐ ☐
	8 ☐ 5		☐ 4 2		3 2 4

6 **P-S / R** Cathy earned £21 378. Brian earned £1450 less than Cathy.
How much did Cathy and Brian earn in total?

7 **P-S** Company A paid £48 362 in tax. Company B paid £949 more than Company A.
Company C paid £3002 less than Company B.
How much tax did the three companies pay in total?

8 **P-S** Use the digits 1, 2, 8, 9 to complete the calculation.
☐☐ + ☐☐ = 119

9 **P-S** Use the digits 1, 2, 3, 7, 8, 9 to complete the calculation.
☐☐☐ + ☐☐☐ = 1020

10 P-S / R

    a Replace each * in this addition with a digit from
    1, 2, 3, 4, 5, 6, 7, 8, 9 to make the calculation correct.
    Use each digit only once.

    b Is there only one solution? Explain.

$$\begin{array}{r} *\,*\,*\,* \\ *\,*\,* \\ +\quad *\,* \\ \hline 6759 \end{array}$$

11 P-S All six of the digits in two 3-digit numbers are different.
What is the largest possible sum of the two numbers?

12 R Ryan rounded a whole number to the nearest 1000 and wrote 5000.
Nadim rounded the same number to the nearest 10 000 and wrote 10 000.
What are the smallest and largest possible values of the original number?

13 R Harry works out $836 - 439$ and writes the answer as 387.

    a Use an addition calculation to check his working.

    b Why can you always use an addition calculation to check a subtraction calculation?

14 Chloe claims that $85 + 964 = 10049$.
Write a subtraction that would help to show her answer is incorrect.

15 R Explain how you know that $523 + 489$ is more than 1000 without working out the
exact answer.

16 R Esther works out that $8524 + 6528 = 15052$.
She says, 'I can use this calculation to work out $15052 - 6528$ without having to do
any working.'

    a Explain how she can do this.

    b What other calculation can she work out without having to do any working?

17 Keith has been asked to add 35 486 to 43 985.

    a Round the numbers to the nearest 10 000 to find an approximation to the answer.

    b Work out the exact sum.

    c Write the two connected subtraction facts.

    d Sally is working out a similar sum.
    Her two starting numbers round to 40 000 and 50 000.
    Work out the smallest possible answer to her sum.

18 P-S Anita thinks of a number and adds 58.
Liam takes the answer to Anita's calculation and subtracts 63.
Charlie uses the answer to Liam's calculation and adds 902.
Ella knows the final answer is 1599.
She also knows what each person has done.
Work backwards to find the number each person was given, and the number Anita started with.

Reflect

19 Do the words in a problem always tell you exactly what calculation you need to do?
Explain.

2.3 Multiplication

- Use an estimate to check an answer to a multiplication
- Use a written method to multiply whole numbers

1 Arnold makes 218 necklaces. Each costs him £13 to make.
   He sells 139 of the necklaces for £21 each. Has he made a profit or a loss? How much?

2 **P-S** Clare has 988 books. Clare has 26 times as many books as Colin.
   How many fewer books does Colin have than Clare?

3 **P-S / R** A production line works continuously for 36 hours.
   It produces 106 pairs of leggings each hour.
   A total of 48 pairs are not good enough to sell.
   How many good pairs of leggings are produced in total, in 36 hours?

4 **P-S** Many schools send students to a summer science fair.
   18 schools send minibuses seating 15 students. 29 schools send full 52-seater coaches.
   11 schools send full 75-seater double-decker buses.
   How many students are at the science fair?

5 38 children attend a nursery school.
   Six times as many children attend the local primary school than attend the nursery school.
   Three times as many students attend the local secondary school than children attend the
   primary school. How many students attend the secondary school?

6 **R** Work out
   a 142 857 × 2   **b** 142 857 × 3   **c** 142 857 × 4
   d Look carefully at parts **a**, **b** and **c** and their answers.
   142 857 × 5 = 7_____
   What do you think the answer will be?
   Work out the answer and see if your prediction is correct.

7 **R**
   a Work out 253 × 7, then multiply your answer by 11 and multiply that answer by 13.
   b Predict the final answer if you started with 387 rather than 253.
   c Work out the answer and see if your prediction is correct.

8 Work out
   a 45 × 45   **b** 44 × 46   **c** 28 × 28
   d 27 × 29   **e** 39 × 39   **f** 38 × 40
   g **R** Look carefully at questions and answers **a–f**.
   Knowing that 25 × 25 is 625, show how you can predict the answer to 24 × 26.

9 P-S / R The digits from 1 to 5 are used once each in this calculation.

$$\square\square\square$$
$$\times \square\square$$

a What is the largest possible answer?

b What is the smallest possible answer?

c Work out where to place the digits so that the answer is:

   i 4248   **ii** 4250   **iii** 16 328

Investigation

10 a Which calculation in each pair gives a bigger answer, and by how much?

   i 12 × 43 or 21 × 34   **ii** 23 × 54 or 32 × 45   **iii** 34 × 65 or 43 × 56

b What do you notice?

c Write another pair of calculations that belong to this family.

d What happens when you skip a digit? For example, 12 × 54 or 21 × 45.

e What happens when you skip two digits?

f Predict what happens when you skip three digits.
   Write a calculation to test your prediction.

---

11 Factorial is a shorthand mathematics notation that works like this:
5 factorial is written 5! and means 5 × 4 × 3 × 2 × 1.
4 factorial is written 4! and means 4 × 3 × 2 × 1.
Work out

a 4!   **b** 5!   **c** 7!   **d** 8!   **e** 9 × 8!

f How else can you write 9 × 8! ?

12 P-S Anna is training for a marathon. Every day she goes for a run.
When the weather is warm or dry, she runs for 5 km.
If it is cold or wet, she runs for 3 km.
She keeps a record of her running.
After 24 days she looks at her records and realises only half of the days were warm or dry.
How far did she run in cold or wet weather?

13 P-S Omar buys 250 cakes for 35p each.
He sells 190 for 49p each and then sells the rest for 29p each.
How much profit does he make?

14 A camera on a phone takes photos that are 5184 pixels by 2592 pixels.
How many pixels are there in one photo?

Reflect

15 Ali says that 452 × 87 = 17 176.
Olivia says she has two simple checks to explain why Ali's answer is incorrect.
One check uses estimating and the other check uses 'final digits'.
Give more details of what Olivia's checks mean.
What are the advantages and disadvantages of each method?

2.4 Division

- Use a written method to divide whole numbers
- Use inverse operations to check an answer

1 Work out $6055 \div 7$.
Write a multiplication calculation to check your answer.
Write multiplication calculations that could check the answers to
a $72479 \div 11 = 6589$ **b** $11754 \div 18 = 653$ **c** $26622 \div 27 = 986$

2 P-S / R In these number wheels, opposite numbers multiply to give the number in the middle.
Copy and complete the number wheels.

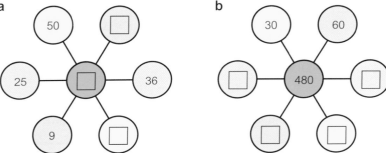

3 P-S The table shows the number of toilets needed in a workplace.

Number of people at work	Number of toilets needed
76–100	5
100+	1 for every extra 25 people

A workplace has 624 employees.
How many toilets are needed?

4 P-S A bottle contains 500 ml of acid.
Hin puts exactly 52 ml of acid into a glass beaker.
Hin then puts exactly 16 ml of acid into each of a number of test tubes.
How many test tubes does Hin need in order to empty the bottle of acid?

5 P-S At the end of each month, a restaurant owner shares the tips equally between the members of staff. Any remainder is put towards the tips for next month.
One month the tips are £856.
There are 18 members of staff.
a How much does each member of staff receive?
b How much is put towards next month's tips?

6 P-S Find a 2-digit number that gives a remainder of 1 when divided by 3 and a remainder of 2 when divided by 5.

7 P-S Find a number between 50 and 60 that gives a remainder of 1 when divided by 2 and also when divided by 3.

8 P-S Find a 2-digit number that gives a remainder of 2 when divided by 3 and also when divided by 7, but that divides exactly by 5.

9 Find the missing digits in these division calculations.

a
$$\frac{8\,6\,\square\,\square}{17)1\,4\,\square\,\square\,1\,4}$$

b
$$\frac{\square\,3\,\square\,5}{5)2\,\square\,\square\,2\,\square}$$

c
$$\frac{4\,\square\,8\,6}{13)5\,\square\,7\,\square\,8}$$

d
$$\frac{4\,2\,\square\,\square\,\square}{7)3\,\square\,\square\,0\,4\,1}$$

10 R Elijah measures his height, and the heights of four friends.
He records 158 cm, 160 cm, 157 cm, 172 cm and 180 cm.
  a Work out the mean height.
  b Elijah includes another friend, who is 163 cm tall.
    By how much does the mean height decrease?

11 From April 2019, people in the UK are allowed to earn £12 500 per year without paying any income tax. Assuming there are 52 weeks in the year, how much is this per week?

Investigation

12 Find the remainder when a 2-digit prime number is divided by 6.
Explain why only some of the possible remainders are obtained.

Reflect

13 How often is multiplication useful when answering a division question?
Never? Sometimes? Often? Always?
Explain.

Hint In which questions did you use multiplication to help you to answer a division question?

2.5 Money and time

- Round money to the nearest pound or penny
- Interpret the display on a calculator in different contexts
- Use a calculator to solve problems involving time and money

1 **R** Olivia adds together 1 hour and 15 minutes and 2 hours and 30 minutes.
She uses her calculator and types 1.15 + 2.30 = 3.45.
Explain what she has done wrong and work out the correct answer.

2 Convert 250 hours to days and hours.

3 Multiply each of these numbers by 10 and 100, giving your answers in appropriate units.
    a 35p   **b** £1.50
    c 4 minutes   **d** 3 minutes and 20 seconds
    e **R** Why were parts **c** and **d** harder than parts **a** and **b**?

4 **P-S** Three online clothes shops place sponsored adverts on a search engine when people search for 'checked trousers'. They pay for every click on their adverts.
The more they pay for their adverts, the higher the adverts appear on the page.

Name of shop	Cost per click	Page position	Number of clicks in a week
Fashion Heights	35p	1	23 142
Legs 11	31p	2	24 783
Walking Smart	28p	3	23 021

    a Work out how much each shop paid for their advert that week.
    b Did the clothes shop that paid the most get the most clicks in a week?

5 **P-S** Carlos buys a new sofa that costs £984.
He pays a **deposit** of £300.
He then pays the remaining amount in 12 equal monthly **instalments**.
How much does Carlos pay each month?

6 **P-S** A supermarket sells the same make of crisps in three different multi-packs:

    Big-pack: £1.48 for 6 packets
    Supa-pack: £2.32 for 10 packets
    Mega-pack: £5.15 for 22 packets.

  Tom has £30. What is the largest number of packets of crisps he can buy?

7 A stop-motion film involves individual photos being joined together.
A 1-second film requires 25 photos.
How many photos are needed for a 45-minute film?

8 Debbie spends £5 and receives five coins in change.
What is the greatest and least possible cost of her purchase?

9 P-S Luna and Lily have some money.
Lily has seven times as much money as Luna.
When added together, they have an amount between £10 and £20.
Lily has an exact number of pounds. How much money does Lily have?

10 P-S Muhammad's class has been collecting small coins for charity.
When they count up the money, Muhammad finds the 5p and 2p coins are worth £1.76 in total, and there are 40 coins.
How many 2p coins are there?

11 P-S Robin's family offer her two ways to earn money at home when she helps with the housework.
A She is offered 1p for the first time she helps, 2p for the second, 4p for the third, doubling each time.
B £1 for every time she helps.
Robin wants to choose option **B** but her sister says option **A** would be better. How many times does she need to help for option **A** to be better?

12 Beth is trying hard to practise the trumpet for 20 minutes every day.
She keeps this up for all of March, April and May.
How long has she practised in total over these three months?

13 P-S Sally has seven hour-long maths lessons every two weeks.
At her cousin's school, they have four 50-minute lessons of maths every week.
Who has more time in maths lessons in a two-week period, and by how much?

14 Some people have tried to create a metric method for measuring time.
They wanted:
    100 metric-seconds in a metric-minute
    100 metric-minutes in a metric-hour
    10 metric-hours in a day.
How many more metric-seconds in a day would this method give, compared to our usual seconds?

Reflect

15 Sarah says that calculations involving money are easier than calculations involving time.
Do you agree? Explain.

2.6 Negative numbers

- Order positive and negative numbers
- Add and subtract positive and negative numbers
- Begin to multiply with negative numbers

1 Work out
  a $-12 + 18$
  b $-18 + 12$
  c $12 - 18$
  d $18 - 12$
  e 2×-5
  f 5×-2
  g 12×-3
  h 3×-12

2 **P-S / R** The answer to a calculation is -12.
  Write four different calculations that each give an answer of -12.

3 The temperatures at some cities were recorded on a cold day in January:
  Edinburgh $-8\,°C$ Belfast $-3\,°C$ Leeds $-10\,°C$ Cardiff $3\,°C$.
  a How much colder is each city compared to Cardiff?
  b How much warmer is each city compared to Leeds?
  c Write the four cities in order of their temperature (coldest first).
  d **P-S / R** The temperature in Brighton was within $6\,°C$ of both Edinburgh and Cardiff.
    What possible temperatures could there have been for Brighton?

4 Work out
  a $-42 + 18$
  b $-18 + 42$
  c $92 - 108$
  d $108 - 92$
  e 2×-35
  f 35×-2
  g 82×-3
  h 3×-82

5 The temperature at 8 am every day for a week at a location in Scotland was recorded.
  The temperatures were:
  $-3\,°C$ $2\,°C$ $1\,°C$ $-3\,°C$ $-1\,°C$ $0\,°C$ $-4\,°C$.
  a What was the median temperature?
  b What was the range of these temperatures?

6 **P-S** Two whole numbers add up to -12. Find both numbers if:
  a one is 4 more than the other
  b one is 18 more than the other
  c one is 50 more than the other
  d one is 3 times bigger than the other
  e one is 11 times bigger than the other.

7 The air temperature drops by 1 °C for every 160 m gain in height.
It is 3 °C at the foot of a mountain.
How high up the mountain would you have to go for the air temperature to drop to −4 °C?

8 Work out −10 + 9 − 8 + 7 − 6 + 5 − 4 + 3 − 2 + 1.

9 **P-S** Use the digits 1, 2, 3 and 4 to make two numbers.
You can create a 3-digit number and a single-digit number or two 2-digit numbers.
Subtract one number from the other to create:
a the smallest possible number
b the largest possible number
c as near to zero as possible.

10 Start with the number 8.
Double the number and subtract 10.
Repeat until you get a negative number answer.
What is the negative number answer?

11 **P-S** Arthur thinks of a number.
Leah doubles Arthur's number and then subtracts 25.
Here is a table showing some results of this process.
Find the missing numbers.

Arthur	5	6	11			
Leah	−15			−11	−39	−25

12 **R** Pairs of numbers that add up to 100 are called complements to 100.
Which of these calculations do complements of 100 help you to answer?
28 + 72   28 − 72   −28 + 72   −28 − 72

13 **a** Work out 2 − 5.
b Write a temperature question that uses the calculation.

14 **a** Use the priority of operations to work out:
  i 4 × 20 − 100   **ii** 20 ÷ 4 − 100   **iii** 20 − 100 ÷ 4   **iv** 20 − 4 × 100.
b Order the calculations from parts **i** to **iv** from smallest answer to largest answer.
c Write another calculation including three different numbers and two different operations that gives the same answer as part **iii**.

Reflect

15 Explain why you can't write a sensible question about a number of apples that uses the calculation in Q13.

2.7 Factors, multiples and primes

- Find all the factor pairs for any whole number
- Identify common factors, the highest common factor and the lowest common multiple
- Recognise prime numbers

1 **P-S** Hayley finds all the factors of a number.
This is her list.

1, 2, 3, 4, □, 9, 12, 13, □, □, 36, 39, □, 78, □, 156, 234, 468

What are the missing numbers?

Investigation

2 The **proper divisors** of a number are its factors, but not the number itself. So the factors
of 10 are 1, 2, 5 and 10, but its proper divisors are only 1, 2 and 5.
Work out the sum of the proper divisors for the numbers between 5 and 30.
Place each number into one of these three categories.

  i **Deficient numbers** are those where the sum is **less than** the number itself.
   For example, the proper divisors of 10 sum to 8, so 10 is a deficient number.

  ii **Perfect numbers** are those where the sum of the proper divisors is **the same as** the
    number itself.

  iii **Abundant numbers** are those where the sum of the proper divisors is **greater than** the
     number itself.

3 **P-S / R** In this number wheel, the highest common factor of opposite numbers is equal to
the number in the middle.

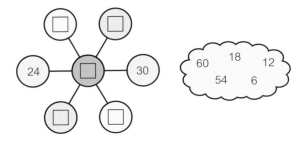

a Use the numbers from the cloud to copy and complete the wheel.

b Explain how you worked out your answers.

4 **P-S** The diagram shows two cogs.
The larger cog has 12 teeth and the smaller cog has 8 teeth.
The cogs start to turn with the red dots next to each other.
What is the smallest number of turns each cog must make before
the red dots are next to each other again?

5 R The diagram shows four numbers linked by lines.

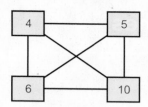

a Work out the lowest common multiple (LCM) of each pair of linked numbers.

b Which pair of numbers has the smallest LCM? Explain why.

c Which pairs of numbers have the same LCM? Explain why.

6 P-S Simon draws this Venn diagram to work out the LCM of two numbers.

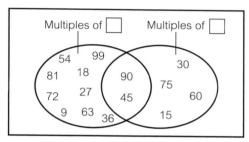

Copy and complete Simon's statement.

The LCM of ☐ and ☐ is ☐.

7 P-S What is the largest gap between two consecutive 2-digit prime numbers?

> **Q7 hint Consecutive** prime numbers are next to each other in the list of prime numbers 2, 3, 5 ...

8 R $165 \div 15 = 11$

a What other factors of 165 can be worked out from this calculation?

b What are the other factors of 165?

c Which of the factors of 165 are prime numbers?

d Explain why 166 will have a remainder of 1 when divided by 11.

> **Q8a hint** You know the factors of 15.

Reflect

9 Write sentences explaining a connection between:

a factors and multiples

b primes and factors

c factors and remainders.

Compare your sentences with others in your class.

2.8 Square numbers

- Recognise square numbers
- Use a calculator to find squares and square roots
- Use the priority of operations, including powers
- Use index notation for powers
- Do mental calculations with squares and square roots

1 **a** List all the factors of the first six square numbers.
   b What is the highest common factor of 16 and 36?

2 Write $<$ or $>$ to make each statement true.
   a $\sqrt{16} \square 6$ **b** $\sqrt{49} \square 4$
   c $\sqrt{121} \square 12$ **d** $2^2 \square \sqrt{9}$
   e $3^2 \square \sqrt{4}$ **f** $4^2 \square \sqrt{16}$

3 Write these numbers in ascending order.
   $\sqrt{100}$, 6^2, $\sqrt{49}$, 3^2

4 Which calculations give the same answer?
   $12^2 \div 6$ $2^2 \times 6$ $24 \div \sqrt{4}$ $6^2 \div 2$ $\sqrt{4} \times 12$

5 Work out these calculations.
   a $10^2 - 45 \times 2$ **b** $15 + 5^2 \div 2$ **c** $(8 + \sqrt{4}) \div 2$

6 Work out
   a 2^2 **b** 20^2 **c** 200^2
   d What do you notice about your answers?

7 **R** A concert has an audience of 900 people.
   Can the seats be arranged in a square? Explain.

8 **P-S** Toby has 52 identical square tiles.
   a He makes the largest possible square using the tiles.
   How many tiles does he use?
   b Toby uses all of his tiles to make two different squares.
   How many tiles does he use in each square?

9 **R**
   a Work out 11^2, 101^2 and 1001^2.
   b Predict the answer to 10001^2. Use your calculator to
   check your prediction.
   c Show that 22^2, 202^2 and 2002^2 follow a similar pattern.

> **Q9b hint** Use the 'squared' key
> on your calculator. Look for a key
> like x^2

10 R Work out 15^2, 25^2, 35^2 and 45^2.

    a Look at the final digits of each answer. What do you notice?

    b Find a way to predict the digits before the final digits.

    c Use your method to predict 55^2 and 65^2.

11 P-S Find the two consecutive square numbers that have a difference of 25.

12 P-S Find the prime numbers whose squares are 165 apart.

13 P-S Find all the 3-digit square numbers that are also a multiple of

    a 5   **b** 7   **c** 13

Investigation

14 The diagram shows two squares.

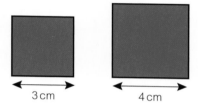

    3 cm   4 cm

    a Work out the area of each square.

    b Work out the total area of the two squares.

    c Sita writes:

    $3^2 + 4^2 = (3 + 4)^2$

    Is Sita correct? Explain.

    d Is Sita's statement true for different size squares?

Reflect

15 All square numbers have an odd number of factors. Explain why.

Hint Think about factor pairs.

2 Extend

1 Work out $1 \times -2 + 3 \times -4 + 5 \times -6 + 7 \times -8 + 9 \times -10$.

2 R   Is the square root of 50 nearer to 7 or 8?
Explain how you know.

3 P-S / R   Dave divided by 11 when he was asked to subtract 11.
He wrote an answer of 247.
What is the correct answer?

4 P-S / R   The passengers in a minibus are five of the Year 7 gymnastics team and ten of the
sixth-form rugby team.
The gymnasts have a mean weight of 45 kg.
The rugby players have a mean weight of 95 kg.
What is the mean weight of all 15 passengers?

5 P-S / R   There are three people running down a long set of steps.
They each start with their right foot on the top step.
Anthony steps on alternate steps.
Bryony has longer legs and so only steps on every third step.
Caleb is far more acrobatic and so he steps on every fifth step.
There are 60 steps in total.
How many steps are stepped on by all three people?

6 P-S   The Earth is rotating slightly slower than it used to.
We occasionally have to add an extra 'leap second' onto the last day in December.
How many seconds are there in a December when a leap second has been added?

7 P-S / R   ABCDE $\times 4$ = EDCBA where A, B, C, D and E represent different digits.
What is the number ABCDE?

8 P-S / R a is the answer to $136\,464 \div 16$.
What number should you start with to end with an answer 100 more than a?

9 P-S   What is the product of the two consecutive numbers that add up to:
  a 151   b 199   c 1001   d 1567?

10 P-S   A watch gains 3 minutes every hour.
It was correct this morning at 8 am.
What time does the watch say when it is really 4:20 pm?

11 P-S / R Four students have a mean test mark of 80%.
What is the minimum mark a fifth student can achieve so that the mean for all five students is not lower than 70%?

12 P-S / R Theo has 9 coins. They total £2.50 in value.
He has only 50p, 20p and 10p coins.
He has more 50p coins than 10p coins.
How many 20p coins does he have?

13 P-S What is the difference between the largest and smallest possible 3-digit numbers where the 3 digits have a product of 18?

14 P-S Temi and Sam have some cards numbered from 1 to 20.
The cards are in numerical order.
Temi takes some cards, starting with number 1.
Sam has the rest of the cards, finishing with number 20.
The total of the numbers on Sam's cards is the same as the total of the numbers on Temi's cards.
How many cards does Sam have?

Investigation

15 A number can be broken into pieces whose sum is the starting number, and then the product of these pieces can be found.
The aim is to find the set of pieces that gives the largest product.
Two examples are shown with a starting number of 12.

12 is $3 + 4 + 5$, and $3 \times 4 \times 5 = 60$

12 is also $2 + 10$, and $2 \times 10 = 20$

So splitting the number 12 into 3, 4 and 5 gives a bigger product than 2 and 10.
Can an even better solution be found?
Now repeat this process for a different starting number.

Reflect

16 Look back at the work you have done in this lesson.
Write a paragraph explaining the new things you have learned about numbers in Unit 2.
Write a sentence explaining anything new you have learned about solving maths problems.

3 Expressions, functions and formulae

Master   Extend p43

3.1 Functions

- Find outputs of simple functions written in words and using symbols
- Describe simple functions in words

1   Work out the outputs of these function machines.

   a   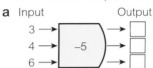   **b** 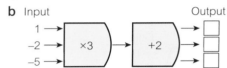

2   **P-S / R**   Alex and Debbie look at this function machine.

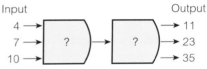

Alex says, 'I think the function is "multiply by 5, then subtract 9".'
Debbie says, 'I think the function is "multiply by 4, then subtract 5".'
Who is correct? Explain your answer.

> **Q2 hint** Try Alex and Debbie's functions on the input numbers.

3   **R**   What single-step function machine has the same output as these two-step function machines?

   a   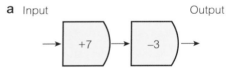   **b** 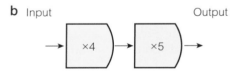

4   **P-S**   Here is a two-step function machine.

   a   An input of 2 gives an output of 10.
      What could the two functions be?
      Write at least three pairs of possible functions.

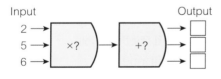

   b   You also know that an input of 5 gives an output of 19.
      What could the two functions be now?
      Is there more than one possible pair of functions?

   c   For the functions you found in part **b**, find the output when the input is 6.

   d   Here is a different two-step function machine.

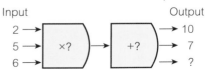

      What is the output when the input is 6?

5 a R The diagram shows a representation of a function. Describe the function in words and symbols.

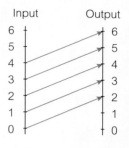

b Draw similar diagrams to represent the functions

   i 'subtract 2'   **ii** 'multiply by 2'   **iii** 'divide by 2'

c Compare your diagrams from part **b** with the diagram in part **a**. What is the same and what is different?

6 P-S The first part of this function machine takes five inputs and adds them together. It gives a single output. What is this function machine calculating?

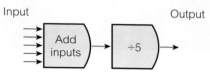

7 P-S Work out the rule for this function machine.

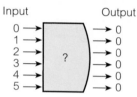

8 R Each of these two-step function machines uses the operations ×3 and +1.

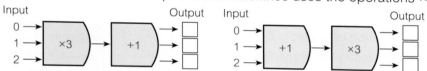

a Work out the outputs for each function machine.

b Is the order of the operations in the two function machines important? Explain.

c Is the order of the two operations important when they are

   i both addition

   ii both subtraction

   iii one addition and one subtraction?

   Show examples to explain.

d Is the order of the two operations important when they are

   i both multiplication

   ii both division

   iii one multiplication and one division?

   Show examples to explain.

Reflect

9 Look back at the functions in this lesson.

   a For each function, does each input map to exactly one output?

   b Which function maps more than one input to the same output?

3.2 Simplifying expressions 1

- Use letters to represent unknowns in algebraic expressions
- Simplify linear algebraic expressions by collecting like terms

1 **P-S** This rectangle and triangle have the same perimeter.

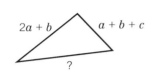

What is the missing side length of the triangle?

2 **R** A teacher asks her students to simplify $3a + 7b - 6a - b$.
Here are some of the answers the students give:

$3a + 6b$	$3b$	$3a - 6b$	$9a + 8b$
$18a - 7b$	$-3a + 6b$	$3a + 6b - 6a$	$6b - 3a$

Which two answers are correct?
For the incorrect answers, what mistake has the student made?

3 Copy and complete:
  a $3z - \square = 0$ **b** $2x - \square = 0$
  c $-4y + \square = 0$ **d** $-t + \square = 0$

4 P-S
  a Copy and complete this addition pyramid.
     Each brick is the sum of the two bricks **below it**.

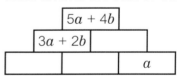

  b How many different possible solutions can you find for this addition pyramid?

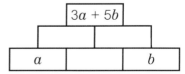

  c Copy and complete this addition pyramid. Is there only one way to do so?

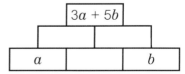

5 **P-S** In a magic square the diagonals, rows and columns all sum to the same total.

a Write the numbers 1–9 in the magic square (using each number only once) so that all the diagonals, rows and columns sum to 15. Three numbers have been written for you.

| 2 | 3 | 6 | 7 | 8 | 9 |

b Write the algebraic expressions in the magic square so that all the rows, columns and diagonals sum to $3c$.

| $c - a - b$ | $c + b$ | $c - a + b$ | $c + a - b$ | $c + a$ | $c + a + b$ |

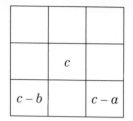

6 **R**

a i Is $3 + 5$ equivalent to $5 + 3$?

ii Is $3 \times 2 + 5 \times 4$ equivalent to $5 \times 4 + 3 \times 2$?

iii Is $3a + 5b$ equivalent to $5b + 3a$?

b Write two pairs of equivalent statements from this set.

$3 - 5$ $\qquad$ $5 - 3$ $\qquad$ $-5 + 3$ $\qquad$ $-3 + 5$

c Write two pairs of equivalent statements from this set.

$3 \times 2 - 5 \times 4$ $\qquad$ $5 \times 4 - 3 \times 2$ $\qquad$ $-3 \times 2 + 5 \times 4$ $\qquad$ $-5 \times 4 + 3 \times 2$

d Write two pairs of equivalent statements from this set.

$3a - 5b$ $\qquad$ $-3a + 5b$ $\qquad$ $-5b + 3a$ $\qquad$ $5b - 3a$

7 **P-S / R** The expression in each box is the sum of the expressions in the two circles joined to the box. Copy and complete the diagrams.
How many different ways can you find to complete each diagram?

a

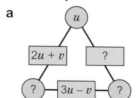

b

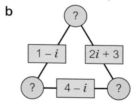

c

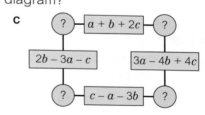

Investigation

8 **a** In Q7 part **b**, is it always possible to answer the question whatever the expressions in the boxes are?

b What about the diagram in Q7 part **c**?

c A similar diagram is made in the shape of a pentagon, with an expression in each box. Explain how you would work out the missing expressions in the circles.
How about a hexagon with an expression in each box?
How about a shape with a larger number of sides?

Reflect

9 What is the same about adding and subtracting expressions and adding and subtracting numbers? What is different?

3.3 Simplifying expressions 2

- Multiply and divide algebraic terms
- Use brackets with numbers and letters

1 Copy and complete:

$$7 \times 635 = 7(\square + 30 + \square)$$
$$= 7 \times 600 + 7 \times \square + 7 \times \square$$
$$= 7a + 7b + 7c \quad \text{where } a = \square, b = \square \text{ and } c = \square.$$

2 **P-S** Write two different multiplications and two different divisions that give these answers.

  a 16y b 10b c 12d d 15x

3 **R**
  a Is 5 × 2 equivalent to 2 × 5?
  b Is 5 ÷ 2 equivalent to 2 ÷ 5?
  c Is 5 × 2a equivalent to 2a × 5?
  d Write all the factor pairs of
    i 12   ii 12b
  e Which has more factors, 8c or 8?
    Explain your answer.

4 **R** This is part of Simon's homework.
  a Explain the mistake that Simon has made.
  b Write down the correct answer.

> Question:
> Expand and simplify
> $4(x + 2) + 3$
>
> Answer:
> $4(x + 2) + 3$
> $= 4x + 2 + 3$
> $= 4x + 5$

5 Expand and simplify these.
  a $2(3x + 4) + 6(x + 2)$
  b $4(x - 3) + 7(2x - 1)$

6 **P-S / R** Show that $8(2x + 5) + 3(4x - 5) = 4(7x + 6) + 1$

> **Q6 hint** Expand and simplify each side.

7 **P-S** Work out the missing value so that $4(x + 3) + 3(x + 4)$ is equivalent to $7(x + 2) + \square$.
  Is there more than one possible answer?

8 **P-S** Work out the missing values so that $2(3x - 5) + 3(4x + \square)$ is equivalent to $2(\square x + 4) + 4x$.
  Is there more than one possible answer?

9 **R** This large rectangle has been split into three smaller rectangles.

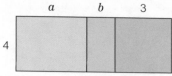

a Write an expression for the width of the large rectangle.

b Use your answer to part **a** to copy and complete:

Area = $\square(\square + \square + \square)$

c Copy and complete:

$4(a + b + 3) = \square + \square + \square$

10 Work out the mean of the expressions in each set.

a $3c$ $5c$ $2c$ $4c$ c

b $2x + 1$ $x - 3$ $8x + 4$ $x - 2$

11 What is the median of the expressions in each set?

a $7a$ $3a$ $2a$ $3a$ $4a$

b $5f$ $8f$ $3f$ $6f$ f f

c $2h$ 0 $-3h$ $-4h$ h $3h$ h

d **R** Explain why you cannot find the median of the expressions in this set.
$2b$ a $3b$ $4a$ $5b$

12 **a** **P-S / R** In how many different ways can the expression $\square(\square x + \square)$ be completed using whole numbers so that it expands to give $24x + 18$?

b What is the highest common factor of 24 and 18?
How does this relate to part **a**?

Investigation

13 **a** Choose three different numbers.
In how many ways can you use these three numbers to complete the expression $\square(\square x + \square)$?

b Expand each of your expressions from part **a**.
Are any of the expressions the same as each other?

c Repeat parts **a** and **b** using a different set of three numbers.
What do you notice about your new answer to part **b**?

d Is there any set of three different numbers which will give a different answer to part **b**?
Give a reason for your answer.

e Now choose four different numbers, and use any three of them to complete the expression.
How does this affect your answers to parts **a**–**d**?

Reflect

14 What is the same about multiplying and dividing expressions, and multiplying and dividing numbers? What is different?

3.4 Writing expressions

- Write expressions from word descriptions using addition, subtraction and multiplication
- Write expressions to represent function machines

1 **a** On Monday a shop sells x newspapers and y magazines.
Write an expression for the total number of newspapers and magazines it sells.

    b Write an expression for the total number of newspapers and magazines sold

      i on Tuesday when they sell 3 fewer newspapers but the same number of magazines

      ii on Wednesday when they sell 4 more newspapers and 7 fewer magazines than on Monday.

2 A rectangle has height b. The width is 5 more than the height.

    a Write an expression for the width.

    b Write and simplify an expression for the perimeter.

3 Write an expression for the perimeter of this rectangle.

4 **P-S** The first side of a triangle has length a. The second side is twice as long.
The third side is 10 units longer than the first side. What is the perimeter of the triangle?

5 **P-S** A regular polygon has s sides. Each side is 3 cm long.
What is the perimeter of the polygon?

6 **a** A plumber charges £70 for a call-out plus £15 for every 15 minutes that they work on the job. Write an expression for the cost of a job that takes h hours.

    b A consultant charges an initial fee of £40 for a consultation plus £120 per hour that the consultation lasts. Write an expression for the cost of a consultation that lasts m minutes.

7 **P-S / R** A Swizzle sweet costs 3 times as much as a Twister sweet.

    a A Twister costs t pence. Write an expression for the cost of a Swizzle.

    b A Swizzle costs s pence. Write an expression for the cost of a Twister.

    c Bella buys a Swizzles and spends the same amount of money on Twisters.
How many sweets does she buy in total?

    d Zack buys b Twisters and spends the same amount of money on Swizzles.
How many sweets does he buy in total?

    e Jaya buys c Swizzles and d Twisters.
How many Twisters could she buy for the same amount of money?

    f Luis buys e Swizzles and f Twisters.
How many Swizzles could he buy for the same amount of money?

8 P-S / R

a Sam says,

'One side of a triangle has length x.
The second side has 3 times the length of the first side.
The third side has 3 times the length of the second side.'

Write an expression for the perimeter of this triangle.

b Explain why Sam cannot be correct.

9 Here is a function machine.

Input   Output

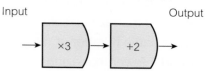

a The input is x.
What is the output?

b The input is $2y + 1$.
What is the output? Simplify your answer.

c P-S   The output is $12a + 2$.
What is the input?

d P-S   The output is $15b + 14$.
What is the input?

10 Here is a function machine.

Input   Output

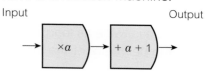

a The input is 2.
What is the output?

b P-S   The output is $5a + 1$.
What is the input?

11 P-S / R

a A function machine gives an output of $12x + 3$ when the input is $3x - 1$.
What could the function for the machine be?
What else could the function be?

b Another function machine gives an output of $10x + 4$ when the input is $2x + 1$
and an output of $13x - 5$ when the input is $3x - 2$.
What could the function for the machine be?

Reflect

12 Describe the effect of the function machine in Q9 in words.
Explain how the expression you wrote in Q9 part **a** gives the same information.
Why is it sometimes useful to write expressions with algebra rather than in words?

3.5 Substituting into formulae

- Substitute positive integers into formulae written with letters

1 A bicycle hire company uses this formula to work out the total cost, £C, to hire a bicycle.

$C = 7d + 15$

where d is the number of days. Work out the cost to hire a bicycle for

a 3 days   b 5 days   c 1 week   d 2 weeks.

2 P-S Weight (W) in newtons is calculated using the formula $W = mg$ where m = mass in kg and g = acceleration due to gravity in m/s^2.

a On Earth, $g = 10$ m/s^2. Work out the weight, in newtons, of

   i a 5 kg dog   ii a 70 kg person   iii a 30 kg monkey.

b On the Moon, $g = 1.6$ m/s^2.

   Work out the weight of the dog, the person and the monkey on the Moon.

3 A formula used in science to work out the potential energy, P, of an object is

$P = mgh$

where m is the mass

        g is the acceleration due to gravity

        h is the height.

Work out the value of P when

a $m = 5$, $g = 10$ and $h = 3$ b $m = 8$, $g = 10$ and $h = 4$

c $m = 2$, $g = 10$ and $h = 8$ d $m = 3.5$, $g = 10$ and $h = 3$.

4 The formula for converting from temperature in Fahrenheit, F, to Celsius, C, is

$C = \dfrac{5(F - 32)}{9}$

Convert these temperatures into °C.

a 41°F   b 59°F   c 77°F   d 23°F

5 Here is a function machine.

a The input is 5. What is the output?

b The input is x. What is the output?

c Substitute $x = 5$ in your answer to part b.

d R How do your answers to parts a and c relate to each other?

   Would the same be true if a number other than 5 was used in parts a and c?

Input   Output

→ [×4] → [−3] →

6 P-S The formula for the number of sheets of paper, N, in r reams of paper is $N = 500r$.

a How many sheets of paper are there in 6 reams?

b How many reams are there when there are 8000 sheets of paper?

c A box of paper contains 5 reams. How many sheets of paper are there in 4 boxes?

d A person wants to order 15 000 sheets of paper. How many boxes should they order?

7 a Which of this set of expressions is the median when $c = 3$?

$$2c + 8 \qquad 3c + 6 \qquad 4c$$

  b P-S / R Is the same term the median for every value of c?
  If so, why? If not, find values of c to make each of the other expressions the median.

8   R The formula for the average speed of an object, s, which travels a distance d in time t is $s = \dfrac{d}{t}$

  a Alice and Bob each run for 10 seconds.
  Alice runs a distance of 60 metres and Bob runs 70 metres.
  Without calculating their speeds, who do you think has the greater speed, and why?
  Now calculate their speeds. Were you correct?

  b Charlie and Dave each run 120 metres.
  Charlie takes 15 seconds and Dave takes 20 seconds.
  Without calculating their speeds, who do you think has the greater speed, and why?
  Now calculate their speeds. Were you correct?

9   R The formula $c = a - b$ connects the values of a, b and c.

  a When b is fixed and a increases, what happens to the value of c?
  Explain your answer. Check by choosing a value for b and some different values for a.

  b When a is fixed and b increases, what happens to the value of c?
  Explain your answer.

10 R The formula $r = \dfrac{p}{q}$ connects the positive numbers p, q and r.

  a When q is fixed and p increases, what happens to the value of r?
  Explain your answer. Check by choosing a value for q and some different values for p.

  b When p is fixed and q increases, what happens to the value of r?
  Explain your answer.

11 A function machine multiplies its input by 6 and then adds 4.

  a What is the output when the input is x?

  b What is the output when the input is $2a$?

  c Substitute x with $2a$ in your answer to part **a**. Do you get the same answer as in part **b**?

Investigation

12 Which is larger, $3n$ or $n + 3$? When?

Reflect

13 a Why are the letters in a formula called variables?

  b Decide whether each statement is true or false.

  i A formula uses letters to represent unknown values.

  ii When you change the value of one variable in a formula, the values of the other variables change.

  iii The relationship between the variables varies as their values vary.

> **Hint** Use examples to help you decide.

3.6 Writing formulae

- Write simple formulae in words
- Write simple formulae using letter symbols

1 P-S / R   Four people can sit around a square table.

When two square tables are placed side by side, six people can sit around them.

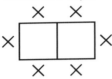

   a How many people can sit around 20 square tables when placed side by side?
   Show your working.
   b How many people can sit around n square tables?

2 A function machine multiplies each input by 5 and then adds 3.
   a What is the output if the input is
      i 5   **ii** −2   **iii** −7   **iv** x
   b Write a formula which connects the output, y, with the input, x.

3 P-S / R   Jon uses matchsticks to make rows of squares joined together.

   For 1 square, he needs 4 matchsticks.
   For 2 squares, he needs 7 matchsticks.
   a How many matches does he need to make a row of 100 squares in this way?
   Explain your working.
   b Find a formula for M, the number of matchsticks needed to make s squares.

4 R   A teacher asks students this question:

   An egg box holds 6 eggs.
   Write a formula that connects the number of eggs with the number of egg boxes.

   One student's answer is:

   $b = 6e$

   What is wrong with this answer?
   Write a better answer to the question.

5 A coach can take 54 passengers. Write a formula that connects the number of coaches, C, with the number of passengers they can take, P.

6 **R** An isosceles triangle has base length 1 cm.
The other two sides each have length x cm.
  a Find the perimeter of the triangle when $x = 3$.
  b A student claims that the formula for the perimeter, p cm, of the triangle is $p = 2(x + 1)$.
  Use your answer to part **a** to show that the student is wrong.
  c Write a correct formula connecting p and x.

7 **P-S / R** Here is a function machine.

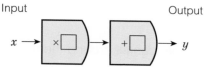

Input   Output

When the input is x, the output is y.
The formula connecting x and y is $y = 4x + 5$.
  a When the input is 7, what is the output?
  b Copy and complete the function machine.

8 Write a formula connecting the perimeter of an equilateral triangle with its side length.

9 Write a formula connecting the perimeter of a square with its side length.

10 a Write a formula connecting the area of a rectangle with its length and width.
  b Write a formula connecting the perimeter of a rectangle with its length and width.

Investigation

11 a Five people attend a party.
  Each person shakes hands with every other person at the party.
  How many handshakes are there in total?
  How many different ways can you find to reach the answer?
  b Six people attend a party and shake hands with every other person at the party.
  How many handshakes are there in total?
  c Find a formula connecting the number of handshakes, H, with the number of people at the party, n. Explain why your formula works, and use your answers to parts **a** and **b** to check that it works when $n = 5$ and $n = 6$.

Reflect

12 a In Q1 and Q3, why is it useful to have a formula to work out the number of people or matchsticks, instead of drawing the diagrams?
  b In Q10, why is it useful to have a formula for the area of a rectangle, instead of a written rule like 'multiply the length by the width'?

3 Extend

1 **P-S / R** What is the perimeter of this shape?

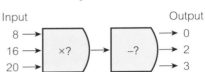

2 **P-S / R** This is a two-step function machine.
  a What is the rule for this function machine?
  b What input would give an output of 8?

3 **R**
  a A formula states $r = s + 2$.
   Is it always, sometimes or never true that r is greater than s? Explain your answer.
  b Another formula states $y = 2x$.
   Is it always, sometimes or never true that y is greater than x? Explain your answer.

4 **R** The formula $p = mn$ connects the whole numbers m, n and p.
  a Let $m = 5$ and $n = 837$.
   m is increased by 1 and n is decreased by 1.
   What do you expect to happen to the value of p?
   Now calculate p before and after you change m and n.
   Are the results what you expected? Explain your results.
   Now find a different way to explain your results.
  b Does the same happen for every choice of starting values of m and n?
  c m is increased by 2 and n is decreased by 2.
   What do you expect to happen to the value of p?

5 **R** The formula $c = \frac{a}{b}$ relates the positive numbers a, b and c.
  a a and b are both increased by 1. What do you expect to happen to the value of c?
   Choose some values of a and b. Calculate c before and after you add 1 to a and b.
   Are the results what you expected?
   Swap your values of a and b and do the same again. Explain your results.
  b Find values of a and b for which the value of c stays the same when both a and b are
   increased by 1.

6 **R**
  a Choose three different whole numbers.
  b Copy and complete '$a = \square$, $b = \square$, $c = \square$' using all three numbers from part **a**.
  c Repeat part **b** to get as many different sets of a, b and c as you can using your three
   numbers.
  d For each set, work out the value of $ab + c$. How many *different values* do you get?
  e By choosing different numbers in part **a**, what is the largest number of different values
   that you can get for $ab + c$? What is the smallest possible number of different values?

7 R

  a Repeat Q6 parts **a–c** to get several sets of values of a, b and c.

  b For each set, work out the value of $a + 2b + 3c$.
How many *different values* do you get?

  c By choosing different numbers in part **a**, what is the largest number of different values that you can get for $a + 2b + 3c$?
What is the smallest possible number of different values?

8 P-S / R

  a Show that $n^2 + n + 11$ is a prime number when $n = 1, 2, 3, 4$ and 5.

  b Is $n^2 + n + 11$ a prime number for every whole number?

  c Repeat parts **a** and **b** with the expression $n^2 + n + 17$.

  d Can you find any other whole number, c, for which the expression $n^2 + n + c$ is a prime number for every whole number n?

9 Here are two function machines.

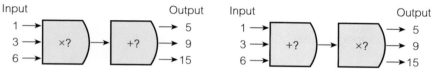

  a What are the functions for the two machines?

  b Do you need three input and output pairs to work out what each machine's function is?
If not, how many do you need?

  c Change the function for the first machine to a different multiplication followed by a different addition.
What is the corresponding function for the second machine?
How do the two functions relate?
Explore different functions for the first machine.

  d The functions are changed so that the inputs 1, 3, 6 now all give an output of 5.
What is the function for the first machine?
What about the second machine?

  e The functions are changed so that the output is always 4. What are the functions now?

  f The functions are changed so that the output is always 3. What are the functions now?

  g Generalise your answers to parts **e** and **f**.
Does your generalisation work for every possible case?

10 In this unit, you have learned about expressions, functions and formulae.
What is the difference between them?
What advantages have you seen for using symbols instead of words to describe mathematical relationships?

4 Decimals and measures

Master   Extend p61

4.1 Decimals and rounding

- Write decimals in order of size
- Round decimals to the nearest whole number and to 1 decimal place
- Round decimals to make estimates and approximations of calculations

1 Write these decimals in descending order.
Then write a decimal at the end of each list, so that they are still in descending order.

  a 0.712, −0.73, −0.724, −0.712, 0.72

  b 12.874, −12.874, 12.92, −12.92, 12.9, −12.9

  c 0.203, 0.291, 0.2, 0.24, 0.29

  d 0.43, 0.491, 0.45, 0.405, 0.49

2 **a** Write these decimals in ascending order.

    i 0.352, 0.37, 0.311, 0.315, 0.376

    ii 18.429, 18.49, 18.4, 18.42, 18.411

    iii 0.13, 0.107, 0.7, 0.17, 0.73

    iv 0.52, 0.514, 0.55, 0.502, 0.562

  b R For each list, suggest a decimal that could be placed between the second and third decimals in the list so that the decimals are still in ascending order.

3 A car part needs to measure between 0.095 cm and 0.105 cm.
The first five parts off the production line measure
    0.098 cm, 0.1 cm, 0.15 cm, 0.09 cm, 0.0955 cm
Which of these parts are acceptable?

4 **R** Emily writes down an answer of 4.3 correct to 1 decimal place.
Which two of these could be her rounded answer?

  A 4.28

  B 4.39

  C 4.358

  D 4.2499

  E 4.3058

5 **R** Tim enters 5.1 × 12.3 on his calculator.
He gets the answer 85.3.
Without working out the exact answer, explain how you know Tim did not enter the calculation correctly.

6 James works out $3.02 \div 0.49$ on his calculator.
His answer is 3.35555…
Use an approximate calculation to show that James must be wrong.

7 **R** A school collects £20 000 for charity, to be split between three charities.
Sian uses her calculator to work out £20 000 $\div$ 3 = £6666.666 667.
She says each charity should receive £6666.67.
Use your calculator to work out £6666.67 $\times$ 3.
Explain why Sian's rounding doesn't work. Suggest a solution.

8 **R** 220 students in Year 7 are going on a school trip.
A coach can seat 3 adults and 50 students.
Keith says they need 4 coaches.
Sally says they need 5 coaches.
Explain who is correct. Show your working.

9 **R** Alana is working out an estimate to $17.4 \div 2.7$.
 a Why is it better for Alana to work out $18 \div 3$ instead of $17 \div 3$?
 b Make similar choices to estimate
   i $27.8 \div 2.9$ **ii** $35.1 \div 3.9$
   iii $60.9 \div 11.1$ **iv** $74.9 \div 4.4$

10 **R** Kiera's answer to a calculation has 1 decimal place.
She decides to round to the nearest whole number.
Kiera's rounded whole number is 20 041.
Write three possibilities for Kiera's decimal.

11 Write a list of five decimals in ascending order.
Make your first decimal 998.78 and your last decimal 998.87.
Your list must include at least one number written to 1 decimal place.

12 **R** A theatre company is visiting a school.
They charge £500 for their visit.
60 students are going to watch the theatre company.
£500 $\div$ 60 = £8.33 when rounded to 2 decimal places.
Why might this answer cause a financial problem?

Reflect

13 When rounding numbers in real life, it is not always
appropriate to round up or round down. Explain why.

> **Hint** Look back at Q7 and Q8 to help you.

4.2 Length, mass and capacity

- Multiply and divide decimals by 10, 100 and 1000
- Convert measurements into the same units to compare them
- Solve simple problems involving units of measurement in the context of length, mass and capacity
- Convert between metric units of length, mass and capacity

1 Work out
   a 4.7 × 10 ÷ 1000   b 4.7 ÷ 10 × 100
   c 0.47 × 10 ÷ 100   d 0.047 × 1000 ÷ 10

2 Write these lengths in millimetres.
   a 7 m   b 55 m
   c 109 m   d 0.83 m

3 Write these measurements in metres.
   a 12 000 mm   b 1400 mm
   c 2750 mm   d 439 mm

4 A washing-up bowl holds 9.5 litres.
   A small bucket holds 9050 ml.
   Which holds more water?

5 Write these lengths in ascending order.
   a 120 cm, 1.31 m, 124 cm, 1.19 m
   b 1.2 km, 1300 m, 1.09 km, 1100 m
   c 1155 mm, 1.23 m, 1209 mm, 1.16 m
   d 1105 mm, 111 cm, 1.13 m, 1210 mm, 128 cm, 1.23 m

6 Which is longest:
   2.67 km, 2760 m or 262 700 cm?

7 Which is shortest:
   0.0058 km, 5.9 m, 621 cm, 5820 mm or 0.057 km?

8 A robin's wing span is between 0.13 m and 0.14 m.
   The robin weighs between 0.02 kg and 0.022 kg.
   a Write a possible wing span of the robin in centimetres.
   b Write a possible mass of the robin in grams.

9 Here are the heights of some teachers in a school.

Mr Smyth: 1.88 m
Ms James: 1.72 m
Dr Shah: 1.78 m
Mrs Johnson: 1.6 m
Mr Ali: 1.82 m

Work out the mean height, giving your answer in centimetres.

10 Some students measure the lengths of their pets' tails.
Here are the results.

33 cm   36 mm   292 mm   0.05 m   28.2 cm   0.278 m

Write the median length in centimetres.

11 In a zoo, the giraffe's height is 10 times the height of the penguin.
The giraffe is 5.1 m tall.
How tall is the penguin? Give your answer in centimetres.

12 P-S An elephant weighs 2700 kg.
A dog weighs 100 times less than the elephant.
A mouse weighs 1000 times less than the dog.
An ant weighs 10000 times less than the mouse.
How much does the ant weigh? Give your answer in milligrams (mg).

> **Q12 hint** A **milligram (mg)** is a thousandth of a gram.
> 1 g = 1000 mg

Investigation

13 a Which of these calculations will give the same result?

A $\boxed{\times 10}$ then $\boxed{\times 10}$

B $\boxed{\times 100}$ then $\boxed{\times 10}$

C $\boxed{\times 10}$ then $\boxed{\times 100}$

D $\boxed{\times 1000}$ then $\boxed{\div 10}$

b Write three different calculations involving 10, 100 and 1000, once each, that give the answer 1. Your calculations can include multiplication, division or both.

c i Sarah says that **C** is the calculation you use to change millimetres to metres.
Is she correct? Explain.

ii What *single* calculation can you use to change millimetres to metres?

Reflect

14 The measures you have used in this lesson are called 'metric' measures.
The metric system is described as a 'base 10' system.
What do you think this means?

4.3 Scales and measures

- Use scale diagrams
- Read scales
- Write decimal measures as two related units of measure
- Interpret metric measures displayed on a calculator

1   Write the length of the pencil in each diagram, to the degree of accuracy given by the scale. The first one is started for you.

a

The scale is marked in whole centimetres.
Length of the pencil to the nearest cm =

b

c

2   Write down the volume shown in each of these measuring cylinders, to the degree of accuracy given by the scale.

a   **b**   **c**

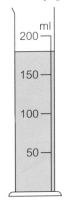   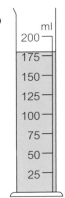   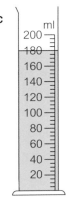

3   What volume is shown in each jug? Use the degree of accuracy of the scale of the jug.

a   **b**   **c**

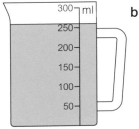   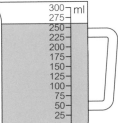   

4 This is an extract from a map where 1 cm represents 4 km.
Work out the distances between

a Swinfield and Westacre

b Morbeach and Swinfield

c Goldbeach and Westacre.

Morbeach
•

4 km

Goldbeach
•

Westacre
•

Swinfield
•

5 This is the answer shown on a calculator screen.

200.5

a Assume the calculation was in pounds. Write this answer in pounds and pence.

b Assume the calculation was in kilograms. Write this answer in grams.

c Assume the calculation was in metres. Write this answer in millimetres.

d Assume the calculation was in hours. Write this answer in minutes.

6 P-S

```
+-------+-------+-------+-------+-------+
0 m        [    ]    0.04 m   [    ]    [    ]    0.1 m
```

a Copy and complete the number line in metres.

b Redraw the same number line, marking the measures in millimetres.

7 Here is a jug.

a The jug shows multiples of 100 ml. Write two millilitre volumes that you can measure using this jug. One must *not* be a multiple of 100 ml.

b R Write two millilitre volumes between 0 and 500 ml you *cannot* measure using this jug. Explain your answer.

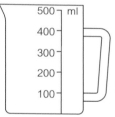

8 This scale shows mass measured in kilograms (kg) on the outer scale, and pounds (lb) on the inner scale.

a Write the measure shown in pounds (lb).

b Write the measure shown in kilograms (kg).

Reflect

9 Look back at Q5. What type of measure is

a easiest to interpret when shown on a calculator

b hardest to interpret when shown on a calculator?

Explain your answers.

4.4 Working with decimals mentally

- Multiply decimals by multiples of 10, 100 and 1000
- Multiply decimals mentally
- Check a result by considering whether it is of the right order of magnitude
- Understand where to position the decimal point by considering equivalent calculations

1 Use the fact $0.83 \times 3.5 = 2.905$ to calculate
   a 0.083×3.5
   b 8.3×35
   c 830×0.035
   d Write down two other multiplications that will have an answer of 2.905.
   e R Explain why $83 \times 35 \neq 29\,050$.

   > **Q1e hint** $\neq$ means 'is not equal to'.

2 Fiona's favourite cheese costs £12.49 per kilogram.
   She wants to buy 700 g.
   a Estimate how much this should cost.
   b Use a calculator to work out the exact value to the nearest penny.

3 a Copy and complete this number pattern.
      $588.8 \div 92 = 6.4$
      $588.8 \div 9.2 = 64$
      $588.8 \div 0.92 =$
      $588.8 \div 0.092 =$
      $588.8 \div 00092 =$
   b Work out $58.88 \div 9.2$.
      Use estimates to check your answer.

4 $4.4 \times 63 = 277.2$
   Use this fact to work out these calculations.
   Check your answers using estimates.
   a 0.44×63 b 0.44×6.3

5 Work out
   a 2×4 b 0.2×4
   c 0.2×0.4 d 0.02×0.4
   e 0.02×0.04 f 5×5
   g 0.5×5 h 0.5×0.5
   i 0.05×0.5 j 0.05×0.05

6 R Kai says that 0.3×0.03 is 0.09.
   Explain how you know he is wrong.

7 Work out 93.5×4.52 on your calculator.
Without using your calculator, copy and complete these related calculations.

a $\square \div 4.52 = \square$ **b** $\square \div 93.5 = \square$

8 **P-S** $17.3 \times 8.6 = 148.78$
Use this fact to work out these divisions.

a $148.78 \div 8.6$ **b** $148.78 \div 0.86$
c $1.4878 \div 8.6$ **d** $148.78 \div 17.3$
e $148.78 \div 1.73$ **f** $1.4878 \div 1.73$

9 **R** Without using a calculator, write these calculations so that their answers are in ascending order.

| $3.45 \div 0.025$ | $3.45 \div 2.5$ | $34.5 \div 2.5$ |

10 **R** 17^2 is 289.
What is

a 1.7^2 **b** 0.17^2?

11 **P-S** $24 \times 32 = 768$
Use this fact to work out these divisions.

a $768 \div 64$ **b** $768 \div 0.64$
c $384 \div 0.64$ **d** $384 \div 6.4$
e $192 \div 6.4$ **f** $192 \div 0.64$

12 **P-S / R** $0.12 \times 120 \div 3.2 = 4.5$
Using this fact, copy and complete

a $0.24 \times 1200 \div 6.4 = \square$
b $0.12 \times 1200 \div \square = 90$
c $12 \times \square \div 320 = 0.45$
d $\square \times 1.2 \div 1.6 = 0.009$

Reflect

13 Write three things that you look for when using a calculation fact to work out other calculations.

4.5 Working with decimals

- Add and subtract decimals
- Multiply and divide decimals by single-digit whole numbers
- Divide numbers that give decimal answers

1 Work out
   a $3 - 0.2$ b $7 - 0.4$
   c $10 - 6.34$ d $100 - 8.5$

2 **P-S** Varsha orders:

Lasagne	£6.95
Ice cream	£1.99
Cola	£1.45

How much change does Varsha get from £20?
Use an estimate to check your answer.

3 Kelly has £503.62 in her bank account.
She spends £206.87.
   a Approximately how much money does Kelly have left?
   b Work out exactly how much money Kelly has left.

4 Anna and Ed have £6.
They spend £5.88.
Anna counts up on this number line to work out the difference between £6 and £5.88.

   a Copy and complete Anna's working.
   Ed writes this subtraction calculation.

   6 . 0 0
  – 5 . 8 8
  ─────────

   b Copy and complete Ed's working.
   c **R** Whose method do you prefer? Explain why.

5 Sohail is a 100 m runner.
His times for the last five races are

   12.5 seconds, 13.4 seconds, 11.9 seconds, 12.5 seconds, 12.2 seconds

Work out his mean time.

6 Write the median and range of these values.

   3.04   3.4   3.401   3.41   3.041

7 **P-S** This magic square has the same total for each row and column.
Work out the missing numbers.

0.2	0.13	0.18
0.15	0.17	

8 There are 8 people in a quiz team.
They win £190 and share the prize equally.
How much should each member receive?

9 **P-S** Two numbers multiply to give 1.
Both numbers have exactly 1 non-zero decimal place.
Work out the two numbers.

Q9 hint Start by finding two whole numbers that multiply to give 100.

10 **P-S** The mean mass of four cats is 3.9 kg.
What is their total mass? Give your answer in grams.

11 **P-S** Charlie is cooking dinner.
The recipe serves 8 people.
It uses three 340 g tins of tuna, two 330 g tins of tomatoes and 2.5 g of paprika.
How much of each ingredient is used per person?
Round answers to 1 decimal place where necessary.

12 **R**
  a Try to work out each of these calculations mentally.
    For any you can't work out mentally, use a written calculation.
    i 2.52 + 1.304   **ii** 2.52 + 1.34   **iii** 2.52 + 1.49
  b Which was the easiest to work out? Explain.
  c Explain what made the others harder.

13 **R** Mia and John are both trying to work out £20 − £2.99.
Mia writes this column subtraction.

$$\begin{array}{r} {}^{1}\cancel{2}{}^{9}\cancel{0}.{}^{9}\cancel{0}{}^{1}0 \\ -\ \ 2.99 \\ \hline 17.01 \end{array}$$

John says it is easier to subtract £3 and then add 1p.
Which method do you prefer? Explain.

Reflect

14 Sometimes using a written method can make the calculation harder.
Create your own subtraction question where it would be more efficient to use a
mental method.

4.6 Perimeter

- Work out the perimeters of composite shapes and polygons
- Solve perimeter problems

1 Work out the perimeter of each shape. Write all your answers in centimetres.

a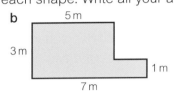

b

c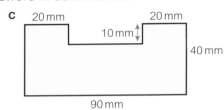

2 **P-S / R** A rectangle has a perimeter of 20.6 cm.

   a Draw three possible rectangles with side lengths marked.

   b A square has the same perimeter.
   What is the side length of the square?

3 **P-S** A rope is cut to fit exactly around the perimeter of these shapes.
   The length of rope is then formed into a square.
   Work out the side length of the square for each shape.

a

b

c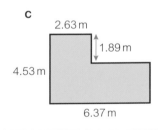

d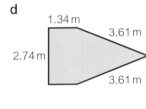

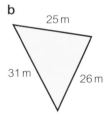

Investigation

4 Draw all possible rectangles that have integer sides *and* a perimeter of 24.
   How can you be sure you have found all of them?

> **Hint**
> An integer is a
> whole number.

---

5 Two different lengths, a and b, are used to construct these shapes.

a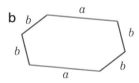

b

c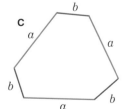

d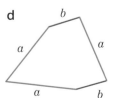

Write a simplified expression for the perimeter of each shape.

6 **P-S** Write a simplified algebraic expression for the perimeter of each shape.

a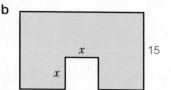

b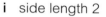

c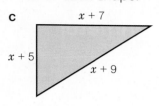

7 A right-angled triangle with sides 6, 8 and 10 has a square, of side length x, cut out of the right-angled corner.

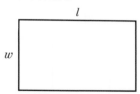

a What is the perimeter of the triangle before the square is cut out?

b Once the square has been cut out, what is the perimeter of the shaded shape if the square has

   i side length 2   **ii** side length 1.5?

c **P-S / R** Explain why the perimeter will always be the same for different values of x.

8 **P-S / R** A square with side 10 cm has a smaller square, of side length d, cut out of one corner. Show that the perimeter is unchanged.

9 **P-S** A rectangle is twice as wide as it is tall. It has a perimeter of 60 cm. Work out the length of the shortest side of the rectangle.

10 **R**

  a Write a formula for the perimeter of this rectangle in its simplest form. Start with $P =$

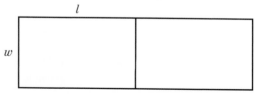

  b Write the formula for the perimeter of this new shape.

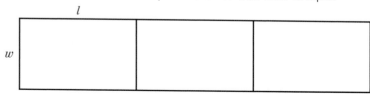

  c Write the formula for the perimeter of this new shape.

  d Predict the formula for the perimeter of a shape made of 10 of these rectangles.

Reflect

11 Write two advantages of using a formula to describe the perimeter of a shape.

4.7 Area

- Find areas of irregular shapes by counting squares
- Calculate the areas of shapes made from rectangles
- Solve problems involving area

1   a   Work out the perimeter and area of a rectangle with
  - i   width 12 cm and height 5 cm
  - ii   width 10 cm and height 7 cm
  - iii   width 4 cm and height 13 cm.

   b   Meera says two rectangles with the same perimeter always have the same area.
     Look back at your answers for part **a** and comment on Meera's statement.

2   a   Work out the perimeter and area of a rectangle with
  - i   length 8 m and height 3 m
  - ii   length 10 m and height 2.4 m
  - iii   length 12 m and height 2 m.

   b   Jack says two rectangles with the same area will have the same perimeter.
     Look back at your answers for part **a** and comment on Jack's statement.

3   **P-S**   Chico orders a mat for a giant chessboard set.
It is a square of side length 9 feet.

> **Q3 hint**
> 1 foot ≈ 30 cm

   a   What is the perimeter of the mat in metres?

   b   What is the area of the mat in m²?

There are 64 squares on a chessboard. Half are black and half are white.

   c   What area of the mat is black? Give your answer in m² correct to 1 decimal place.

   d   What is the area of one of the squares on the mat?
     Give your answer in m² to 1 decimal place.

4   **R**   Give an example to show why each of these statements is wrong.

> **Q4a hint**
> What if one side
> is a decimal?

   a   The perimeter of a rectangle cannot be an odd number.

   b   When the length and the width of a rectangle are doubled, the area
     is also doubled.

   c   Ignoring the units, the area and the perimeter of a square are always different.

5   **P-S / R**   Karen has 20 m of fence to make the largest possible rabbit enclosure.
She comes up with these three ideas.

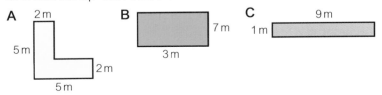

   a   Show that each rabbit enclosure uses 20 m of fencing.

   b   Which design, **A**, **B** or **C**, gives the rabbits the most space?

6 a Work out the area of this shape by adding together the areas of A and B.

b Work out the area of the same shape again, by finding the area of the whole rectangle and subtracting the area of C.

c R Which method do you prefer? Why?

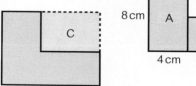

7 Work out the areas of these shapes.

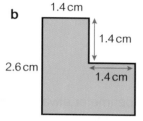 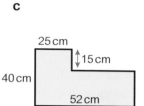 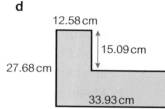

8 In the UK, the A series of paper sizes is used.

a A6 paper is 105 mm × 148 mm. What is its area in mm^2?

b A5 paper is 148 mm × 210 mm. What is its area in mm^2?

c A4 paper is 210 mm × 297 mm. What is its area in mm^2?

d A3 paper is 297 mm × 420 mm. What is its area in mm^2?

e A2 paper is 420 mm × 594 mm. What is its area in mm^2?

f Continue the pattern to work out the area of A1 and A0 paper.

Investigation

9 a Draw a rectangle. Work out its area.

b Now draw a rectangle with twice the length and twice the width. Work out its area.

c What would you need to multiply the smaller area by to reach the larger area?

d What would happen if the second rectangle was half the length and half the width?

10 P-S A rectangular pond 10 m by 8 m has square paving slabs all the way around the edge. Each slab is 50 cm by 50 cm. What is the total area of the paving in m^2?

11 P-S A 20 cm square is cut out of a rectangle that is 25 cm by 30 cm. What area is left?

12 P-S A 10 cm square has a 1 cm border drawn inside it. What area does the border take up? What is the area of the smaller square inside the border?

13 R Simon is working out the perimeter and area of a rectangle. He writes, 'Area = 18 cm, Perimeter = 22 cm^2'. What is wrong with his answers?

Reflect

14 What is the same and what is different about perimeter and area?

4.8 More units of measure

- Choose suitable units to measure length and area
- Use units of measurement to solve problems
- Use metric and imperial units

1 Here are some equivalent metric and imperial measures.

    1 mile ≈ 1.6 km
    1 ft ≈ 30 cm
    1 lb ≈ 450 g
    1 pint ≈ $\frac{1}{2}$ litre
    1 gallon ≈ 4.5 litres

    Convert these amounts into the units shown.

    a 4 lb ≈ □ g   **b** 6 pints ≈ □ litres   **c** 4 gallons ≈ □ litres

2 **P-S** A ferry can carry vehicles totalling 7000 tonnes.
    Can it carry
    430 cars, with mean weight of 1500 kg each *and*
    137 lorries, with mean weight of 40 tonnes each?

3 **P-S** For a long-distance camping trip, students need
    a rucksack that has a capacity of at least 65 litres.
    Peter buys a rucksack measuring 34 cm by 26 cm by 75 cm.
    Is Peter's rucksack big enough?

> **Q3 hint** 1 ml = 1 cm³,
> 1 litre = □ ml.

4 A rectangle measures 80 cm by 1.2 m.
    What are its area and perimeter?

5 A park has a large grass area.
    It is a rectangle measuring 900 m by 1.5 km in size.
    What are its area and perimeter?

Investigation

6 Sketch a rectangle with side lengths of 80 cm and 60 cm.
    Work out the area of the rectangle in cm².
    Now re-label the sides in metres instead of centimetres.
    What is the area in m²?
    Paige says you need to divide the cm² by 100 to get the area in m².
    Is this correct?
    Test your idea on some different sized rectangles.

7 **R** Callum is adding up these lengths:
600 m, 800 m, 1.8 km, 2 miles, 4.8 km
  a Callum enters 600 + 800 + 1.8 + 2 + 4.8 on his calculator.
  What has he done wrong?
  b Lucas says,
    'All the units have to be the same so let's change them all into miles.'
    Is this a good strategy? Explain.
  c Work out the correct answer.

8 **P-S** Faizal asks some friends how far they walk to school.
  Arthur: 500 m
  Ben: 2.8 km
  Carley: 3 miles
  Dawn: 1 mile
  Elle: 650 m
  Work out the mean distance.

 9 **R** 1 hectare of French farmland costs, on average, 6000 euros.
  0.405 hectares is approximately 1 acre.
  Isabelle sees this sign:

  Is this a good sale price?

 10 Work out the area of each of these rectangles.

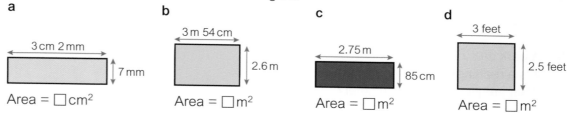

a Area = ☐ cm²
b Area = ☐ m²
c Area = ☐ m²
d Area = ☐ m²

  Write your answers in the units given.
  Give your answers to parts **c** and **d** correct to 2 decimal places.

Reflect

11 Why can you compare two measures given in feet and centimetres, but not litres and centimetres?
  Is it ever possible to compare a litres and a centimetres measure? Explain.

4 Extend

1   **P-S / R**   The area of this L shape is 32 cm².

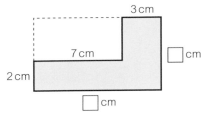

Work out its perimeter.

2   **P-S**   Here are four measures:

    3.14, 3.10, 3.014, 3.1041

There is a fifth measure missing.
The mean of all five measures is 3.1041.
Work out the fifth measure.

3   **P-S**   Work out twice the difference between these amounts:
- three times 2.9
- 2.1 doubled then doubled again.

4   **P-S / R**   A 20 cm by 30 cm rectangle has a rectangle drawn inside, 3 cm from the edge all the way around.
A 10 cm by 60 cm rectangle has a rectangle drawn inside, also 3 cm from the edge all the way around.
Sam says both larger rectangles have the same area, therefore the interior rectangles have the same area. Is Sam correct? Show how you know.

5   **P-S**   Esther and Jake go out on their bikes at 12 midday.
Esther cycles 36 km in 2 hours. She stops for a drink for 15 minutes.
Then Esther cycles for another 45 minutes, covering an additional 10 km.
Jake cycles 15 miles to a friend's house. It takes him 1 hour.
Jake spends 1 hour at his friend's house. Then he cycles home.
Who cycles further in the 3 hours?

6   **P-S**   A rectangle is twice as wide as it is tall. It has an area of 32 cm².
What is its perimeter?

7   A sheet of A4 paper is 210 mm by 297 mm.
How many 20 mm squares could fit on an A4 sheet?

8   **P-S**   A square has another square cut out from it.
The side lengths of both squares are whole numbers of centimetres less than 10 cm.
The shape left behind has an area of 65 cm².
What is the perimeter of the larger square?

9 A large rectangular field, 1 mile wide and 3 miles long, has a road cut through the middle. The road is 10 m wide.

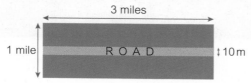

3 miles

1 mile | R O A D | ‡ 10 m

What area of the field is not turned into road?
Give your answer in m².

10 P-S A cube has side lengths of 5 cm.
What is the total of the areas of all the faces on the cube?

11 P-S Here are some imperial units of length.
There are 8 chains in a furlong, 22 yards in a chain, and 3 feet in a yard.
An acre is a unit of area of a rectangle that is a chain by a furlong.
1 foot is equivalent to 30 cm.
Work out the size of an acre in m².

12 P-S There are 8 pints in a gallon.
1 pint is 568 ml.
How many litres are in 1 gallon?

13 P-S / R Wei measures his classroom to be 12 feet wide and 15 feet long.
Carpet tiles are 40 cm by 40 cm.
How many tiles does he need to carpet the room?

Investigation

14 a Imagine 32 cm of string that you can make a rectangle from.
Write down the measurements of some different sizes of rectangles that are possible.
Work out the area for each rectangle.
What is the largest rectangle you can create?

b Repeat part **a** with 100 cm of string.

c What is similar about your largest rectangles from parts **a** and **b**?

d Imagine 64 square centimetres, like tiles, that you can arrange to make different shapes.
Sketch some possible rectangles that you could create from all of these 64 tiles.
Work out the perimeter for each one. What is
  i the largest possible perimeter   **ii** the smallest possible perimeter?

e Repeat this with 100 square centimetres.

f What is similar about your answers to parts **d** and **e**?

Reflect

15 Write five new things about measures that you have learned in this Depth unit.

5 Fractions and percentages

Master   Extend p75

5.1 Comparing fractions

- Use fraction notation to describe parts of a shape
- Compare simple fractions
- Use a diagram to compare two or more simple fractions

1 R   Rob says, '$\frac{5}{7}$ of this shape is shaded.'

Is Rob correct?
Explain your answer.

2 a   What fraction of this shape is shaded?

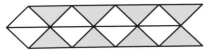

   b P-S / R   How many *more* triangles must be shaded so that $\frac{3}{4}$ of the shape is shaded?
   Explain how you worked out the answer.

3 P-S   Use the grid to decide which is larger, $\frac{3}{4}$ or $\frac{4}{5}$

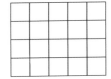

4 R   Gill says, '$\frac{1}{15}$ is greater than $\frac{1}{14}$ because 15 is greater than 14.'
Is Gill correct? Explain your answer.

5 R   Bikram says $\frac{2}{3}$ of this shape is shaded.
Theo says $\frac{3}{4}$ of this shape is shaded.

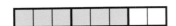

Explain who is correct and why.

6   Put these fractions in order (smallest first).
   $\frac{1}{54}$ $\frac{1}{24}$ $\frac{1}{154}$

7 Esther colours in $\frac{2}{3}$ of this shape.

How many extra squares need to be coloured in so that $\frac{3}{4}$ is coloured?

8 Put these fractions in order (smallest first).

$1\frac{1}{2}$ $\qquad\qquad\qquad$ $1\frac{1}{5}$ $\qquad\qquad\qquad$ $1\frac{1}{3}$

9 Which fraction is closer to 1: $\frac{19}{20}$ or $\frac{23}{22}$?

10 Which fraction is closer to $\frac{1}{2}$: $\frac{29}{60}$ or $\frac{49}{100}$?

11 Find three different unit fractions that lie between $\frac{1}{39}$ and $\frac{1}{49}$

Investigation

12 a Make two copies of the grid shown.

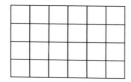

Use the grids to show two different non-unit fractions with different denominators. Which is larger?

b Repeat part **a** for a different pair of fractions.

c Without drawing a grid, write an inequality for two different non-unit fractions.

$\frac{\square}{\square} > \frac{\square}{\square}$

Reflect

13 Copy and complete this sentence with the word **larger** or **smaller**.
For unit fractions, the larger the denominator, the _____ the fraction.
Give examples to support your answer.

5.2 Simplifying fractions

- Change an improper fraction to a mixed number
- Identify equivalent fractions
- Simplify fractions by cancelling common factors

1 **R** Choi simplifies $\frac{18}{30}$ like this.

$$\frac{18}{30} = \frac{9}{15}$$

Buck says, 'What you've written is correct,
but it's still not good enough.'
Explain what Buck means.

2 Simplify these fractions fully.

   a $\frac{24}{60}$ **b** $\frac{60}{120}$ **c** $\frac{120}{210}$ **d** $\frac{210}{336}$

3 **P-S** The bar chart shows the composition of a piece of Cheddar cheese.
The total mass of the piece of cheese is 120 g.

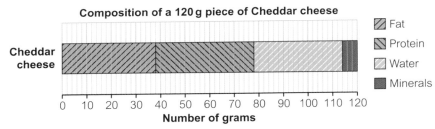

What fraction of the piece of cheese is protein?
Give your answer in its simplest form.

4 Which is larger: $1\frac{4}{5}$ or $\frac{11}{5}$?

5 Change these fractions into mixed numbers.

   a $\frac{13}{11}$ **b** $\frac{15}{13}$ **c** $\frac{17}{15}$ **d** $\frac{19}{17}$

6 Which is larger: $\frac{23}{5}$ or $4\frac{2}{5}$?

7 **P-S** Which fraction is the odd one out? Why?

   $\frac{4}{5}$ $\frac{12}{15}$ $\frac{18}{15}$ $\frac{40}{50}$

8 Which two fractions are the nearest in value to each other?

   $\frac{12}{15}$ $\frac{8}{10}$ $\frac{14}{20}$

9 Which of these fractions simplify to $\frac{4}{7}$?

$\frac{48}{84}$ $\qquad\qquad$ $\frac{32}{52}$ $\qquad\qquad$ $\frac{60}{105}$ $\qquad\qquad$ $\frac{54}{91}$

10 Change these fractions into mixed numbers, simplifying the fractions where possible.

a $\frac{14}{12}$ $\qquad$ **b** $\frac{18}{14}$ $\qquad$ **c** $\frac{30}{20}$ $\qquad$ **d** $\frac{28}{24}$

11 Which is nearer to $3\frac{2}{15}$: $\frac{17}{5}$ or $\frac{49}{15}$?

12 Which is larger: $\frac{7}{9}$ or $\frac{39}{50}$?

13 P-S Which is the odd one out?

a $\frac{13}{17}$ $\qquad\quad$ $\frac{39}{51}$ $\qquad\quad$ $\frac{65}{80}$ $\qquad\quad$ $\frac{91}{119}$

b $\frac{25}{28}$ $\qquad\quad$ $\frac{75}{84}$ $\qquad\quad$ $\frac{275}{308}$ $\qquad\quad$ $\frac{50}{57}$

c $\frac{81}{85}$ $\qquad\quad$ $\frac{243}{256}$ $\qquad\quad$ $\frac{405}{425}$ $\qquad\quad$ $\frac{567}{595}$

14 The pie chart shows the time Rahul spends in different lessons at school each week.

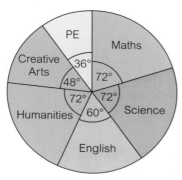

a What fraction of Rahul's week is spent in English lessons?

b The school calls Maths, English and Science 'core lessons'.
What fraction of his week does Rahul spend in 'core lessons'?

c Rahul's favourite lessons are Creative Arts and PE.
What fraction of Rahul's week is *not* in his favourite subjects?

Reflect

15 a Which of these fractions is easiest to visualise?

$\frac{49}{63}$ $\qquad\qquad$ $\frac{2}{10}$ $\qquad\qquad$ $\frac{42}{72}$ $\qquad\qquad$ $\frac{24}{32}$

Explain why.

b Simplify the fractions.
Does this make them easier to visualise, or not?

5.3 Working with fractions

- Add and subtract simple fractions
- Calculate simple fractions of quantities

1 **P-S** Hamish adds together two different fractions with the same denominator. His answer is $\frac{1}{3}$. Write down two fractions that Hamish might have added.

2 Work out
   a $\frac{1}{17} + \frac{5}{17} + \frac{9}{17}$
   b $\frac{1}{37} + \frac{5}{37} + \frac{9}{37}$
   c $\frac{1}{41} + \frac{5}{41} + \frac{9}{41}$

3 A pizza is cut into 8 equal pieces.
   James and John each have 3 pieces and Tim has the rest.
   a What fraction of the pizza does each person have?
   b What fraction of the pizza do James and Tim have in total?

4 Priti has a bag of 25 sweets.
   There are 16 red sweets, 6 yellow sweets and the rest are green.
   a Write the fraction for the total of red and yellow sweets.
   b Write the fraction for the total of yellow and green sweets.
   c Write the fraction for the total of red, yellow and green sweets.

5 Eliot says that $\frac{10}{11} - \frac{3}{11} = \frac{7}{11}$. What addition calculation could Eliot use to check his answer?

6 Jack scores $\frac{63}{80}$ in his Science test. His brother scores $\frac{57}{80}$. How much better did Jack do?

7 Beth ices 25 cupcakes. She ices 18 with white icing and the rest with chocolate icing.
   a What fraction does Beth ice with chocolate icing?
   b She puts a sweet on the top of $\frac{1}{2}$ of the white icing cakes.
      How many more cakes have a sweet than have chocolate icing?

8 Work out
   a $\frac{5}{6}$ of 24
   b $\frac{3}{8}$ of 72
   c $\frac{4}{13}$ of 52

9 Which of these calculations gives an answer that is different from the other two?

    $\frac{4}{9}$ of 36 $\frac{2}{5}$ of 45 $\frac{2}{3}$ of 24

10 **P-S** Arthur, Bethan and Charlie have £120. Charlie has $\frac{2}{3}$ of the money. Bethan has $\frac{3}{4}$ of the remainder. How much money does Arthur have?

11 What is the difference between $\frac{5}{8}$ of 24 and $\frac{4}{7}$ of 28?

12 Work out what number needs to be added to each of these to give the answer 10.

   a $5\frac{3}{4}$
   b $6\frac{7}{8}$
   c $6\frac{11}{12}$
   d $8\frac{13}{18}$

13 P-S In a bag of 120 sweets, $\frac{2}{5}$ of the sweets are red, $\frac{3}{8}$ are orange and the rest are green. How many more red sweets are there than green sweets?

14 What is $\frac{1}{2}$ of $\frac{1}{3}$ of $\frac{1}{4}$ of 24?

15 P-S / R Keith goes for a cycle ride. He checks his distance and finds that he has covered $\frac{3}{8}$ of his total journey with 5 km more to travel until he is half-way. How long is Keith's cycle ride in total?

16 P-S / R In a 10-km race Anita runs 4 km, walks $\frac{3}{20}$ of the remainder and jogs the rest. How far does Anita jog?

17 P-S / R Sally knows her journey to school very well. She knows that she meets some traffic lights when she is $\frac{1}{3}$ of the way to school, and passes a garage when she is half-way. The distance between the traffic lights and the garage is 2 miles. How far is Sally's total journey?

18 A shop sells a jumper for £48. During a sale the shop takes $\frac{1}{4}$ off all the prices. How much does the jumper sell for in the sale?

19 P-S / R Harry thinks of a number. He increases it by one quarter, and then reduces that answer by one third. He finishes with 45. What number did Harry start with?

20 P-S / R A set of data contains five values with a median of 6.
  a $\frac{2}{5}$ of the values are less than the median. What could the data values be?
  b $\frac{1}{5}$ of the values are less than the median. What could the data values be?
  c None of the values are less than the median. What could the data values be?
  d If there are six values instead of five, what fraction of the values could be less than the median?

21 Find the mean of these numbers: $\quad \frac{4}{71} \quad \frac{11}{71} \quad \frac{2}{71} \quad \frac{7}{71}$

Investigation

22 George and Anne are simplifying fractions. They are working on $\frac{16}{64}$. George says that both parts divide by 16 so the answer is $\frac{1}{4}$. Anne says you could get the same answer just by crossing off both 6s. They realise the crossing off method should not work, but they find two other 2-digit fractions where it does work.
Find the fractions where crossing off single digits gives a correct equivalent fraction.

Reflect

23 On Monday Nina completed some addition calculations with fractions.
Here are three of her answers.
  a $\frac{1}{5} + \frac{2}{5} = \frac{3}{5}$ **b** $\frac{2}{7} + \frac{3}{7} = \frac{5}{7}$ **c** $\frac{3}{11} + \frac{6}{11} = \frac{9}{11}$
On Tuesday Nina was attempting some subtraction calculations.
Explain how her answers from Monday would help her correct these.
  a $\frac{3}{5} - \frac{2}{5} = \frac{2}{5}$ **b** $\frac{5}{7} - \frac{2}{7} = \frac{4}{7}$ **c** $\frac{9}{11} - \frac{3}{11} = \frac{3}{11}$

5.4 Fractions and decimals

- Work with equivalent fractions and decimals
- Write one number as a fraction of another

1   In a rugby match the Newcastle Falcons won 13 out of the 20 line-outs.
    a What fraction of the line-outs did they win?
    b Write your answer to part **a** as a decimal.

2   **P-S**   A theme park's website gives information on different types of events.
    There are 9 thrill rides, 9 laughs and frights, 6 attractions and 6 young fun.
    a What fraction of the events are *not* attractions?
    b Write your answer to part **a** as a decimal.

3   **P-S**   The Millennium Stadium in Cardiff is made from 4000 tonnes of concrete,
    12 000 tonnes of structural steel and 40 000 tonnes of steel reinforcement.
    What fraction of the stadium is made from
    a concrete
    b steel reinforcement?
    Give each fraction in its simplest form.

4   In a class of 30 children, 10 wear glasses.
    a What fraction do *not* wear glasses?
    b $\frac{1}{5}$ of the class are wearing a hat.
      How many children are *not* wearing a hat?
    c None of the children without glasses is wearing a hat.
      How many children are wearing glasses *and* a hat?

5   Change these fractions to decimals.
    a $\frac{3}{50}$ b $\frac{12}{200}$
    c $\frac{35}{500}$ d $\frac{180}{2000}$

6   Change these decimals to fractions.
    a 0.5   b 0.05   c 0.005
    d 0.2   e 0.12   f 0.112

7   Change these decimals to fractions.
    a 1.51   b 2.505   c 8.403

8 Write these pairs of numbers in order, smallest first.
   a $\frac{1}{10}$, 0.085   **b** $\frac{6}{25}$, 0.23

   c $\frac{17}{50}$, 0.39   **d** $\frac{22}{200}$, 0.12

9 Convert $\frac{18}{300}$ into a decimal.

10 Convert 0.768 into a fraction.
   Simplify your fraction as much as possible.

11 What fraction is 56 cm out of 2 m?
   Write your answer as a decimal.

12 What fraction is 35 minutes out of 2 hours?

13 What fraction is 25 cm out of 10 km?

14 Add together $\frac{1}{10} + \frac{2}{100} + \frac{5}{1000}$.
   Give your answer as a decimal.

15 **P-S** A jumbo jet has a mass of 150 tonnes when empty, and 320 tonnes when loaded with
   fuel for take-off.
   What fraction of the take-off mass is the fuel?

16 Write these decimals as fractions.
   a 0.4   **b** 0.04   **c** 0.004

17 **R** Alex knows that 0.5 is equivalent to $\frac{1}{2}$.
   He knows that 0.05 is 0.5 divided by 10.
   How does that help Alex find the fraction equivalent to 0.05?

Reflect

18 Luke says,
   'Give me any decimal with 1, 2 or 3 decimal places and I can write it as a fraction.'
   Is Luke correct? Give some examples.

5.5 Understanding percentages

- Understand percentage as 'the number of parts per 100'
- Convert a percentage to a fraction or decimal
- Work with equivalent percentages, fractions and decimals

1 By volume, dry air contains approximately 78% nitrogen, 21% oxygen and the remainder is other gases and water vapour.
What fraction of dry air is
a nitrogen
b oxygen
c other gases and water vapour?
Give each fraction in its simplest form.

2 R The decimal 6.2 is written as which percentage of 1?

$$\boxed{62\%} \quad \boxed{0.062\%} \quad \boxed{620\%} \quad \boxed{6.2\%} \quad \boxed{0.62\%}$$

Explain why.

3 Convert these to percentages to find the largest in each group.
a $\frac{3}{4}$ and $\frac{7}{10}$
b $\frac{18}{40}$, $\frac{35}{50}$ and $\frac{44}{80}$
c $\frac{17}{20}$, $\frac{28}{50}$, $\frac{81}{90}$ and $\frac{240}{300}$

4 Write each fraction as a decimal and as a percentage.
a $\frac{3}{15}$ b $\frac{39}{65}$
c $\frac{13}{10}$ d $\frac{81}{75}$
e $\frac{189}{135}$ f $\frac{45}{100}$

5 The heights of some students are measured.
a 30 students are measured.
What percentage of students will be taller than the median?
b 100 students are measured.
What percentage of students will be shorter than the median?

6 P-S Look at the diagram.

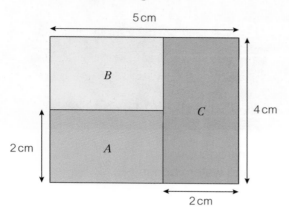

Out of the whole rectangle, write

a the fraction that is area A

b the percentage that is area B

c the fraction that is area C writing your answer as a decimal.

7 A survey asks people their favourite flavour of ice cream and produces this pie chart. 30% of the people chose chocolate.

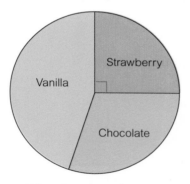

a What fraction chose vanilla?

b Write, as a decimal, the fraction who chose strawberry.

Reflect

8 Kai gets $\frac{41}{50}$ in his Geography test.

Milo scores $\frac{22}{25}$ in his History test.

They wonder who got the higher mark.

a Convert both scores into percentages.

b Convert the scores into fractions with the same denominator.

c Did you find it easier to work out the percentage or the fraction?
Would your answer change if the Geography test was out of 45 instead of 50?

5.6 Percentages of amounts

- Use different strategies to calculate with percentages
- Express one number as a percentage of another

1 Rewrite these statements, giving the numbers as percentages.
   a 23 out of 40 students have a bicycle.
   b 27 out of 80 people went abroad this year.
   c 237 out of 250 people watch football on TV.
   d 72 out of 125 students have a mobile phone.

Q1a hint

$$\frac{23}{40} \overset{\times 5}{=} \frac{\square}{200} \overset{\div 2}{=} \frac{\square}{100}$$

2 a The tower of a wind turbine weighs 35 tonnes.
      The total weight of the wind turbine is 50 tonnes.
      Write the weight of the tower as a percentage of the total weight of the wind turbine.
   b The tower of a wind turbine costs £37 500.
      The total cost of the wind turbine is £250 000.
      Write the cost of the tower as a percentage of the total cost of the wind turbine.

3 Ralph takes part in a charity fun run. 80% of his donations go to a children's hospice.
   Ralph gets £519.29 in donations. How much does the children's hospice get?
   Round your answer to a suitable amount.

4 Charlene grows some sunflowers. Her tallest plant was 120 cm tall two weeks ago.
   One week ago it was 132 cm tall.
   a How many centimetres has it grown by?
   b Write this increase as a percentage of 120 cm.
   c This week the plant is 156 cm tall. What percentage is this compared to two weeks ago?

5 Michael's baby is 4 kg when she is born.
   One week later she weighs 4.2 kg, and two weeks later she weighs 4.5 kg.
   Write both of these weights as a percentage of her birth weight.

6 What is 175% of £120?

7 What is 40% of 50% of £60?

8 What is 25% of 30% of £200?

9 Increase £40 by one quarter and then find 30% of your answer.

10 How much longer is 45% of 80 m than 85% of 40 m?

11 Elijah's coffee shop sells 250 drinks on a Monday. It sells 450 drinks on a Friday.
    a Write the extra sales on Friday, compared to Monday, as a fraction of Monday's sales.
    b What percentage are Friday's sales compared to Monday's sales?

12 P-S Omar is training for a long-distance cycle race. In week 1 he cycles 50 km.
In week 2 he increases his distance by $\frac{1}{5}$. Week 3 is 10% longer than week 2.
What percentage is Omar's week 3 compared to his week 1 distance?

13 Julie is training to run a marathon. Last week she ran 20 km. This week she runs 25 km.
What percentage is this week's distance compared to last week's?

14 Evie scores $\frac{30}{50}$ in her first Maths test. In the second Maths test she scores 96%.
Write Evie's second score compared to her first score as a decimal, then as a percentage.

15 P-S Five years ago 50 litres of diesel cost £35. Today 35 litres of diesel costs £50.
Write the new price per litre of diesel as a percentage of the old price per litre of diesel.

16 R A register is taken twice a day at school, and statistics compiled every four weeks.
  a Why is it impossible for a student to have 99% attendance?
  b What is the highest attendance that is not perfect?

17 P-S / R Alice took two reading tests. The first was out of 40 and the second out of 50.
She got 90% of the total marks available. She scored 35 on the first test.
What did Alice score on the second test?

18 P-S An online shop charges 10% postage on orders up to (and including) £40, and 5% on
orders over £40. Ben's order totals £39.50.
He spends 70p more. How much does Ben save?

19 P-S The cells in a biology experiment are growing at a rate of 20% per week.
They cover 1 cm² of the dish at the start of the experiment.
How long will it take until they cover 10 cm²?

20 Which chocolate bar has the greater mass of cocoa?
Brand A: 70% cocoa, and bars of 125 g   Brand B: 85% cocoa, and bars of 90 g

21 The graph shows the number of absences
for a group of 100 students.
  a What percentage of the absences
     occurred on Monday?
  b Write the smallest proportion of
     absences as a decimal.
  c What fraction of the absences occurred
     on Thursday or Friday?

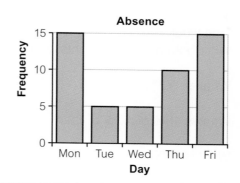

22 Which of these statements make sense? Explain why you think this.
A puppy's weight increases by 120%.
A company makes a 130% profit.
A person gives 110% effort.

5 Extend

1 **P-S** What fraction is half-way between

    a $\frac{1}{6}$ and $\frac{1}{8}$ **b** $\frac{1}{7}$ and $\frac{1}{11}$?

2 Work out 30% of 200 plus 200% of 30.

3 **P-S** What number increases by 300% when squared?

4 Find the median of 21%, $\frac{23}{99}$ and $\frac{69}{300}$.

5 **P-S** Find a whole number x so that $\frac{1}{x} + \frac{x}{2} = \frac{33}{8}$

6 **P-S** A cube is enlarged so that every length becomes 10% longer.
What is the new volume of the cube as a percentage of the original volume of the cube?

7 **P-S** People have landed on the Moon, which is 384 thousand kilometres from the Earth.
We now look to Mars, which is 55 million kilometres away.
What percentage of the distance to Mars have we travelled by landing on the Moon?

8 Find the highest common factor (HCF) and the lowest common multiple (LCM) of 24 and 42.
What fraction is the HCF of the LCM?

9 **P-S** Look at the triangle.

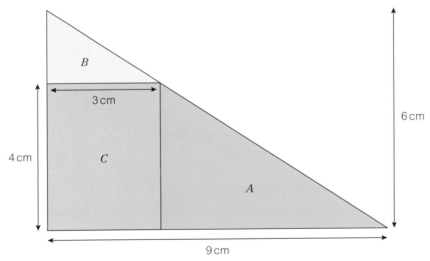

    a What percentage of the whole triangle is taken by region C?
    b Write the area of the whole triangle taken by region B as
      i a fraction
      ii a percentage.

10 a Use a calculator to write $\frac{1}{11}$, $\frac{2}{11}$ and $\frac{3}{11}$ as decimals.

  b Describe the pattern you see.

  c Without using your calculator, predict how you could write $\frac{8}{11}$ as a decimal.

  d How could you write $\frac{13}{11}$ as a decimal?

11 P-S / R The rectangle contains four fractions and the oval contains four whole numbers.

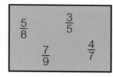 

  a Choose a fraction from the rectangle and multiply it by a whole number from the oval.

  b Which fraction and whole number, when you multiply them together, will give you

    i the largest answer possible

    ii the smallest answer possible?

12 R Work out

  a $\frac{1}{2}$ of £30 and then $\frac{1}{3}$ of the answer.

  b $\frac{1}{3}$ of £30 and then $\frac{1}{2}$ of the answer.

  c What do you notice about your answers to parts **a** and **b**?

  d What is the overall fraction of £30 that you have found?

  e How can you combine $\frac{1}{2}$ and $\frac{1}{3}$ to give you this overall fraction?

13 P-S Peter, Jay and Ruth are in a race.
Jay runs 10% faster than Peter, and Ruth runs 10% faster than Jay.
When Ruth has completed 100 m, work out how far

  a Jay has completed

  b Peter has completed.

14 P-S Lucas has a 20% staff discount in the shop where he works.
In a sale week the shop reduces all the prices by $\frac{1}{4}$.
Lucas's staff discount still applies.
What percentage of the original price does Lucas pay?

15 Which is larger, $\frac{5}{24}$ or $\frac{6}{29}$?
What have you learned in this lesson that would help you answer the question?

6 Probability

Master   **Extend p87**

6.1 The language of probability

- Use the language of probability
- Use a probability scale with words
- Understand the probability scale from 0 to 1

1 How would you describe the probability of each event?
Choose from: impossible, unlikely, even chance, likely, certain.

  a Getting a 'head' when you flip a coin.

  b A coin landing on its edge when you drop it onto a table.

  c It raining at least 50 times in Bristol next year.

  d Getting a 6 when you roll an ordinary dice.

2 The one-armed bandit machine has a paper strip stuck to its wheel.
You pull the handle once and the strip shows your winnings.
An unhappy face means you lose.

Use words to describe the probability that the wheel lands on

  a a yellow square

  b a yellow or a blue square

  c a black square.

3 **P-S** Virginia rolls a 12-sided dice once.
The dice has each of the numbers 1–12 on its faces.
Describe a possible event with each of these probabilities.

  a impossible

  b 50%

  c unlikely

  d 1

4 The probability of it raining on Tuesday is 0.7.
The probability of it raining on Wednesday is 80%.
On which day is it more likely to rain?

5 Write an equivalent fraction value for each word on the probability scale.

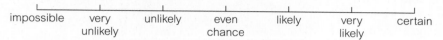

impossible   very   unlikely   even   likely   very   certain
           unlikely   chance   likely

6 Write an equivalent probability word for each percentage on the probability scale.

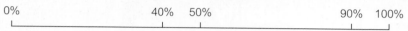

0%   40%   50%   90%   100%

7 R Here are two spinners.
Explain why the probability of the first spinner landing on A is the same as the probability of the second spinner landing on R.

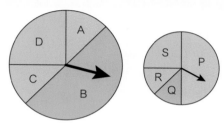

8 R A bag contains some blue counters (B), green counters (G) and yellow counters (Y).

A counter is taken at random from the bag.
One of the three colours is twice as likely to be picked than the other two are.
Which colour? Explain why.

9 P-S Esme is practising her spelling of the days of the week. She chooses a day at random.
Use a word to describe the probability that the day Esme chooses
a has a letter 'T' in it
b has a letter 'A' in it.

Reflect

10 Lucy and Isla support the same football team.
After 10 matches, they look back on their team's performance.
Lucy says it is likely the team will win their next match.
Isla says the probability they will win is $\frac{7}{10}$.
Who has made the more precise statement? Explain your answer.

6.2 Calculating probability

- Identify outcomes and equally likely outcomes
- Calculate probabilities
- Use a probability scale from 0 to 1

1 When Jamie's computer is switched on, it randomly chooses one of two background images – the sky or the beach.
Jamie switched on his computer on Wednesday and on Thursday.
a Write the possible outcomes for the background images.
b Work out the probability that the background image will be the beach on both days.

2 R Maya is using this spinner.

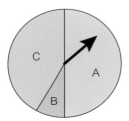

She says, 'There are three choices on this spinner, so the chance of each one is $\frac{1}{3}$.'
Explain why Maya is wrong.

3 R Ollie says, 'The probability of a football team winning is $\frac{1}{3}$ because winning is only one out of the three possible outcomes: win, lose, draw.' Explain why Ollie is wrong.

4 The letters M, A, R, T, I, A and N are put on cards. One card is selected at random.
Put these events on a probability scale.
a A vowel is selected.
b A letter from the word MATHS is selected.
c A letter drawn with no curves is selected.

5 A fair 10-sided spinner is numbered from 0 to 9.
Work out the probability, as a percentage, that the spinner lands on
a a number less than 5   b a multiple of 4   c a prime number.

Investigation

6 Kathryn puts some red, white, blue and pink counters in a bag. She gives the bag to Clive, who takes a counter out at random, records the colour, and then puts it back.
After some time Clive concludes that the probabilities for each colour are
red: 36%   white: 34%   blue: $\frac{1}{5}$ pink: $\frac{1}{10}$
Kathryn tells him there are fewer than 100 counters in the bag.
Work out how many counters of each of the colours are in the bag.

7 A spinner is designed.

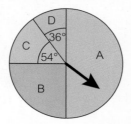

Work out the probability, as a decimal, that the spinner lands on

a A   **b** B or C   **c** D or A   **d** A or C or D

8 **P-S / R**   A fair 8-sided spinner is going to be marked with letters.
Jake has marked some events on a probability scale.

Design a possible spinner for these probabilities.

9 **P-S**   A bag contains 4 red counters and 1 yellow counter.
One counter is selected at random.

  a What is the probability that a yellow counter is selected?
  b 5 more yellow counters are added. How does the probability of selecting yellow change?
  c How many red counters need to be added to make the probability of selecting red the same as the initial state?

10 **P-S**   A set of 26 cards, one with each letter of the alphabet on, is placed in a bag.
One is selected at random. What is the probability of

  a choosing a letter from Anna's name
  b choosing a letter that doesn't appear in this part of the question
  c choosing a vowel, if the letters VWXYZ are removed?

11 There are 30 students in a class.
The probability of choosing someone who wears glasses is 20%.

  a How many students wear glasses?
  b 3 students with glasses have dark hair. 25% of the rest of the class have dark hair.
    How many students in the whole class have dark hair?
  c Is a student more likely to have dark hair if they wear glasses or not?

12 **P-S**   In a bag there is a basketball, a tennis ball and a golf ball.
Because of their size, it is twice as likely to pick out the tennis ball compared to the golf ball, and three times more likely to choose the basketball compared to the tennis ball.
Work out the probability of each ball being chosen.

Reflect

13 Look back at your answers to Q9–10. How did you decide whether to write the probabilities as a fraction, a decimal or a percentage?

6.3 More probability calculations

- Calculate more complex probabilities
- Calculate the probability of an event not happening

1   The probability that Dana will *not* get a seat on the 8:10 am train to work is 0.28.
    Work out the probability that she *will* get a seat.

2   Students in Steve's class choose their favourite colour. Here is a graph of their results.

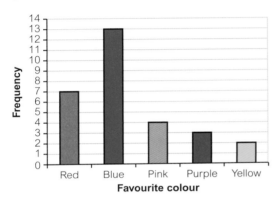

What is the probability that a student selected at random chose

a red or pink

b pink or purple

c blue or pink or purple?

3   Matt has a special dice numbered from 1 to 8.
    When he rolls the dice, what is the probability that the number is

a even or prime

b odd or larger than 5

c even or odd?

4   **P-S / R**   Ruby places the letters A, B or C on each space in the spinner.

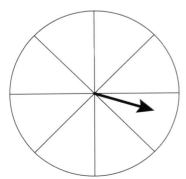

The probability of getting A or B is $\frac{5}{8}$ and the probability of getting B or C is $\frac{6}{8}$.
Work out how many of each letter she places on the spinner.

5 Gavin has a fair coin and a fair dice. He tosses both at once.
He knows the coin is either heads or tails, and the dice lands on one of six numbers.
He thinks there will be eight possible outcomes.

a Write a list of all the possible outcomes and show that there are more than eight.

> **Hint** Start with 1H.

b Work out the probability that the coin lands on heads *and* the dice lands on a 5 or a 6.

6 A spinner is designed.

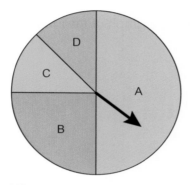

What is the probability of
a not getting B
b getting A or D
c not getting A or D?

7 There are 4 bananas, 3 apples and 2 oranges in a fruit bowl.
Eli chooses one at random.
a What is the probability he chooses a banana?
b What is the probability he chooses an apple or an orange?
c His sister takes an orange.
What effect does this have on the probability that Eli chooses an orange?

8 P-S   There are 30 students in Cora's tutor group.
12 were born in the autumn term and 30% were born in the spring term.
a How many students were born in the summer term?
b What is the probability that someone chosen at random was born in the autumn term?
c It is claimed that $\frac{1}{3}$ of the students born in the spring and summer terms will be amazing at sport, but only $\frac{1}{4}$ of the autumn term students.
What is the probability that a student chosen at random will be amazing at sport?

9 There are red, green and yellow counters in a bag.
One is selected at random.
Explain two ways to work out the probability of *not* choosing yellow.

6.4 Experimental probability

- Estimate probability based on experimental data
- Make conclusions based on the results of an experiment

1   **R**   Tom is looking at the weather records from August.
He uses these records to make a prediction for the weather in November.
Why is this prediction unlikely to be accurate?

2   Records show that in Cyprus it was sunny on 888 days out of the last 1000 days.
   a Estimate the probability that it will be sunny in Cyprus tomorrow.
   b R   Is this a good model for predicting the weather in Cyprus for Christmas Day?
     Give a reason for your answer.

3   Gemma collected 10p coins in her piggy bank. She took a coin out of the piggy bank at
random, looked at it and then put it back in the piggy bank.
She did this several times and recorded 20 old coins and 10 new coins.
   a How many times did Gemma take a coin from her piggy bank?
   b Estimate the probability that the next coin she takes out will be an old coin.

4   **P-S**   An optician's records show that 17 of the last 50 customers bought tinted lenses, and
23 of them bought two pairs of glasses.
   a Estimate the probability that the next customer orders
     i   tinted lenses   **ii** two pairs of glasses.
   b R   The optician's assistant worked out $17 + 23 = 40$ and estimated that
     the probability of a customer ordering tinted lenses or two pairs of glasses is $\frac{40}{50}$.
     Explain why he might be wrong.

5   Rojas recorded the numbers of people entering a lift on the
ground floor of a department store on Saturday morning.
   a The lift arrives at the ground floor.
     Estimate the probability that
     i   3 people enter
     ii 3 or 4 people enter
     iii nobody enters
     iv more than 6 people enter
     v   some people enter.
   b The lift left the ground floor 50 times the following
     Saturday morning.
     Estimate the number of times 3 people entered the lift.
   c R   Are your estimated probabilities a good model for lift activity on Monday?
     Explain your answer.
   d R   Are your estimated probabilities a good model for people entering the lift on the top
     floor? Explain your answer.

People	Frequency
0	2
1	5
2	5
3	8
4	7
5	6
6	3
7	2
8	2

6 R Rosie and Daisy roll some dice.
Rosie carries out 30 rolls and finds that her dice lands on a 6 four times.
Daisy carries out 300 rolls and finds that her dice lands on a 6 thirty-eight times.
Whose results are more reliable?

7 R Owen has a drawing pin.
He says that it will land either point down or point up.
Since there are only two choices, each must have the same probability.
Owen tests his idea by tossing the drawing pin 100 times.
His results are point down 65 and point up 35.
Why is the experiment important?

8 R Mary is trying to improve her skills at long jump.
Here are the records of her last 40 jumps.

Distance (m)	Frequency
4.5–5.0	8
5.0–5.5	10
5.5–6.0	12
6.0–6.5	7
6.5–7.0	3

a Looking in total at her 40 jumps, what is the probability that she jumped
  i less than 6 metres
  ii between 5 and 6 metres?
b Why is using the record of her last 40 jumps unlikely to be a good method to predict her jump tomorrow?

9 R Chris supports his local football team.
They win their first five games.
Chris says this means they must win next week's game.
Is he correct? Explain why.

Reflect

10 Julia says that tomorrow it will either rain or it won't rain, so the probability of it raining is $\frac{1}{2}$.
What have you studied in this lesson that might help you convince Julia she is wrong?

6.5 Expected outcomes

- Use probability to estimate the expected number of outcomes
- Apply probabilities from experimental data in simple situations

1 In 2011, the probability of a driver making an insurance claim was 0.13.
In 2012, there were 33 million insured drivers in the UK.
Estimate the number of drivers making an insurance claim in 2012.

2 **R** In a game, people are invited to pay 20p to roll three dice.
If they get three 6s, they win £50.
The probability of rolling three 6s is $\frac{1}{216}$.
Is this game likely to make money? Explain your answer.

3 Raffle tickets numbered 1 to 100 are folded, and prizes awarded to any people picking a
ticket that ends in a 0 or a 5.
Each prize is worth 40p.
How much should the tickets cost to raise at least £10? Explain your answer.

4 In cricket, a googly is a way of bowling the ball.
The probability that Nate bowls a googly is 0.15.
How many googlies would you expect Nate to bowl in 40 deliveries?

5 **R** The probability that a computer microchip is faulty is 0.22 when the production process
is working properly.
A company employee found that six microchips were faulty out of a batch of 20.
Do you think that the production process is working properly? Explain your answer.

6 Archie rolls a fair dice 300 times.
How many 6s should he expect?

7 John tosses two fair coins 40 times.
How many times should he expect both to land on tails?

8 Esther intends to spin this spinner 50 times.
The percentages show how much of the
spinner is taken by each region.
  a How many times should she expect the
spinner to land on A?
  b How many times should she expect the
spinner to land on C?
  c How many times should she expect the
spinner *not* to land on B?

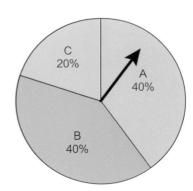

9 A fair dice is rolled 300 times.

    a How many 5s would you expect to see in the results?

    b The dice lands on a 3 forty-five times.
      How many fewer is this than expected?

    c R The dice doesn't land on 4 at all in the 300 rolls.
      Jason says he is surprised by this.
      Is he right to be surprised?
      Use probabilities and expected values to explain.

10 R Jenny has a coin she suspects is biased.
She flips it and records the results.
After 10 flips she has 4 heads.
After 20 flips she has 9 heads.
After 50 flips she has 20 heads.
Jenny says that 4 out of 10 is not $\frac{1}{2}$ so this is enough evidence her coin is biased.
Do you agree?

11 P-S / R Callum has two spinners.

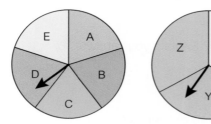

He spins the first one 50 times and the second one 30 times.
Should he expect to see more As or more Xs?

Reflect

12 Hiro rolls a dice 24 times and looks at his results.
He says, 'Getting a prime number has probability 3 out of 6, which is $\frac{1}{2}$, so I should
expect to get a prime number 12 times in my results.'
When he looks at his results, he has rolled a prime number 10 times.
Is the dice biased?

6 Extend

1   **P-S**   What angles should be used to design the sectors of a spinner so that the probability of red is $\frac{1}{4}$, the probability of green is $\frac{1}{3}$, and the only other colour on the spinner is blue?

2   **P-S**   There are 20 counters in a bag. 8 are white on both sides. 5 are black on both sides. The remainder are white on one side and black on the other. A counter is selected at random.
   a What is the probability that the counter is
      i a different colour on each side   **ii** white on at least one side
      iii black on at least one side?
   b R   Why do the answers for parts **ii** and **iii** add up to more than 1?

3   **P-S**   A spinner is designed to randomly choose a number from 1 to 3.
   The probability of number 2 being selected is twice as much as number 1.
   The probability of number 3 being selected is three times as much as number 1.
   a What is the probability of number 3 being selected?
   b What is the probability of an even number being selected?

4   A school summer fair has a tombola. Tickets numbered from 1 to 1000 are in a bucket.
   People pay to choose a numbered ticket, and win a prize if the number ends in a 0 or a 5.
   a How many winning tickets are there?
   b Finn buys 5 tickets. How many prizes should he expect to win?
   c Dylan buys 10 tickets. Is he guaranteed to win more prizes than Finn?

5   A school runs a fundraising prize draw called the 100-Club. The top prize is £100.
   The probability of winning is $\frac{1}{100}$. People pay £1 per week to play.
   The prize draw runs once a week for 40 weeks every year.
   You enter the draw every week it runs for five years.
   a How many times would you expect to win?
   b How much profit would you expect to make?

6   **P-S**   It appears that Thea's teacher chooses students at random to answer questions.
   But Thea notices that students in the front row are chosen three times more often than students in the middle row, and those in the middle row are chosen three times more often than those in the back row. What is the probability that someone in the back row will be chosen?

7   **R**   When a plate is dropped on the floor, there is a 40% chance that it breaks.
   Over one day 6 plates were broken. How many were dropped?

8   **P-S**   Red, green and blue counters are placed in a bag. One is selected at random.
   The probability that the counter is red is 20%.
   The probability that a green counter is selected is $\frac{3}{4}$.
   a What is the probability of selecting a blue counter?
   b What is the smallest number of counters that could be in the bag?
   c There are 3 blue counters in the bag. How many green counters are there?

9 **P-S / R** There are red and blue counters in a bag. The probability of choosing a red counter is $\frac{3}{8}$. What is the minimum number of blue counters that need to be added to the bag so that the probability of choosing a red counter is $\frac{1}{4}$?

10 Drawing pins can land point up or point down.
Amy tosses a pair of drawing pins 100 times and records these results.

Both point up	36
Both point down	16
One each way	48

Work out the probability that exactly one drawing pin would land point up.

11 **P-S** A set of cards, numbered from 1 to 9, is put in a bag and one is selected at random. What is the probability of

a choosing an odd number

b choosing a number lower than the mean

c choosing a number that is not a multiple of 3?

12 **P-S** Annie, Barney and Charlie each have a chair to sit on. They choose chairs at random. What is the probability that they sit in alphabetical order?

13 **P-S** The letters of ANNE are each printed on a different card, and the cards shuffled. Two are selected at random. What is the probability the cards chosen are A and N?

14 **P-S / R** Rory never runs on Monday.
The probability of him running on Tuesday is the same as on Wednesday.
He is twice as likely to run on Thursday as on Tuesday.
He is twice as likely to run on Friday as on Thursday.
On Saturday and Sunday, the probability of him running is 10%.
He only ever runs once in a week.
What is the probability that Rory runs on Friday?

15 **P-S** Eloise thinks of a 2-digit number. She tells Lily that it is not a cube, a prime or a square. Lily guesses Eloise's number. What is the probability that Lily guesses correctly?

Investigation

16 Is it more likely to snow at Christmas or Easter? How would you investigate?

Reflect

17 A class at school spend some time rolling dice and recording their results.
This is the data they collect.

Number	1	2	3	4	5	6
Frequency	95	84	89	111	116	105

Use what you have learned in this lesson to comment on the fairness of their dice.

7 Ratio and proportion

Master   Extend p99

7.1 Direct proportion

- Use direct proportion in simple contexts
- Solve simple problems involving direct proportion
- Use the unitary method to solve simple word problems involving direct proportion

1 Last year a school bought ties for each of the 250 students in Year 7. This cost £1125. This year they need 280 ties. How much will they cost?

2 **P-S** Jonathon's car can travel 315 miles on 35 litres of petrol.
Sandra's car can travel 240 miles on 30 litres of petrol.
Whose car is more economical?

3 **P-S** Here is a recipe for pancakes for four people.
Sophie makes pancakes for 14 people.
She has 800 g of flour, 1200 ml of milk and 10 eggs.
Does she have enough ingredients?

Serves 4 people
200 g flour
350 ml milk
2 eggs

4 **P-S** A shop-keeper wants to charge 1.5 times as much per toilet roll for offer B than offer A.
What is the price for offer B?

Offer A
8 toilet rolls
£2.40

Offer B
3 toilet rolls
?

5 **R** Here are some multipacks of crisps.
Each pack is the same brand and contains the same size of smaller packs.

SMALL MULTIPACK
5 packets of crisps
£1.50

MEDIUM MULTIPACK
10 packets of crisps
£2.98

LARGE MULTIPACK
20 packets of crisps
£5.50

Which is best value for money? Explain your answer.

6 **P-S / R** A shop has Easter eggs on offer.

OFFER A
3 for £10.50

OFFER B
5 for £17.50

OFFER C
6 for £20.40

a Which offer is the best value for money?
b Write your own offer, D, that is better value than A but worse value than C.

7 A school canteen has 3 cooks and serves 30 people in 30 seconds.
How long would it take to serve 500 people?

8 **R** A school is having a new fence put around the playing field.
The two people working can construct 5 m of fence every 30 minutes.
a How long will it take them to construct 200 m of fencing?
Rob thinks that 20 people working should be able to construct 50 m of fence every 30 minutes.
b Why might Rob be wrong?

9 This design needs 16 tiles to cover a 40 cm by 40 cm area.
How many tiles would be needed to cover
a 40 cm by 120 cm
b 80 cm by 200 cm
c 50 cm by 50 cm?

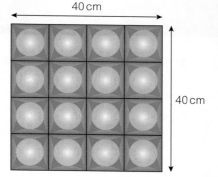

40 cm

40 cm

10 **R** Stevie is struggling to find an easy way to mentally divide 464 by 8.
Her friend suggests halving then halving again, and then halving again.
a Explain why her friend is correct.
b Explain how to extend this method to dividing by 16.
c What is 464 ÷ 16?

11 James measures the length of some string in both centimetres and inches.
a He doubles the length of the string.
What happens to the measurements in centimetres and inches?
b He divides the length of the string by three.
What happens to the measurements in centimetres and inches?

12 **P-S** 3 apples cost the same as 4 oranges. 3 oranges cost the same as 5 bananas.
How many bananas would cost the same as 9 apples?

13 **P-S / R** Harriet has a recipe that serves 8 people. She needs to adapt it to serve 12 people.
She divides each recipe item by 8 to work out the recipe for 1 person, then multiplies by 12.
Her sister suggests that she halves the recipe so that it serves 4 people, then multiplies by 3. Which method is better? Explain.

Reflect

14 **a** In which questions did you
  i divide to find 1 item, and then multiply
  ii use halving or doubling?
b How did you decide which method to use?

7.2 Writing ratios

- Use ratio notation
- Reduce a ratio to its simplest form
- Reduce a three-part ratio to its simplest form by cancelling

1 The bar chart shows the number of boys and girls at an after-school club.

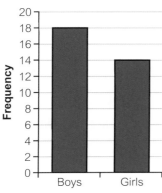

What is the ratio of boys to girls?

2 **P-S / R** These are the points scored in different matches by a netball club's 'A' team and 'B' team.

'A' team	8	12	15	18	16	10	17	22	21	16	21
'B' team	10	17	9	6	18	10	14	18	15	11	15

  a Write the teams' mean scores as a ratio A : B.
  b What does this tell you about the teams' performances?

3 **P-S** A farmer has some sheep and some cows.
  a Write down the ratio of heads to feet for all their animals.
  b Another farmer has 100 animals.
    At least one is a sheep and at least one is a duck.
    The farmer only has sheep and ducks.
    What is the maximum and minimum possible ratios of heads to feet for the 100 animals?

4 Write down the ratio of white beads to red beads to black beads in the following designs.
  a
  b
  c

5 A charity divides its budget like this:
  35% for wages
  40% for resourcing
  25% for marketing
  Write the ratio spent on wages to resourcing to marketing in its simplest form.

6 Write each ratio in its simplest form.

    a $5:15:45$ **b** $14:28:77$

    c $18:99:117$ **d** $500:675:350$

7 **P-S** Karen is 12 years old.
Jane is 3 years older than Karen and 3 years younger than Sarah.
Write the ratio of Karen's age to Jane's age to Sarah's age in its simplest form.

8 Michael has 240 Twitter followers.
Godfrey has twice as many followers as Michael and $\frac{1}{3}$ fewer than David.
Write the ratio of the number of Michael's to Godfrey's to David's Twitter followers as a ratio in its simplest form.

9 Write down the ratio of edges to corners to faces on

    a a cube

    b a cuboid

    c a tetrahedron.

> **Key point** A **tetrahedron** is a triangular-based pyramid.

10 Some metals are combined to form alloys.
Write the composition of each alloy as a ratio in its simplest form.

    a 100 g of brass is made from 65 g of copper and 35 g of zinc.

    b 800 g of bronze is made from 700 g of copper and 100 g of tin.

    c 300 g of white gold is made from 135 g of gold, the rest silver.

    d Alnico is a mix of four metals, used to make powerful magnets. 300 g of alnico is made from 27 g of aluminium, 63 g of nickel, 72 g of copper and the rest is iron.

Investigation

11 24 counters are split into two groups, so that the number of counters in at least one of the groups is a factor of 24.

    a Work out all possible groupings.

    b Write each of the groupings as a ratio in its simplest form.

Reflect

12 Tim has mixed red and white paint in the ratio $5:2$ to create pink.
His sister Janet has mixed red and white paint in the ratio $7:3$.
Their shades of pink look very similar, but are slightly different.
Use what you have learned in this unit to explain the difference.

> **Hint** Write each ratio in the form $35:$ something.

7.3 Using ratios

- Use ratios and measures
- Divide a quantity into two parts in a ratio given in words
- Divide a quantity into two parts in a given ratio
- Solve word problems involving ratio

1   Alice and Bob share some money in the ratio 50 : 70 and Alice receives £650.
How much money does Bob receive?

2   A hairdresser makes hair colouring by mixing dye with peroxide solution in the ratio 1 : 2.
He wants 0.45 litres of hair colouring.

> **Q2 hint** Start by changing 0.45 litres into millilitres.

   a   How much dye does he use?

   b   How much peroxide solution does he use?

   c   Show how you checked your answers to parts **a** and **b**.

3   Gilding metal is made from zinc and copper in the ratio 1 : 19.
How much copper is in 1.2 kg of gilding metal?
Show how you checked your answer.

4   Brass is made by combining copper and zinc in the ratio 13 : 7.

   a   How much zinc is needed to combine with 52 g of copper?

   b   How much brass is made?

5   **P-S**   Jenny gives some of her earnings to charity.
The ratio of the amount she keeps to the amount she gives to charity is 9 : 1.
In 2012, Jenny earned £18 000. In 2013, she earned £23 000.
How much more did Jenny give to charity in 2013 than in 2012?

6   **R**

   a   Write the ratio 4 m : 200 cm in its simplest form.

   b   Does it matter whether you convert 200 cm to m or 4 m to cm?

7   Simplify

   a   2 m : 150 cm   b   250 cm : 4 m   c   2 km : 1200 m   d   1.2 cm : 36 mm

   e   1 day : 6 hours   f   8 hours : 2 days   g   63 kg : 200 g   h   2 weeks : 14 days

8   A patio is created using 1 m square tiles.
What is the ratio of the number of edge tiles to the number of middle tiles when the whole patio is:

   a   4 m by 8 m   b   4 m by 12 m   c   5 m by 5 m?

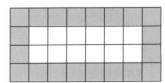

9   The diagram shows the amount of each ingredient in 800 ml of salad dressing.

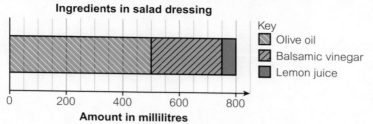

Ingredients in salad dressing

Key
Olive oil
Balsamic vinegar
Lemon juice

Amount in millilitres

a Write the ratio of olive oil to balsamic vinegar to lemon juice in its simplest form.

b Work out the amount of balsamic vinegar needed for 2.4 litres of salad dressing.

11 **R** $a:b = 1:2$ and $b:c = 3:4$. What is the ratio $a:b:c$?

12 **P-S**   Freya and Tom share some chocolate in the ratio $3:4$.
    Tom receives 35 g more chocolate than Freya.
    How much chocolate do they have in total?

13 **P-S / R**   Safety rules for a school trip insist that there are at least 2 staff on every 50-seat
    coach. There is also 1 member of staff on every minibus. The minibus can seat 15 people.
    The overall ratio of staff to students for a school trip must be at least $1:20$.
    A trip is suggested using 1 coach and 2 minibuses.
    Will the overall ratio of staff to students be safe?

14 **P-S**   James, Osaka and Karim share some money in the ratio $9:4:2$.
    Osaka has £15 more than Karim. Work out how much each person has.

15 **P-S**   A recipe for shortbread uses sugar to butter to flour in the ratio $1:2:3$.
    Using 200 g of flour will make 20 pieces of shortbread.
    How much shortbread can be made from 300 g of sugar, 200 g of butter and 1 kg of flour?

16 **P-S / R**   Amy, Brian and Chaya share some sweets between them in the ratio $3:4:5$.
    Explain why it is not possible for Chaya to have 5 more sweets than Amy.

17 **P-S**   White gold is made using gold and silver in the ratio $9:11$.
    Silver is a tenth of the cost of gold.
    What is the ratio of the value of white gold : pure gold?

7.4 Ratios, proportions and fractions

- Use fractions to describe and compare proportions
- Understand and use the relationship between fractions, ratio and proportion

1 Bronze is $\frac{1}{8}$ tin and the rest copper. Write the ratio of tin : copper in its simplest form.

2 In a wallpaper design, $\frac{3}{5}$ of the design is squares and $\frac{2}{5}$ of the design is triangles.
   Write the ratio of squares to triangles in its simplest form.

3 $\frac{7}{10}$ of the Earth is water and $\frac{3}{10}$ is land. Write this as a ratio.

4 In a class of students, $\frac{5}{6}$ are right handed and $\frac{1}{6}$ are left handed.
   Write the ratio of right-handed students to left-handed students.

5 R   James says that a $\frac{1}{2}$ and $\frac{1}{2}$ mixture is the same as a 1 : 2 ratio. Explain why he is incorrect.

6 For a charity art exhibition, James gives 12 paintings, Jaya gives 8 and Fernando gives 5.
   a Write the numbers of paintings as a ratio.
   b What proportion of the paintings does each artist give?

7 The table shows the number of
   teaspoons of different spices
   used in two different curry recipes.
   Which curry has the greater
   proportion of chilli in the spice mix?

Spice mix	Chicken curry	Egg curry
Turmeric	1	2
Chilli	2	1
Coriander	6	3
Cumin	5	1
Garam masala	4	1

8 R   The table shows the number
   of visitors to the top three zoos in
   the UK in 2011 and 2012.

Zoo	2011	2012
Chester	1 425 319	1 405 233
London	1 090 741	974 433
Whipsnade	502 785	476 226

   a David said,
      'In 2012, more than half of the visitors to the top three zoos went to Chester.'
      Is this correct? If not, suggest what David meant to say.
   b Jem said,
      'In 2011, a third of the visitors to the top three zoos went to Whipsnade.'
      Is this correct? If not, suggest what Jem meant to say.

9 P-S   A recycling plant separates materials from fridges.
   In a fridge, 50% of its mass is iron, 10% is other metals and the rest is plastic.
   a Write the ratio of the mass of iron to other metals
      to plastic in its simplest form.
   b What fraction of the mass of the fridge is plastic?

> **Q9b hint** Write your answer in its simplest form.

10 Concrete is made by combining cement, sand and aggregate in the ratio $1:3:3$.
What fraction of concrete is cement?

11 P-S Jane and Mark have an equal number of stickers.
Jane gives $\frac{1}{5}$ of her stickers to Mark.

Q11 hint Draw a bar model to help.

Jane [bar model]
Mark [bar model]

  a Write the ratio of the number of Jane's stickers to
Mark's stickers. Write the ratio in its simplest form.
  b Mark has 12 more stickers than Jane.
How many stickers does Jane have now?
  c How many stickers do they have altogether?

12 P-S Simon and Clare have an equal number of video games.
Simon gives $\frac{2}{5}$ of his video games to Clare.

  a Write the ratio of the number of video games that Simon has to the number Clare has now.
  b Clare has 24 more video games than Simon. How many video games does Simon have?
  c How many video games do they have altogether?

13 The table shows the number of visitors
to the top three attractions in London.

  a For each attraction, write the ratio of
visitors in 2011 to 2012 in its
simplest form.

Attraction	2011	2012
British Museum	5.8 million	5.6 million
Tate Modern	4.89 million	5.3 million
National Gallery	5.3 million	5.42 million

  b Has the proportion of visitors going to the British Museum increased?

14 P-S In a car-park, $\frac{1}{5}$ of the spaces are reserved for cars with children.
Write the ratio of spaces for cars with children, to cars without children, in its simplest form.

15 P-S / R Sally has a mix of red and blue counters, with $\frac{1}{3}$ being red.
Keith has a mix of red and yellow counters, with $\frac{2}{3}$ being red.
In total Keith has twice as many counters as Sally.
If all the counters are put together, what fraction will be yellow?

16 P-S / R Tim has some white and black counters, with $\frac{1}{3}$ being white.
Tom has some white and black counters, with $\frac{2}{3}$ being white.
Tom has twice as many black counters as Tim.
In total, what is the ratio of white to black counters?

17 P-S / R In a class of 30 students 10 wear glasses, and 13 have dark hair.
$\frac{1}{2}$ of the students with glasses also have dark hair.
For the group of students with dark hair, what is the ratio of glasses to no glasses?

Reflect

18 In this lesson, you were asked questions about ratios and proportions.
Are ratio and proportion the same thing or different? Explain.

7.5 Proportions and percentages

- Use percentages to describe proportions
- Use percentages to compare simple proportions
- Understand and use the relationship between percentages, ratio and proportion

1 In the 2012 Olympic Games, the Netherlands won gold, silver and bronze medals in the ratio 6:6:8. What proportion of the medals were
  a gold   **b** bronze?
  Write your answers as percentages.

2 **P-S** Jenna practises two stunts on her skateboard. The table shows the success of her attempts.
  a In what proportion of attempts was she successful?
  b At which stunt was she more successful?

	Stunt 1	Stunt 2
Failed	5	7
Nailed it!	15	18

3 The table shows the number of matches two football teams win, lose and draw in one season.

	Win	Lose	Draw
Team A	5	8	3
Team B	6	11	3

  a Write the proportion of matches lost by each team as a percentage.
  b Which team lost the higher proportion of matches?

4 **P-S / R** Jennie and Claire make lemonade.
  The ratio of lemon to water in Jennie's lemonade is 2:3.
  The ratio of lemon to water in Claire's lemonade is 9:11.
  Use proportions to explain which lemonade is stronger.

  > **Q4 hint** Write the proportions as percentages.

Investigation

5 There are 20 counters in a bag.
  The counters are red, blue or green.
  There are more red than blue, and more blue than green.
  Consider all possibilities and describe the number of blue counters as a percentage of all 20 counters.

6 Esther has created a fruit drink called Aponge.
  The drink is a mixture of apple juice and orange juice. 40% of the mixture is orange juice.
  a Write the ratio of apple juice to orange juice in its simplest form.
  b Esther wants to make 1 litre of Aponge. How much apple juice will she need?
  c Esther has 2.4 litres of apple juice and 1500 ml of orange juice.
    i How much Aponge can she make?
    ii How much apple juice will she have left over?

7 For each diagram, write

   a the fraction of counters that are black or red

   b the percentage of counters that are black or red

   c the ratio of black and red to white counters.

   Give all answers in their simplest form.

8 Bill and Loice are the only two goalkeepers on a hockey team.
In their last match Bill played for 35% of the time.

   a Write down the ratio of Bill playing to Loice playing.

   b P-S The match lasted for 50 minutes.
     How long did Loice play for?

9 James, Carl and Bree share some chocolates so that:
   James has 30%
   Carl has 0.45 of the chocolates
   Bree has the rest.
Write this as a ratio in its simplest form.

10 P-S / R When analysing experiments, Amber is looking to see which results occur more than 95% of the time. Do any of these results match her criterion?

   a Omar scores 18 out of 20.   **b** Zane achieves 48 out of 50.

   c Adele's ratio of winning:losing is 19:6.   **d** Jaya is successful $\frac{198}{200}$ times.

11 P-S In a pond, 35% of the fish are goldfish, 50% are carp and the rest are minnows.

   a Write the ratio of fish in its simplest form.

   b There are 14 goldfish and 20 carp. How many minnows are there?

12 P-S / R The pie chart shows the proportions of different items that make up a family's recycling.

   a Measure the angles in the pie chart.

   b Write the ratio of cans, glass, boxes and
     newspapers recycled as a ratio in its simplest form.

   c In July, the family recycled 24 cans.
     How many boxes did they recycle?

   d In August, they recycled 160 items.
     Did they recycle more boxes in July or August?

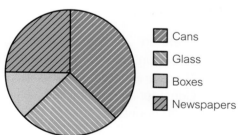

Reflect

13 Look back at the questions you have answered.
When is it better to use ratios to make comparisons?
When is it better to use proportions?

7 Extend

1 P-S   Arthur and Beth are counting their money.
They find that if Arthur gives Beth £5 then they would both
have the same amount of money, but if Beth gives Arthur
£5 then he would have three times as much money as her.
Write the ratio of the amount of money Arthur has to the amount of money Beth has.
Write the ratio in its simplest form.

> **Q1 hint** Work out how much money each person has first.

2 The purity of gold alloys is measured using the carat
system. The relationship between the percentage of
gold and the number of carats is shown in the table.
Work out the carat rating of the following gold alloys.
  a Red gold: 3 parts gold and 1 part copper
  b Green gold: made from 150 g gold, 30 g silver,
    12 g copper and 8 g cadmium
  c White gold: made from 45 g gold and 15 g nickel

Percentage of gold	Carat
58.33–62.50%	14 C
75.00–79.16%	18 C
91.66–95.83%	22 C
95.83–99.95%	23 C
99.95–100%	24 C

3 A square is split into 9 identical smaller squares.
The middle square is removed and stuck onto the outside of the larger square.

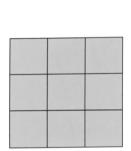 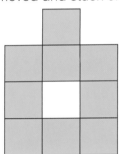

What is the ratio of the external perimeter of the new shape to the perimeter of the
original square?

Investigation

4 You are given 24 squares and asked to arrange them to make a rectangle.
For each possible rectangle work out the ratio of the length of its longest side to its perimeter
in its simplest terms.

---

5 A grasshopper takes 2 seconds to make 5 jumps.
How long will it take it to make 12 jumps?

6 P-S / R   Concrete can be made by mixing cement, sand and stone, in the ratio 3 : 7 : 8.
To make 1 cubic metre requires 7 bags of cement.
Cement, sand and stone come in the same size of bags.
How much sand is needed to make 12 cubic metres of concrete?

7 P-S / R A porridge recipe, to serve four people, uses 440 g oats and 1.1 litres of milk. James is trying to make porridge for 37 people. He has 4 kg of oats and 9 litres of milk. How much more of each ingredient does he need to buy?

8 P-S / R On a farm there are some chickens and some cows.
The ratio of chickens to cows is $31 : 12$.
In total the animals have 440 feet.
How many chickens are there?

9 R In a fruit salad containing identically sized pieces of apple, melon and pineapple the proportion of ingredients can be described as:

the ratio $5 : 6 : 9$

percentages of 25%, 30% and 45%

fractions of $\frac{1}{5}$, $\frac{3}{10}$ and $\frac{9}{20}$

A total mass of 1 kg of fruit salad is required.
a Work out how much of each ingredient is needed following each of the descriptions above.
b Which description did you find the easiest to work with and why?

10 P-S A running club has over 500 members in three categories of members: juniors, adults and seniors. The ratio of juniors to adults is $8 : 25$. The ratio of adults to seniors is $19 : 7$. What is the lowest possible total number of members in the running club?

11 P-S A school counts Years 7 to 9 as juniors, and Years 10 and 11 as seniors.
This year there are 200 students in each junior year, and 150 students in each senior year.
Next year the school is expecting 250 students to join Year 7.
What is the ratio of
a juniors to seniors this year and next year
b juniors this year to juniors next year?

12 R The ratio $a : b$ is $2 : 3$, the ratio $b : c$ is $2 : 5$ and the ratio $c : d$ is $2 : 7$.
What is the ratio $a : d$?

13 P-S A rectangle is stretched so that it is 3 times wider and twice as high.
What is the ratio of the area of the stretched rectangle to the area of the original rectangle?

14 P-S / R In Year 8 there are 120 children.
On a cold day everyone is wearing either a hat or a scarf, but not both.
The ratio of hats to scarves is $8 : 3$ for the boys and $6 : 7$ for the girls.
The ratio of boys to girls is $11 : 13$.
Work out the ratio of boys to girls just for the children wearing hats.

Reflect

15 Financial ratios and proportions are used a lot by businesses to show how well they are performing.
Use what you have learned in this unit to give some examples of the types of ratio and proportion you think may be used by a business to demonstrate its performance.

8 Lines and angles

Master   Extend p113

8.1 Measuring and drawing angles

- Use a protractor to measure and draw angles
- Recognise acute, obtuse and reflex angles

1 A large jet plane takes off at an angle of about 8°.
Draw an accurate diagram to show this angle.

2 Which of these six angles is the largest?

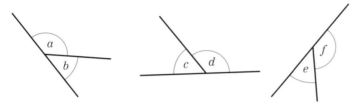

3 **P-S** This spinner has four sectors.
Each sector wins a prize.

    a Which prize do you have the best chance of winning?
    b Which prize do you have the least chance of winning?

4 **R** If you add two acute angles, do you get an obtuse angle?

5 How many *different* angles are shown on this diagram?
Measure each one.

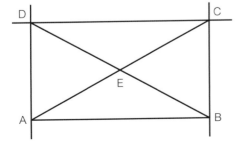

6 Road signs on hills warn of how steep each hill is. The percentage represents the height compared to the base of a right-angled triangle drawn under the hill.
Draw a triangle for each of these hills and measure the angle the hill makes with the horizontal.

7 An angle of latitude shows the angle between the equator and a line drawn from the centre of the Earth to a point on the Earth.

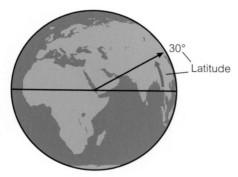

Draw angles to represent the latitude of these three cities.
  a Mumbai, 19° **b** Frankfurt, 50° **c** Stockholm, 59°

8 **P-S / R** Tim measures the angles of a triangle to be 140°, 110° and 150°. What error has Tim made with his protractor? What are the correct angles?

9 What is the maximum number of obtuse angles that can fit on a pie chart?

10 What is the maximum number of obtuse angles a triangle can have?

11 R
  a 180° on a straight line is split into two angles. What types of angles could they be?
  b 180° on a straight line is split into three angles. What types of angles could they be?
  c 180° on a straight line is split into four angles. What types of angles could they be?

12 Parts **a** to **e** consider three angles around a point.
  If the layout is possible, draw it and mark on the angles.
  If it is not possible, write 'not possible'.
  a Two acute angles and one reflex angle
  b Three acute angles
  c One acute angle, one obtuse angle and one reflex angle
  d One acute angle and two obtuse angles
  e Three right angles

13 Consider the capital letters that use only straight lines and no curves.

    a Which letters use only right angles?

    b Which letters use obtuse angles?

    c Which letters use both obtuse angles and acute angles?

14 Chloe finds a large compass rose on the pavement. She stands on it facing north.

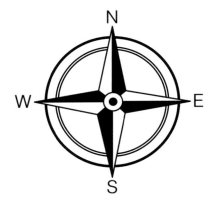

Start each time facing north. In which direction is Chloe facing after she does:

a three half-turns

b one quarter-turn, then two quarter-turns, then three quarter-turns (all in the same direction)

c a quarter-turn clockwise, then a three-quarter-turn anti-clockwise, then a half-turn?

15 P-S How many right angles are there on the surface of a cube?

16 Name the angles in the diagram that are part of triangles that include vertex D.

> **Q16 hint** The **vertices** (plural of vertex) of a triangle are its corners.

What types of angles are they: acute, obtuse, reflex or right angles?

Reflect

17 Explain why it is impossible to have two obtuse angles only

    a in a right angle

    b on a straight line

    c around a point.

8.2 Lines, angles and triangles

- Estimate the size of angles
- Describe and label lines, angles and triangles
- Identify angle and side properties of triangles

1 Draw a rectangle ABCD where AB is 6 cm and BC is 8 cm. Measure
  a the length of diagonal AC   **b** the size of each angle in triangle ABC.

Investigation

2 Using a scale of 1 cm : 2 m, draw a scale drawing of a room measuring 8 m by 10 m.
  a Measure the length of the diagonal on your diagram.
  b Calculate the length of the diagonal in the room.

3 Sketch a square EFGH.
  What type of triangle is EFG?

> **Q3 hint** 'Sketch' means 'draw a rough diagram'. It does not have to be accurate.

4 **R** James says the answer to Q3 is 'right-angled' but John says it is 'isosceles'.
  Can they both be correct?

5 **a** Sketch a right-angled scalene triangle.
  b R Is it possible to draw a scalene triangle with two right angles? Explain your answer.

6 **a** Draw an acute angle PQR.   **b** Draw an obtuse angle XYZ.

7 What is the correct mathematical name for these triangles?

a   b   c   d   e

8 Which one of these angles is
  a 40°   **b** 60°

9 **P-S a** Sketch a triangle ABC so that angle ABC is 40° and angle BCA is a right angle.
  b Sketch a triangle PQR so that angles QRP and PQR are both 60°.

Investigation

10 How many different isosceles triangles can you create using only angles that are multiples of 20°?

Reflect

11 **a** Which pairs of words can apply to a single triangle?
  b Is it possible for three of these words to apply to a single triangle? Explain.

> scalene   isosceles
> right-angled   equilateral

8.3 Drawing triangles accurately

* Use a ruler and protractor to draw triangles accurately

1   Draw these three triangles accurately.
    Measure side A in millimetres in each one.

a

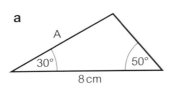

b

8 cm

c

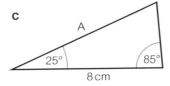

2   Draw two triangles with different length sides but each with 90°, 60° and 30° angles.

3   Draw two triangles with different length sides but each with 50°, 60° and 70° angles.

4   A regular pentagon has angles of 108° at
    each vertex.
    Draw a regular pentagon with 5 cm sides.

> **Q4 hint** Start with an isosceles triangle with
> an 108° angle and 5 cm either side of it.

5   Draw an equilateral triangle with 6 cm sides.
    Measure the height.

> **Q5 hint** The height is the measurement
> inside the triangle from the top to the base,
> making a right angle with the base.

6   Draw the two possible isosceles triangles with
    sides of 4 cm and 3 cm.

7   Draw this triangle accurately.

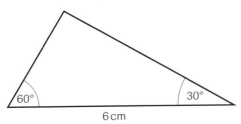

Work out the difference in length between the longest and shortest sides.

8   Re-draw the triangle from Q7, swapping over the two angles.
    What is the same about your two versions of the triangle?

9   Draw an isosceles right-angled triangle with two sides of 5 cm.
    Measure the length of the hypotenuse.

10 Draw a triangle with sides of 3 cm, 4 cm and 5 cm.
    Draw three equilateral triangles, one based on each side of the original triangle.

11 Draw two isosceles triangles with sides of 7 cm, 7 cm and 4 cm.
Draw them so they have the 4 cm side in common.

12 Draw this diagram accurately.
Measure the perimeter of the quadrilateral you have drawn.

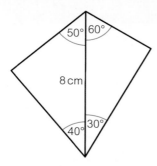

13 **P-S** This diagram has a vertical line of symmetry.
Make an accurate drawing of the diagram and measure the perimeter of the shaded shape.

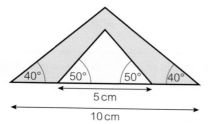

14 Draw these triangles accurately. Measure any missing sides and angles.

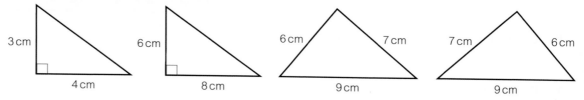

---

15 Imagine you are given a 12 cm piece of string.
What triangles can you make that have each side as a whole number of centimetres?

16 Liam says, 'You can draw many different triangles all with the same size angles but different length sides.'
Sam says, 'You can also draw many different triangles all with the same length sides but different angles.'
Are they both correct? Explain your answer.

8.4 Calculating angles

- Use the rules for angles on a straight line, angles around a point and vertically opposite angles
- Solve problems involving angles

1 Give an example of the sizes of angles that split a circle into a reflex, an obtuse and an acute angle.

2 **P-S** Three angles fit on a straight line. The angles are in the ratio $1:2:3$.
What is the size of the smallest angle?

3 **P-S** Four angles fit around a point. The angles are in the ratio $1:2:5:7$.
What is the size of the largest angle?

4 **P-S** Draw a pie chart with four sectors in the ratio $1:2:3:4$.

5 Look at the diagram.
Work out the sizes of angles a, b and c.
What rule did you use in each case?

6 Work out the sizes of all the missing angles in this diagram.

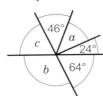

7 **P-S** Work out the size of the smallest angle in this diagram.

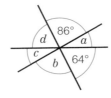

8 **P-S** There are three angles on a straight line.
One is a right angle and the remaining two are in the ratio $1:5$.
What is the size of the smallest angle?

9 **P-S** There are three angles around a point.
One takes $\frac{1}{3}$ of the whole and one takes 30%.
Work out the size of the remaining angle.

10 **P-S / R** There are five angles around a point.
When written in numerical order, the angles increase in steps of $10°$.
What is the size of the median angle?

11 P-S / R There are four angles on a straight line. One is 60°.
When written in numerical order, the other three angles increase in steps of 20°.
What is the size of the smallest angle?

12 a There are 30 equal angles drawn around a point.
What is the size of each angle?

b There are 180 equal angles drawn around a point.
What is the size of each angle?

c There are 360 equal angles drawn around a point.
What is the size of each angle?

d R Calculate the size of each of 3600 equal angles drawn around a point.
Explain why this might be impossible to draw.

13 P-S / R Rebecca is designing a pattern.
She marks angles of 12° around a point, starting as
shown in the diagram and continuing all the way round.
She marks a point on each line so that all of the points
are the same distance from point A.
She then joins up all of these new points to make a
regular polygon.

a How many sides does the regular polygon have?

b The regular polygon has sides with length 4 cm.
What is the perimeter of the polygon?

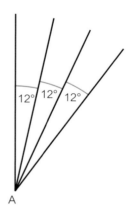

14 P-S / R

a Is it possible to draw

i three angles on a straight line with a mode of 40°

ii four angles around a point with a range of 0°

iii five angles on a straight line with a mean of 45°

iv seven angles around a point with a median of 121°?

b Draw a set of angles around a point so that the mode, median, mean and range are all
equal to 60°.

Reflect

15 Steve likes right angles. He says he remembers 180° for a straight line because it is two
right angles, and 360° around a point is from four right angles.

Ruth finds it easy to remember 180° for a straight line and then mentally joins two straight
lines back to back to make 360° around a point.

Tom finds the 360° around a point easiest to remember, then cuts it in half to make two
straight lines (so each is 180°) and half again to make right angles.

Who are you most like? How do you remember the size of a right angle, the angles on a
straight line and the angle around a point?

8.5 Angles in a triangle

- Use the rule for the sum of angles in a triangle
- Calculate interior and exterior angles
- Solve angle problems involving triangles

1 Work out the sum of the three exterior angles shown on this diagram.

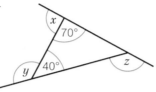

2 This is a scissor truss. It is used to build a cathedral or vaulted ceiling.

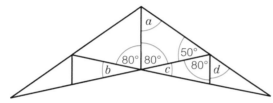

Work out the size of each unknown angle.

3 **P-S** Three triangles are drawn inside a rectangle. Work out the size of angle a.

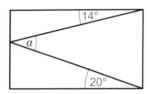

4 **P-S** Work out the size of angle d.

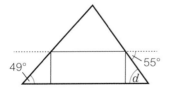

5 **P-S** The diagram shows two isosceles triangles. There are three sides with the same length.

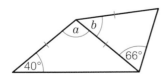

Work out the sizes of angles a and b.

6 **P-S** The angles in a triangle are in the ratio of $1 : 3 : 8$. Work out the size of the median angle.

7 P-S The angles in a triangle are in the ratio of $1:2:6$.
Work out the size of the largest external angle.

8 P-S One angle in an isosceles triangle is $37°$.
Work out the two possible differences between the other two angles.

9 Work out the size of angle x.

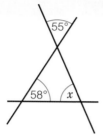

10 P-S In triangle ABC, AB = AC
and angle CAB = $40°$.
Line DC **bisects** angle ACB.
Work out the sizes of angles x, y and z.

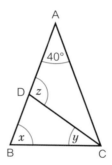

> **Q10 hint** If a line
> **bisects** an angle,
> then it divides
> the angle into
> two equal-sized
> smaller angles.

11 P-S / R The interior angles of a regular hexagon are $120°$.
Find the marked angle inside this regular hexagon.

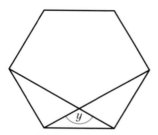

Reflect

12 Look at the diagram.
Explain how you would work out the interior and
exterior angle at point B.
Can you see a way to find the exterior angle
without first finding the interior one?

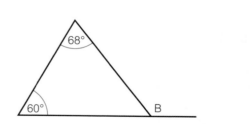

8.6 Quadrilaterals

- Identify and name types of quadrilaterals
- Use the rule for the sum of angles in a quadrilateral
- Solve angle problems involving quadrilaterals

1 **P-S** Look at the diagram.
Work out the missing angle.

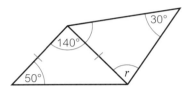

2 **P-S** This pattern is made up of three identical red rhombus tiles and three identical blue rhombus tiles.

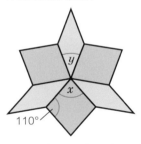

    a Work out the size of angle x.

    b What is the size of angle y?
      Show your working.

3 Look at the diagram. Work out the size of angle a.

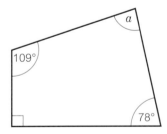

4 Look at the diagram.
    a Work out the size of
      i angle b **ii** angle c.
    b Add angles b and c together.
    c Was it easier to work out angles b and c
      in part **a**, or to find angle a in Q3?

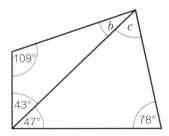

5 Find the missing angles r, s, t and u.

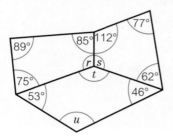

6 **P-S / R** In the diagram the inner shape is a square and the outer shape is a rectangle.

   a Work out the sizes of angles a, b, c and d.

   b Which angles are easiest to find? Why?

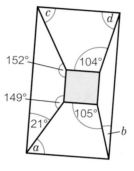

7 **P-S / R** The diagram shows a small square inside a larger square.

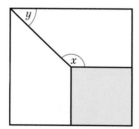

   Find the values of angles x and y.

8 **P-S / R** The diagram shows a square inside a larger quadrilateral.

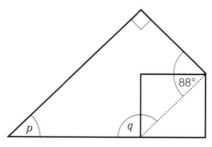

   a Find the sizes of angles p and q.

   b Which angle could you find first?

Reflect

9 In this section, you have used the fact that angles in a quadrilateral always add to 360°. What additional information do you know about angles in a parallelogram, a rhombus, a kite and a trapezium?

8 Extend

1 P-S The angles in a quadrilateral are in the ratio $3:5:7:21$. Find the difference between the largest and smallest angles.

2 P-S What is the mean angle in any quadrilateral?

3 P-S Find the size of angle e.

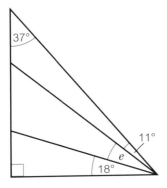

4 P-S / R A square is drawn inside a kite. Find the size of angle c.

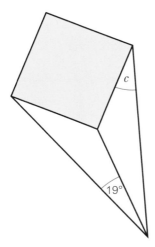

5 P-S / R The smallest angle of triangle B is equal to 75% of the smallest angle in triangle A. Find the size of the middle-sized angle in triangle B.

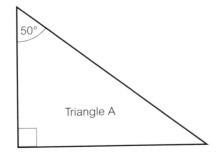 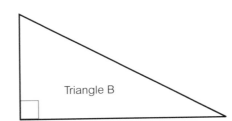

Triangle A   Triangle B

6 **P-S / R** The diagram shows triangle A.

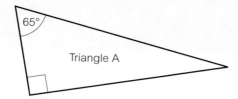

Triangle A

Triangle B is created so that its smallest angle is $\frac{3}{5}$ of the smallest angle of triangle A.
Another angle in triangle B is $\frac{5}{9}$ of the largest angle of triangle A.
Find the largest angle in triangle B.

7 **P-S / R** A square is drawn inside a non-isosceles trapezium.
The two triangles formed on either end have the same three angles.

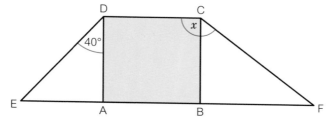

Work out the size of angle x.

8 **P-S / R** An equilateral triangle is drawn inside a larger triangle.
Lines XB and XA are the same length.

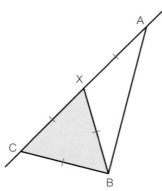

Find all the angles and explain how you know that triangle ABC is a right-angled triangle.

Investigation

9 Eight isosceles triangles are constructed inside a circle so that they form a regular octagon. Use what you've learned in this unit to find the internal angle of the regular octagon. Explain how this method could be used to find the internal angle of any size of regular polygon.

Reflect

10 List all the things you need to consider when finding a missing angle.

9 Sequences and graphs

Master   Extend p127

9.1 Sequences

- Recognise, describe and continue number sequences
- Generate terms of a sequence using a one-step term-to-term rule
- Find missing terms in a sequence

1 Decide whether each of these sets of numbers is finite or infinite.
  a multiples of 5
  b birthday dates
  c even numbers
  d temperatures throughout one day
  e integers less than 100
  f Are there more odd numbers than multiples of 5?

2 **P-S** Write two different ways to continue each of these number sequences.
  Write down the term-to-term rule you used and the next three numbers.
  a 1, 3, ...   **b** 1, 5, ...   **c** 3, 6, ...   **d** 8, 4, ...

3 Look at the sequences in Q2.
  a Which sequences are ascending?
  b R Another sequence has first term 8. You are not given the second term.
    Is it possible to decide whether this sequence is ascending? Explain.

4 **P-S** One grain of rice is placed on the first square of a chessboard, two grains on the
  second, four grains on the third, and so on, doubling the number on each square.
  a How many grains will be on the fifth square?
  b Which square will have 64 grains?

5 A car hire company offers a special six-month deal.
  For the first month it costs £300 to hire the car.
  For the second month the cost reduces by £20.
  Then it reduces by an extra £20 each month.
  a How much will it cost to hire the car in
    i the third month   **ii** the fifth month?
  b R Why is the deal for only six months?

6 **P-S** Work out the three missing terms in each sequence.
  a $\frac{1}{3}, \frac{2}{3}, 1, 1\frac{1}{3}$, __, __, __
  b __, $\frac{3}{4}, \frac{1}{2}$, __, 0, $-\frac{1}{4}$, __
  c $\frac{1}{2}, \frac{1}{3}, \frac{1}{4}$, __, __, __
  d __, 11, __, __, 17
  e 4, __, __, 19, __
  f -2, __, __, __, -10, -12
  g __, __, 8.9, __, 8.3
  h 0.5, __, __, __, 1.7

7 **R** Look back at the sequences in Q6.
The sequence in part **a** is infinite.
It goes towards positive infinity.

Q7 hint

$-\infty$ 0 $+\infty$

  a Which other sequence(s) go towards positive infinity?

  b Which sequence(s) go towards negative infinity?

  c The sequence in part **c** is infinite too. What value does this sequence go towards?

8 **P-S / R** The ages of Alice, her mother and her great-grandmother give the first numbers in a sequence with a term-to-term rule, multiply by 3. Alice's great-grandmother will be celebrating her 100th birthday next week. How old is Alice?

9 These sequences of fractions have a different rule for the numerator and the denominator. Write the next three terms of each sequence.

  a $\frac{1}{6}, \frac{3}{12}, \frac{5}{18}, \frac{7}{24}, \dots$ **b** $\frac{12}{30}, \frac{15}{60}, \frac{18}{120}, \frac{21}{240}, \dots$ **c** $\frac{3}{4}, \frac{9}{16}, \frac{27}{64}, \frac{81}{256}, \dots$

10 **P-S** Part of a sequence is 32, 39, 46.

  a What are the two terms before these numbers in the sequence?

  b What are the next two terms of this sequence?

  c A new term is inserted between each number: 32, …, 39, …, 46.
    Write the new term-to-term rule and the two missing terms.

  d The first term of the sequence in part **c** is a positive even number less than 10.
    Write the first 10 terms of the sequence.

11 R Harry writes the first 10 terms of a sequence using a term-to-term rule.
The first term is 38. The next term in the sequence is 11 less than the previous term.
Are there more positive or negative numbers in his list? Explain.

Investigation

12 A sequence is generated from this rule:
    Is the number even?
        Yes: halve it.   **No:** add 1.
    STOP when you reach 1.

  a What sequence would you create when you start at: **i** 20   **ii** 19   **iii** 18?

  b What starting number, under 50, would generate the longest sequence?

13 What is the first term in each of these sequences that is more than 100?

  a 1st term, 5   term-to-term rule: add 7

  b 1st term, 3   term-to-term rule: double and add 1

  c 1st term, 1   term-to-term rule: triple and subtract 1

14 **P-S** Write a single-digit even first term, and a term-to-term rule, so that the fifth term of the sequence is more than 100.

Reflect

15 What is always the same and what can be different about infinite sequences?

9.2 Pattern sequences

- Find patterns and rules in sequences
- Describe how a pattern sequence grows

1 For each sequence
   i   write the terms generated from each pattern
   ii write the 10th term in each sequence.

a

b

c

d

e

2 For each sequence
   i   draw the next pattern
   ii   copy and complete the table
   iii write the first term and the term-to-term rule.

a

Term number	1	2	3	4	5
Number of lines	6	11			

b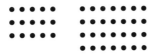

Term number	1	2	3	4	5	6
Number of dots	1	6	15			

3 **R** Frank generates a sequence by measuring the perimeters of these squares.
Will 22 be one of the terms in the sequence? Explain.

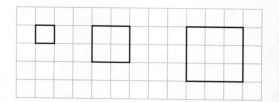

Investigation

4 A robotic rabbit is in a field. It is lonely.
It learns how to make a new robotic rabbit when it is 2 months old.
From then on, it can produce one new robotic rabbit each month.
Each new robotic rabbit works the same way, and can produce a new one when it is 2 months old.
The robotic rabbits never die.
How many robotic rabbits will there be after 6 months?

Hint Draw a diagram to show how many rabbits there are each month.

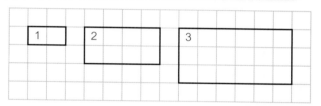

5 **P-S** A sequence is generated by measuring the perimeter of this sequence of rectangles. Each rectangle has a width that is twice its height.
What term in the sequence will be closest to 100?

6 Look at this sequence of expanding rectangles.
  a How many blue squares are in the next pattern?
  b How many white squares are in the next pattern?
  c How many squares in total are in the next pattern?
  d **P-S** One of the patterns has 132 squares.
    How many of the squares are
    i blue   **ii** white?

7 **R** Use grid paper to draw the first three shapes in each of two pattern sequences, where the shapes have perimeters 8, 14, 20, ...
Only one of your pattern sequences can be rectangles.
Do the 10th shapes in both pattern sequences have the same or different perimeters? Explain.

Reflect

8 In Q1, how does the shape that the dots are arranged in relate to the first term and the term-to-term rule?
Describe a similar pattern sequence that begins with dots in an octagonal arrangement.

Hint What would be the first term and the term-to-term rule?

9.3 Coordinates and midpoints

- Generate and plot coordinates from a rule
- Solve problems and spot patterns in coordinates
- Find the midpoint of a line segment

1 Draw a grid with x- and y-axes from −5 to 5.

  a Plot and label these points.

    A(3, 0)   B(2, 2)   C(0, 3)   D(−2, 2)

    E(−3, 0)   F(−2, −2)   G(0, −3)   H(2, −2)

  b Join the points in alphabetical order.
    What shape have you made?

2 Sarah writes sequences of pairs of coordinates.
  Look at the term-to-term rule for the x-coordinates and for the y-coordinates.
  Write the next three pairs of coordinates in each sequence.

  a (2, 1), (4, 2), (6, 3)   **b** (12, 3), (8, 5), (4, 7)

  c (5, 0), (3, −2), (1, −4)   **d** (−13, 13), (−7, 8), (−1, 3)

3 **P-S** Copy and complete the missing coordinates in each sequence of x- and y-coordinates.

  a (18, 4), (☐, 8), (10, ☐), (6, 16)

  b (3, 0), (0, ☐), (☐, 6), (−6, 9)

  c (−1, 5), (☐, ☐), (☐, 1), (5, −1)

4 **a** **P-S** Copy and complete the missing coordinates in each sequence.

    i (☐, 4), (−1, 4), (☐, ☐), (3, 4)

    ii (−2, 2), (☐, ☐), (2, 2), (☐, 2)

  b Draw a grid with x- and y- axes from −5 to 5.

    i Plot the points from part **a i** and label them A, C, E, G.

    ii Plot the points from part **a ii** and label them B, D, F, H.

  c Join A to B, C to D, E to F and G to H.

  d **R** Describe the pattern of the coordinates of midpoints for each line.

5 Jan is designing a building using a computer. She wants to place a stairwell at the midpoint of a wall. The wall goes from (5, 4) to (33, 6). What are the coordinates of the stairwell?

6 Find the midpoint of the line segment joining each pair of points.

  a A(2, 4) and B(2, 12)

  b X(11, 4) and Y(5, 4)

  c M(2, 5) and N(6, 9)

  d P(6, −2) and Q(4, 4)

  e G(−5, 2) and H(−1, −4)

  f V(20, −10) and W(−3, 1)

7 P-S

   a Work out the midpoint of the line segment joining (1, 5) and (−4, −2).

   b A line segment RS has a midpoint, M, at (7, 10). R is the point (5, 3).
      What are the coordinates of S?

8 The diagram shows three corners of a
   parallelogram ABCD.

   a What are the coordinates of point D?

   b P-S Work out the coordinates of the midpoints of

     i AB   **ii** CD   **iii** BC

     iv AD   **v** AC

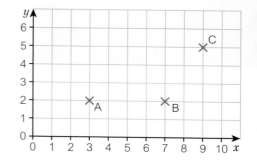

9 Plot points so that:

   a The y-coordinate is double the x-coordinate. Mark this point A.

   b The y-coordinate is 3 more than the x-coordinate. Mark this point B.

   c The x-coordinate is positive and the y-coordinate is negative.
     The x- and y-coordinates add to −3. Mark this point C.

   d Join points to make line segments AB, BC and CA.
     Find the midpoint of each line segment.

10 P-S Where will the line joining (3, 5) to (4, 8) cross the y-axis?

11 P-S Where will the line joining (3, 4) to (5, 5) cross the x-axis?

12 P-S M(6, 6) is the midpoint of the line segment joining A to B.
   Find the coordinates of B when A is at

   a (3, 4)   **b** (2, 4)   **c** (−2, 0)   **d** (−2, 16)

13 R The points A(4, 4), B(4, 12), C(8, 12) and D(8, 4) are joined to form a rectangle.
   Point X is the midpoint of AC.

   a Explain how to find the coordinates of X.

   b Point Y is the midpoint of BD.
     Explain how you know the coordinates of Y.

14 P-S / R The points A, B, C and D lie on a straight line.
   B is the midpoint of AD and C is the midpoint of BD.
   C is (7, −1) and D is (10, −2).
   Find the coordinates of A.

Reflect

15 Ben says he can use his knowledge of averages to find midpoints of lines.
   What average can Ben use?
   Describe how this average can be used to find the midpoint of a line segment from (3, 8)
   to (5, 16).

9.4 Extending sequences

- Describe and continue special sequences
- Use the term-to-term rule to work out more terms in a sequence
- Recognise an arithmetic sequence and a geometric sequence

1 Fibonacci numbers are formed as follows.
The first number is 1. The second number is 1.
The following numbers are created by adding the two previous numbers.
So the third number is $1 + 1 = 2$, the fourth is $1 + 2 = 3$, and so on.
a Work out all the Fibonacci numbers up to 200.
b Show that the tenth Fibonacci number is divisible by the fifth, and that the twelfth number is divisible by the sixth.

2 Carol invests £250.
a After a year, her investment doubles, but she has to pay £40.
How much does she have at the end of the first year?
b The next year, the same thing happens again.
How much does she have at the end of the second year?
c Work out the totals for the ends of the next two years.
Do the amounts form an arithmetic sequence?

3 Work out the first five terms of each arithmetic sequence.
a first term = 15   common difference = −3
b first term = −50   common difference = −5
c first term = 0.05   common difference = 4
d first term = 9.5   common difference = 0.2
e first term = −12   common difference = 0.3
f R What type of sequence do you get from
   i a positive common difference   **ii** a negative common difference?

4 R The number of people reading a blog increases by 100 each day.
a On the first day 300 people read the blog. How many will be reading it after 28 days?
b Is the sequence of the number of people reading the blog arithmetic or geometric? Explain.

5 R For each sequence
   i decide whether it is arithmetic or geometric
   ii describe the sequence by giving the first term and the term-to-term rule
   iii write the next two terms.
a 5, 25, 125, 625, …   **b** 128, 64, 32, 16, …
c 0.5, 0.3, 0.1, −0.1, …   **d** 0.1, 0.2, 0.4, 0.8, 1.6, …
e $1, \frac{1}{2}, \frac{1}{4}, \frac{1}{8}, \dots$

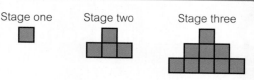

Stage one   Stage two   Stage three

6 A sequence is created like this:
Start with 1 square, add 3 underneath,
then add 5 underneath.

  a Write the sequence of numbers of new squares added to each pattern.

  b Write the sequence of numbers of total squares in each pattern.

  c What type of numbers make up the sequence in part **b**?
  Explain why you get these numbers.

  d Is the sequence in part **b** arithmetic, geometric or neither?

7 **R** The table shows the UK population in 1950 and 2000.

Year	UK population (to the nearest million)
1950	51 000 000
2000	59 000 000

  a Assuming that the population growth is an arithmetic sequence, draw a graph to predict the population in 2050.

  b Do you think it is sensible to predict the population like this? Explain your answer.

  c The population in 2010 was actually 62 000 000
  Does this change your prediction for the population in 2050?

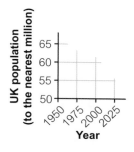

8 **a** Copy and complete this table.

  b Draw a line graph to show the relationship between the side length of a square and its perimeter. Label the horizontal axis 'Side length' and the vertical axis 'Perimeter'.

Side length of a square	1	2	3	4	5
Perimeter of a square					

  c Is the sequence of the perimeter of squares arithmetic or geometric?

9 **a** Draw a grid with x- and y-axes from 0 to 15.

  b Plot the points (2, 6), (6, 8), (10, 10) and (14, 12) on your grid. Join the points.

  c Use the line on your graph to continue this sequence of x-coordinates: 2, 4, 6, ...

  d Are the sequences of x- and y-coordinates arithmetic or geometric sequences?

10 **R** An arithmetic sequence is a linear sequence.
Why do you think it is called a linear sequence?

> **Q10 hint** Look at the graphs in Q8 and Q9 to help you.

11 **R**

  a Draw a grid with x- and y-axes from 0 to 20.
  Plot the points (1, 1), (2, 4), (3, 9) and (4, 16) on your grid.

  b Use your graph to explain why the relationship between x and y is not linear.

  c How could you have realised the relationship was not linear without plotting a graph?

12 Write three facts you know about arithmetic sequences.
Compare your facts with others in your class.

9.5 Straight-line graphs

- Recognise, name and plot graphs parallel to the axes
- Recognise, name and plot the graphs of $y = x$ and $y = -x$
- Plot straight-line graphs using a table of values

1   **R**   Look at these points.

P(5, 2)   Q(12, 5)   R(5, −3)   S(5, 0)   T(−2, 5)

Which of them are on the line

a $x = 5$ **b** $y = 5$

2   These four points form a rectangle.
Write the equation of the line that forms
each side of the rectangle.

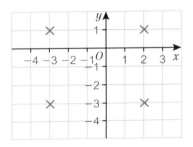

3   Match the equations of the graphs to the lines.

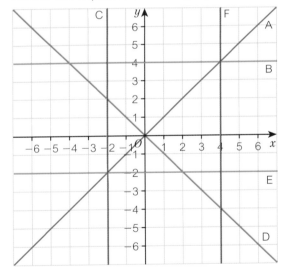

$x = -2$

$y = x$

$y = 4$

$y = -x$

$y = -2$

$x = 4$

4   **a**   Copy and complete the table of values for the equation
$y = 2x - 3$.

x	0	2	4	6
y				

b   Draw a grid with x- and y-axes from −10 to 10 and plot the graph of $y = 2x - 3$.

c   Copy and complete the table of values for the equation
$y = 6 - x$.

x	0	5	10
y			

d   Plot the graph of $y = 6 - x$ on your grid from part **b**.

e   Write the coordinates of the point where the two graphs intersect.

5 P-S What is the angle between the graphs of $y = x$ and $y = -x$?

6 R
  a Write the equation of a line that passes through the point $(3, -2)$ that is
   i vertical **ii** horizontal.
  b Are there any other horizontal or vertical lines that pass through the point $(3, -2)$? Explain.

7 The table shows the relationship between miles and kilometres.

Miles	0	50	100
Kilometres	0	80	160

  a Plot a graph using these values to work out
   i how many kilometres are the same as 60 miles
   ii how many miles are the same as 60 km.
  b How many kilometres are the same as 250 miles?

8 A manufacturer claims that a car does 60 miles to the gallon.
  a Draw the graph of $d = 60f$ where f = fuel used and d = distance travelled.
  b Use the graph to work out
   i how much fuel is needed for a journey of 150 miles
   ii how far the car can travel on 3.5 gallons.

Investigation

9 **a** Make a table of values for each graph. Use the x-values 0, 1, 2, 3, 4.
   i $y = x$ **ii** $y = 2x$ **iii** $y = 3x$
  b For each table, complete the statement
   'When the x-value increases by 1, the y-value increases by □.'
  c **i** Predict what you think will happen in a table for $y = 4x$.
   ii Check your answer by making a table of values.
  d **i** Plot all the graphs from part **a** on the same pair of axes.
   ii Which graph is steepest?
  e Look at these tables of values.
  Graph **A**

x	−1	0	1
y	−6	0	6

  Graph **B**

x	−1	0	1
y	−5	0	5

   i Which graph is steeper, **A** or **B**?
   ii Plot the graphs to check your answer.

Reflect

10 In this lesson, you have drawn a lot of linear (straight-line) graphs.
  A graph of linear function has *only one* y-coordinate for each x-coordinate.
  Look back at the linear graphs you have drawn in this lesson.
  Give two examples of equations of graphs of linear functions.
  Give an example of the equation of a graph that is not a linear function. Explain.

9.6 Position-to-term rules

- Generate terms of a sequence using a position-to-term rule
- Use linear expressions to describe the *n*th term of simple sequences.

1 **R** The **general term** of a sequence is $10n$.

> **Key point** The *n*th term is sometimes called the **general term**.

   a Is 35 a term in this sequence?
Explain your answer.

   b Which term number has the value 60?

   c Which term will be the first one larger than 105?

2 The general term of a sequence is $5n - 3$.
Which number term is

   a 22   **b** 47

   c 112   **d** 9997?

3 Work out the first five terms of the sequence for each general term.

   a $3n + 4$ **b** $2n + 5$

   c $4n - 2$ **d** $n + 12$

   e $5n - 3$ **f** $3 - n$

   g **R** How does the common difference relate to the general term in each sequence?

4 **R** Look at this sequence of dominoes.

   a Draw the next domino in the sequence.

   b In words, write a rule to explain how to work out the number of dots in the bottom section when you know the number of dots in the top section.

   c Write your rule from part **b** using algebra.

5 **a** The *n*th term of a sequence is $2n + 3$.
Copy and complete the table to find the first six terms of the sequence.

Position	1	2	3	4	5	6
Term						

   b Write the first six terms in each sequence.

      i $2n + 2$

      ii $2n - 5$

      iii $2n + 10$

   c **R** What do you notice about the common difference in all these sequences?

6 **P-S** Write the nth term for a sequence where the terms

    a include 24 and 33

    b are not whole numbers.

7 **P-S** The general term of a sequence is $-2.5n - 15$.

    a Is the sequence finite or infinite?

    b Which term has the highest value?
    What is this value?

8 **P-S** For how many terms is $2n + 3$ larger than $5n - 10$?

9 **R** How do you know that $5n + 3$ will always be larger than $3n + 2$?

Investigation

10 a Write the nth term of this sequence:

    2, 4, 6, 8, 10, …

    b Here is another sequence:

    3, 5, 7, 9, 11, …

    Compare the first terms of this sequence and of the sequence in part **a**; compare the second term of this sequence and the sequence in part **a**, and so on.
    Describe in words how this sequence relates to the sequence in part **a**.

    c Use your answers to parts **a** and **b** to write the nth term of the sequence

    3, 5, 7, 9, 11, …

    d Here is another sequence:

    0, 2, 4, 6, 8, …

    Describe in words how this sequence relates to the sequence in part **a**.

    e Use your answers to parts **a** and **d** to write the nth term of the sequence

    0, 2, 4, 6, 8, …

    f Use the sequence in part **a** to write the nth terms of these sequences.

    i 5, 7, 9, 11, …

    ii 12, 14, 16, 18, …

    iii −3, −1, 1, 3, …

Reflect

11 Which information is enough to allow you to work out *all* the terms in a sequence?

    | the position-to-term rule | | the general term | | the first term | | the common difference |

    | the 100th term | | the first term and the term-to-term rule |

9 Extend

1 The first two terms of a sequence are 1 and 3.
The sequence could be arithmetic *or* geometric.
a For an arithmetic sequence starting 1, 3, …
  i write the next two terms
  ii work out the nth term.
b For a geometric sequence starting 1, 3, …
  i write the next two terms
  ii describe the sequence, giving the first term and the term-to-term rule.

2 These diagrams are made by creating triangles from dots.

a How many dots would be used in the sixth diagram?
b P-S   Which diagram is the first to use more than 100 dots?

3 P-S   Cells in a laboratory are grown on a large flat dish.
The area they cover doubles every day.
After 10 days the cells cover an area equivalent to an
A3 sheet of paper.
What fraction of the paper will they cover after 5 days?

> **Q3 hint** They double every day, so the cells are not growing according to a linear relationship.
> On day 9 they will cover $\frac{1}{2}$ the paper, which doubles to the whole sheet on the final day.

4 P-S   Write the missing terms in these arithmetic sequences.
  a 3, ☐, ☐, 18
  b 3, ☐, ☐, ☐, 18
  c 3, ☐, ☐, ☐, ☐, 18

5 P-S   A frog is swimming in a well.
The water level is 20 m below the ground level.
The frog climbs out of the well.
During the day, the frog can climb 5 m up the sides of the well, but during the night the frog slips back 3 m.
How long does it take the frog to climb out of the well?

6 Consider the numerator and denominator separately to find the nth term for these sequences. The sequences forming the numerator and denominator are arithmetic.
  a $\frac{3}{5}, \frac{8}{12}, \frac{13}{19}, \frac{18}{26}, \cdots$
  b $\frac{27}{28}, \frac{24}{26}, \frac{21}{24}, \frac{18}{22}, \cdots$
  c $\frac{8}{10}, \frac{10}{15}, \frac{12}{20}, \frac{14}{25}, \cdots$
  d $\frac{15}{20}, \frac{19}{31}, \frac{23}{42}, \frac{27}{53}, \cdots$

7 For each of the sequences in Q6 find the term which is nearest to $\frac{1}{2}$.

8 A forest fire is modelled on a hexagonal grid, with each hexagon representing one tree. The 'fire' is measured by the area it covers. It begins with a solitary tree but each hour spreads to all the trees bordering the original tree.

The first three hours are shown.

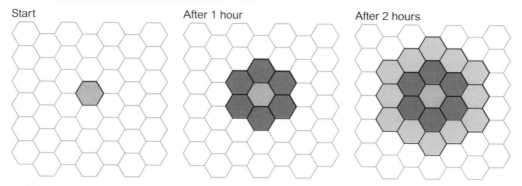

Start   After 1 hour   After 2 hours

   a Write an expression for the number of new trees on fire after n hours.
   b How many hours does it take until 30 new trees catch on fire?
   c How many hours does it take until 100 trees are on fire in total?

9 **P-S** A straight line goes through the points (7, 20) and (15, 42).
   a Find the value of y when $x = 11$.
   b Find the value of x when $y = 53$.

10 **R** The four points A(2, 6), B(5, 9), C(8, 6) and D(5, 3) are plotted on graphs.
   The midpoints of AB, BC, CD and DA are joined to make a quadrilateral.
   Explain how you know this quadrilateral is a square.

Investigation

11 Strontium-90 is a radioactive isotope found in used nuclear fuel.
   It has a half-life of 29 years. This means that after 29 years, half of the atoms will have decayed, forming a new element.
   After another 29 years, half of the remaining atoms will have decayed.
   Strontium-90 can be very harmful to animals and humans.

   a If a field is exposed to 128 grams of strontium-90, how many years would you wait before planting in the field again?

   b Will nuclear waste ever stop being radioactive?

   Hint Use this table to help keep track of the amount of strontium-90. How else could you display this information?

Time (years)	0	29	58	87	116	145	174
Amount of strontium-90 left (g)	128	64					

Reflect

12 List all the words and phrases you can think of that you can use to describe a sequence of numbers. You should have at least eight words and phrases in your list.
   Compare your list with others in your class.

10 Transformations

Master   Extend p141

10.1 Congruency and enlargements

- Identify congruent shapes
- Use the language of enlargement
- Enlarge shapes using given scale factors
- Work out the scale factor given an object and its image

1 This is the logo for a new brand of clothing.
   Copy the logo on to a square grid.
   Enlarge the logo using a scale factor of 3.

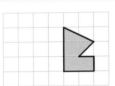

2 The diagram shows three squares A, B and C
   on a square centimetre grid.
   What is the scale factor of enlargement from:
   a A to B   **b** A to C   **c** B to C?

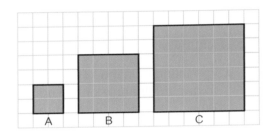

d Copy and complete this table.

Square	Perimeter (cm)	Area (cm²)
A	8	4
B		
C		

e Copy and complete this table. Write each ratio in its simplest form.

Squares	Ratio of side lengths	Ratio of perimeters	Ratio of areas
A:B	1:2		
A:C			
B:C	2:3		

f R What do you notice about the ratios you found in part **e**?

3 **P-S** An architect makes a scale model of a building.
   The base of the model is a rectangle with length 50 cm and width 40 cm.
   The real building will be an enlargement of the model, with base length 200 m.
   a What is the scale of the model?
   b What will the width of the real building be?

4 **a** **P-S / R** A and B are two quadrilaterals. They each have four right angles.
One side of A is 5 cm long, and one side of B is 5 cm long.
Do A and B have to be congruent? Explain why or why not.

b DEF and PQR are two triangles. They each have a right angle and an angle of 30°.
One side of DEF is 5 cm long and one side of PQR is 5 cm long.
Do DEF and PQR have to be congruent? Explain why or why not.

c Would your answer to part **b** be the same if you were told that the right angles,
30° angles and 5 cm length sides are as shown in this diagram?

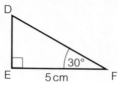 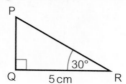

5 **R** The rectangle on the left is enlarged to give
the rectangle on the right.
Some students are asked to work out the value of h.
Alison says that $h = 12$. Becky says that $h = 16$.
Who is correct? What did the other student do wrong?

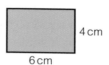 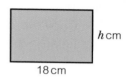

Investigation

Diagrams not drawn
accurately

6 **a** The triangle on the left is enlarged
to give the triangle on the right.
What is the scale factor of the enlargement?

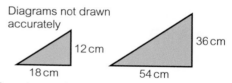

b What is the ratio of the base to the height of the triangle on the left, in its simplest
form? What is the ratio of the base to the height of the triangle on the right, in its
simplest form? How do these compare?

c Draw other triangles and enlargements of them. Do you get the same final answer to
the questions in part **b**? Explain why the final answers are or are not the same.

d Is what you have discovered also true for enlargements of other shapes?

---

7 The shape on the left is enlarged to give
the shape on the right.

a What is the scale factor?

b What is the value of x?

Diagrams not
drawn accurately

 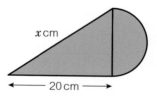

Reflect

8 **a** Two shapes are congruent.
What is definitely the same about them and what might be different?

b One shape is an enlargement of another.
What is definitely the same about them and what might be different?

10.2 Symmetry

- Recognise line and rotational symmetry in 2D shapes
- Solve problems using line symmetry
- Identify all the symmetries of 2D shapes
- Identify reflection symmetry in 3D solids

1 R

  a A quadrilateral has exactly 1 line of symmetry.
    What type of quadrilateral is it?

  b A quadrilateral has exactly 2 lines of symmetry.
    What type of quadrilateral is it?

  c A quadrilateral has exactly 3 lines of symmetry.
    What type of quadrilateral is it?

  d A quadrilateral has exactly 4 lines of symmetry.
    What type of quadrilateral is it?

2 This triangular prism has reflection symmetry.
The two planes of symmetry are shown in the diagrams.

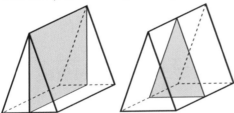

Which of these 3D solids have reflection symmetry?

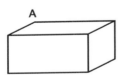

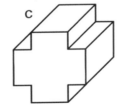
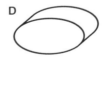

3 Architects and engineers use a variety of metal beams in construction.
These diagrams show three different types of beam used.
How many planes of symmetry does each beam have?

  a

  b
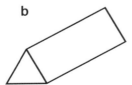
  c
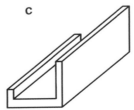

4 P-S / R Fred has a rectangular field.

  a What is the perimeter of the field?

  b What is the area of the field?

  c Fred decides to split his field into two parts by building
    a fence along a line of symmetry of the field.
    For each of the two ways that he can do this, work out:

    i the dimensions of the two parts of the field (their length and width)

    ii the perimeters of the two parts

    iii the areas of the two parts.

  d How do the dimensions, perimeters and areas of the two parts of the field relate to those
    of the original field?

  e Would your answers to part **d** be the same or different if the original field was a square?

100 m

200 m

5 R A student knows that a line of symmetry always splits a shape into two congruent parts.
They claim that these are lines of symmetry of a rectangle, because they each split the
rectangle into two congruent parts.

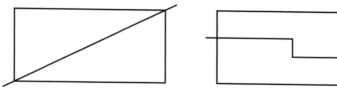

What has the student done wrong?

6 a Complete the table.

Shape	Order of rotational symmetry	Number of lines of symmetry
Equilateral triangle		
Square		
Regular pentagon		
Regular hexagon		
Regular octagon		

  b P-S / R What pattern do you notice? Will this pattern continue? How do you know?

7 P-S

  a Draw a shape which has rotational symmetry of order 3 but no lines of symmetry.

  b Draw a shape which has rotational symmetry of order 4 but no lines of symmetry.

8 R A class is asked, 'What is the order of rotational symmetry of the letter "L"?'
Most students say,
'It doesn't have rotational symmetry', but a few say 'It has rotational symmetry of order 1'.
Which group of students is correct?

9 P-S / R

  a Is there a hexagon that has rotational symmetry of order 3?
    If so, draw one. If not, explain why not.

  b Repeat part **a** for hexagons that could have rotational symmetry of orders 2 and 4.

10 P-S / R

    a Is there a hexagon that has exactly 3 lines of symmetry?
       If so, draw one. If not, explain why not.

    b Repeat part **a** for hexagons that could have 1 and 2 lines of symmetry.

11 P-S

    a This cuboid has 3 planes of symmetry.
       Draw diagrams to show the planes of symmetry.
       For each diagram, imagine the cuboid is cut along the
       plane of symmetry.
       What shape are the new faces made by the cut?

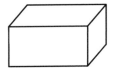

    b How many planes of symmetry does a cube have?

    c Draw diagrams to show each plane of symmetry.

    d Imagine that the cube is cut along each plane of symmetry.
       What shape is the new face made by each cut?

12 R

    a Maeve cuts a solid shape along a plane of symmetry.
       The new faces are triangles. What shape could the solid be?

    b Roy cuts a solid shape along a plane of symmetry.
       The new faces are hexagons. What shape could the solid be?

13 P-S / R In Q11, you found the planes of symmetry of a cube.
Find a solid made out of equilateral triangles that has exactly the
same planes of symmetry. How is this solid related to a cube?

> **Q13 hint** You might find it helpful to use 3D modelling equipment as you explore this problem.

Investigation

14 a A polygon has rotational symmetry of order 3.
      How many sides could the polygon have?

    b Repeat part **a** for polygons with rotational symmetry of order 4 and order 5.
       Suggest how many sides a polygon with rotational symmetry of order 100 could have.

    c A polygon has exactly 3 lines of symmetry.
       How many sides could the polygon have?

    d Repeat part **c** for polygons with exactly 4 lines of symmetry and exactly 5 lines of
       symmetry. Suggest how many sides a polygon with exactly 100 lines of symmetry
       could have.

Reflect

15 a Does a shape that has lines of symmetry always have rotational symmetry of order
      greater than 1?

    b Does a shape which has rotational symmetry of order greater than 1 always have lines
       of symmetry?

10.3 Reflection

- Recognise and carry out reflections in a mirror line
- Reflect a shape on a coordinate grid
- Describe a reflection on a coordinate grid

1 The diagram shows six congruent shapes on a coordinate grid.
Copy and complete these statements:

a A is the reflection of B in the line ___.

b A is the reflection of C in the line ___.

c E is the reflection of F in the line ___.

d B is the reflection of D in the line ___.

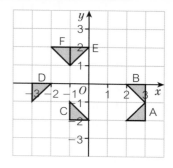

2 Make a copy of this diagram.

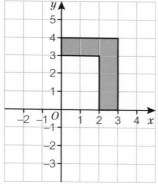

a Reflect the shape in the line $y = 1$.

b Reflect the image from part **a** in the line $x = 1$.

3 Make three copies of this diagram and use one copy for each part of this question.

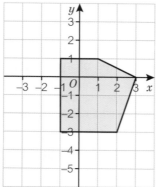

a Reflect the shape in the line $x = 1$.

b Reflect the original shape in the line $y = -2$.

c Reflect the original shape in the line $y = x$.

4   The diagram shows six congruent shapes
    on a coordinate grid.
    For each of the shapes B, C, D, E, F and G,
    copy and complete the statement:
    'Shape ___ is the reflection of shape A in
    the line ___.'

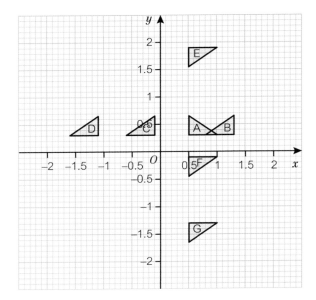

5   P-S / R
    a i   What are the images of the points (3, 4), (4, 1), (0, 3), (1, 0) and (2, 2) when they are
           reflected in the line $x = 0$?
       ii What stays the same and what changes when a point is reflected in this line?
       iii Give a rule (as a function machine, in words or in symbols) for the image of the point
           (a, b) when it is reflected in the line $x = 0$.
       iv Which points are unchanged by the reflection?
    b Repeat part **a** when the points are reflected in the line $y = 0$.
    c Predict what the rule will be when the points are reflected in the line $x = 1$.
       Now repeat part **a** to see if your prediction was correct.
    d Predict what the rule will be when the points are reflected in the line $y = 2$.
       Repeat part **a** to see if your prediction was correct.
    e i   What is the image of the point (a, b) when it is reflected in the line $x = c$?
       ii Which points remain unchanged?
       iii What is the image of the point (a, b) when it is reflected in the line $y = d$?
       iv Which points remain unchanged?

6   P-S / R   The vertices of a square have coordinates (2, 1), (2, 3), (4, 3) and (4, 1).
    a Draw the image of the square when it is reflected in the line $x = 0$.
    b Draw the image of the original square when it is reflected in the line $x = 1$.
       How does this relate to the reflection in part **a**?
    c Predict what the image of the original square will be when it is reflected in the line $x = 2$.
       Draw the image to check or correct your prediction.
       What is the effect of moving the vertical line of reflection one unit to the right?
    d What is the image when the original square is reflected in the line $x = 3$?
       How does this relate to the original square?
    e The original square is reflected in the line $y = c$ for a certain value of c.
       The image is the same as the original square. What is the value of c?

7 R A rectangle has vertices at (2, 4), (6, 4), (6, 6) and (2, 6).

a Find all the reflections that take the rectangle to itself.

b How many reflections are there?

c How does this relate to the lines of symmetry of the rectangle?

> **Q7 hint** A transformation **takes the rectangle to itself** if the image of the rectangle is the same as the original rectangle.

8 P-S / R

a What are the images of the points (3, 4), (4, 1), (2, 0) and (1, 1) when they are reflected in the line $y = x$?

b Give a rule for the image of the point (a, b) when it is reflected in the line $y = x$.

c Repeat parts **a** and **b** for reflection in the line $y = -x$.

9 P-S A square has vertices at (2, 3), (2, 5), (4, 5) and (4, 3).

Find the equations of all lines of reflection that take the square to itself.

Investigation

10 a Draw the image of this shape when reflected in the line $x = 0$.

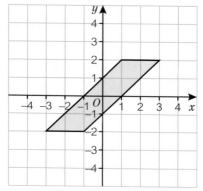

b Find a different line of reflection that gives the same image.

c Find three different shapes that also reflect to the same image when reflected in the lines from parts **a** and **b**.

d What do these shapes all have in common?

Reflect

11 a What happens to vertical and horizontal lines when they are reflected in a line $x = $ something (for example $x = 2$) or $y = $ something?

b What happens to vertical and horizontal lines when they are reflected in the line $y = x$?

10.4 Rotation

- Describe and carry out rotations on a coordinate grid

1 The diagram shows four triangles.
Describe the rotation that takes

  a A onto B

  b B onto C

  c B onto D

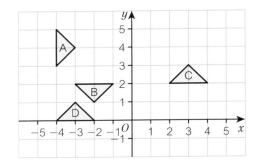

2 Describe the rotation that takes

  a A onto B

  b C onto D

  c B onto C

  d E onto F

  e F onto G

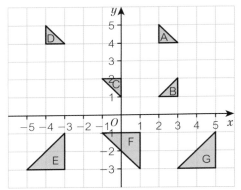

3 Write the coordinates of the vertices
of this triangle after a rotation of

  a 180° about (0, 1)

  b 90° anticlockwise about (2, 2)

  c 90° clockwise about (−1, −1).

  d In part **a**, what is the distance between the vertex of
  the object at (2, 1) and the centre of rotation (0, 1)?
  What is the distance between the image of this
  vertex and the centre of rotation?

  e R Why are the two distances in part **d** equal?

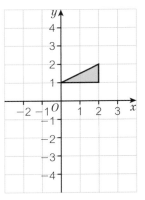

4 Write the coordinates of the vertices
of this triangle after a rotation of

  a 180° about (0, 0)

  b 90° clockwise about (0.5, 0)

  c 90° anticlockwise about (0, 0.4).

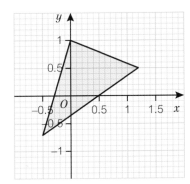

5 a A square has vertices at (2, 3), (6, 3), (6, 7) and (2, 7).
Describe all of the rotations that take the square to itself.

b R What is the order of rotational symmetry of the square?
How does this relate to the answer to part **a**?

6 In this question, your aim is to find the
image of this triangle when it is rotated
about the point (a, b), where a is the
x-coordinate and b is the y-coordinate.

a The triangle is rotated by 180°.
Write the coordinates of the vertices of the
triangle when the centre of rotation is:

i (0, 0)   **ii** (1, 0)   **iii** (2, 0)

iv (3, 0)   **v** (0, 1)   **vi** (0, 2)

Write your answers in a table like this:

Centre	Image of (3, 2)	Image of (5, 2)	Image of (5, 3)
i (0, 0)			

b In part **a i–iv**, the triangle is rotated 180° about a point $(a, 0)$.
What do you notice about the y-coordinates of the vertices of the rotated triangle?

c After rotation about the centre $(a, 0)$, the image of the point (3, 2) is $(2a - 3, -2)$.
Find similar expressions for the coordinates of the images of the points (5, 2) and
(5, 3) after rotation of 180° about the centre $(a, 0)$.

d In part **a v–vi**, the triangle is rotated 180° about a point $(0, b)$.
What do you notice about the x-coordinates of the vertices of the rotated triangle?

e After rotation about the centre $(0, b)$, the image of the point (3, 2) is $(-3, 2b - 2)$.
Find similar expressions for the coordinates of the images of the points (5, 2) and
(5, 3) after rotation of 180° about the centre $(0, b)$.

f Do your answers to parts **b–e** still work if a or b is negative?

g By trying more examples as in part **a**, find the coordinates of the vertices of the
triangle when it is rotated 180° about:

i $(a, 1)$ **ii** $(a, 2)$ **iii** $(a, 3)$ **iv** (a, b)

7 When an object is rotated by 180°, what happens to the image if the centre of rotation is
moved one unit upwards or one unit to the right?

10.5 Translations and combined transformations

- Translate 2D shapes
- Transform 2D shapes by combinations of rotations, reflections and translations

1 **P-S / R**   Rohan translates a shape 2 squares right and 3 squares up.
He then translates the image 5 squares left and 1 square down.
   a What single translation has the same effect as these two transformations combined?
   b Janet wants to translate a shape 7 squares left and 4 squares up using exactly two
   transformations. She starts with a translation 3 squares left and 2 squares down.
   What translation must she do next?
   c Explain how you can answer parts **a** and **b** without drawing and translating shapes.

2 **R**   Look at this diagram.
Write true or false for each statement.
If a statement is false, explain why.
   a B is a translation of A.
   b C is a rotation of A.
   c D is a reflection of A.

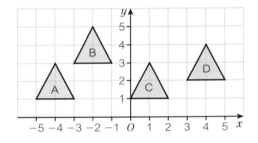

3 **P-S**   Make two copies of this diagram.
   a i On the first copy, transform the object by carrying out a
   translation 6 right and 2 down, followed by a rotation of
   $180°$ about $(2, -1)$.
   ii Describe fully the single transformation that will take the
   image back to the object.
   b i On the second copy, transform the object by carrying
   out a rotation $90°$ clockwise about $(-3, -1)$, followed by
   a rotation $90°$ anticlockwise about $(2, -1)$.
   ii Describe fully the single transformation that will take the
   image back to the object.

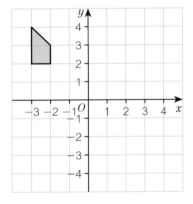

Investigation

4 The diagram shows kite 1.
Kite 1 is reflected in the x-axis to form kite 2.
Kite 2 is reflected in the y-axis to form kite 3.
Kite 3 is reflected in the x-axis to form kite 4.

   a For kites 1, 2, 3 and 4, write the coordinates of points
   A, B, C and D.

   b What reflection would take kite 1 onto kite 4?

   c Experiment with reflecting a different shape in the line
   $y = x$ and then in the line $y = -x$. What do you notice?

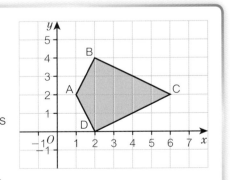

5 **P-S / R** What single transformation is the same as

a reflecting in the line $x = 3$ then reflecting in the line $y = 5$

b reflecting in the line $x = a$ then reflecting in the line $y = b$

c reflecting in the line $x = 0$ then reflecting in the line $x = 1$

d reflecting in the line $x = 0$ then reflecting in the line $x = 3$

e reflecting in the line $x = 0$ then reflecting in the line $x = b$?

Q5b hint Start by testing reflections in specific pairs of lines, like $x = 2$ and $y = 4$.

f Check that your result from part **e** works when b is negative.

g What single transformation is the same as reflecting in the line $x = 1$ followed by reflecting in the line $x = 0$? Is the answer the same as the answer to part **c**?

6 **P-S / R** Look at these diagrams.

The left-hand diagram shows a rectangle with its vertices labelled.

The right-hand diagram shows the image of the rectangle after it has been reflected in the y-axis.

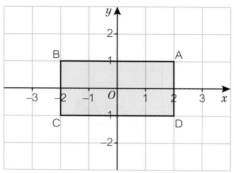 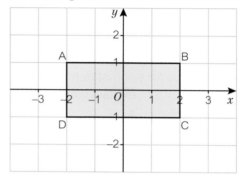

In this question:

X means 'reflect in the x-axis'.

Y means 'reflect in the y-axis'.

R means 'rotate by 180° about the origin'.

I means 'leave everything untouched'.

a Draw the image of the original rectangle after transformation X.

b Draw the image of the rectangle from part **a** after transformation Y.

c Which single transformation is the same as doing X followed by Y?

d Copy and complete this table, showing the result of doing one transformation followed by another. Some entries have already been filled in for you.

e Comment on anything you observe about your completed table.

f When combining transformations, why is the order in which they are done important?

		Second transformation			
		I	R	X	Y
First transformation	I		R		
	R				X
	X			I	
	Y				

Reflect

7 Look at all the objects and their images in this lesson. What can you say about the object and image in translations, reflections, rotations or combinations of these?

10 Extend

1 The four lines $x = 0$, $x = 1$, $y = 0$ and $y = 1$
are all lines of symmetry of a pattern.
Part of the pattern is shown in the diagram.
Copy the grid and show what the whole pattern looks like.

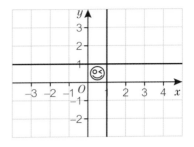

  a How many lines of symmetry are there all together?
  b What are the equations of the lines of symmetry?
  c What is the order of rotational symmetry of this pattern?
  d What is the centre of rotation?

2 P-S / R
  a A shape has exactly 3 lines of symmetry, all passing through a single point.
    i What is the angle between the lines of symmetry?
    ii Does the shape have to have rotational symmetry? If the shape does have rotational
    symmetry, what orders of rotational symmetry could it have?
  b Is there a hexagon that has exactly 4 lines of symmetry?
  If so, draw one. If not, explain why not.

3 P-S / R In this question,
  R means 'rotate by 180° about the origin'
  S means 'rotate by 180° about (1, 0)'.

The graph has an arrow on it, pointing from (0, 0) to (1, 0).
  a Where does the image of the arrow point after transforming by
    i R   **ii** R followed by R
    iii R followed by S   **iv** S followed by R followed by S?
  b Find a sequence of R's and S's which makes the arrow point from (4, 0) to (5, 0).
  c Is there a sequence of R's and S's which makes the arrow point from (−4, 0) to (−5, 0)?
  Either find a sequence or explain why it is impossible to do so.
  d Is there a sequence of R's and S's which makes the arrow point from (5, 0) to (6, 0)?
  Either find a sequence or explain why it is impossible to do so.

4 **a** What is the image of the point (0, 0) after a rotation by 180° about (a, b)?

> **Q4a hint** Look back at your answer to Q6 in Lesson 10.4.

  b **i** What are the images of the points (1, 0), (2, 0) and (3, 0) after a
       rotation by 180° about (a, b)?
    ii What is the image of the point $(x, 0)$ after this rotation?
  c **i** What are the images of the points (0, 1), (0, 2) and (0, 3) after a
       rotation by 180° about (a, b)?
    ii What is the image of the point $(0, y)$ after this rotation?
  d R By looking at the images of other points after a rotation by 180° about (a, b), find a
  rule which gives the image of the point (x, y) after this rotation.

5 **P-S / R**   The diagram shows shapes A and B.
Shape A is transformed by transformation T,
and then rotated 90° clockwise about (1, −1).
The image of shape A after this combined
transformation is shape B.
Describe transformation T.

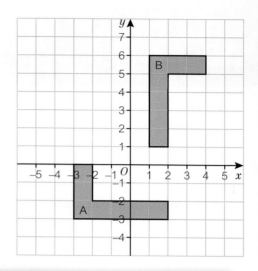

Investigation

6   Here is part of a wrapping paper pattern, drawn along the *x*-axis of a graph.

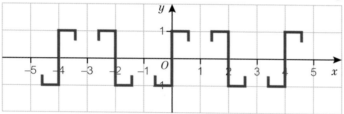

There are lines of symmetry at $x = -3$, $x = -1$, $x = 1$ and so on.
The pattern can be rotated by 180° about the points (−4, 0), (−2, 0), (0, 0), (2, 0) and
so on without changing it: it has rotational symmetry of order 2 *about the points* (−4, 0),
(−2, 0) and so on.
None of these points of rotational symmetry lies on a line of symmetry.
The pattern can also be translated by 4 to the right without changing it.
What other types of patterns can you find? Find one with

a   no rotational symmetry

b   no lines of symmetry

c   the *x*-axis as a line of symmetry.

d   Explain how you know that this pattern is the same type of pattern as the first one.

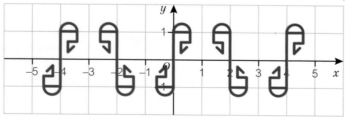

Reflect

7   Where have you seen repeating patterns around you?
What sorts of symmetry do they have?
What different types of patterns can you find?

UNIT 1 Analysing and displaying data

1.1 Mode, median and range

1 a Team D   b Team A

2 a £21 000
   b £32 000
   c The median, as it tells us the middle salary; the range tells us how spread out they are, but gives no indication of what the salaries themselves are.

3 Any number, 150 or lower.

4 a Group 1: 12 kg, Group 2: 12.45 kg,
      Group 3: 12.4 kg, Group 4: 12.6 kg
   b Group 1: 3, Group 2: 4, Group 3: 4, Group 4: 3
   c Group 1: $\frac{3}{7}$, Group 2: $\frac{1}{2}$,
      Group 3: $\frac{4}{9}$, Group 4: $\frac{3}{7}$

5 The range tells us nothing at all about the median. The median is likely to be near 100 g, as that is what is written on the wrappers.

6 a Sometimes true; for example, true in the data set 1, 2, 3, but not in the data set of **Q2**.
   b Sometimes true; for example, true in the data set 1, 2, 2, 3, but not in the data set 1, 1, 2, 5.
   c This depends very much on what 'the middle of the data' means! If 'the middle of the data' means half-way between the smallest and largest values, then sometimes true, as in the answer to part **a**; if 'the middle of the data' means the median, then always true by definition.
   d Always true: it's either the middle value (if an odd number of values) or between the middle two values (if an even number of values), so it's always between the smallest and the largest value. If 'between' is understood to mean 'strictly between' (so not equal to either extreme value), then this is sometimes true; for example, the data set 1, 1, 2 has the median equal to the smallest value. There is the potential here for a discussion about the importance of precise language in mathematics.
   e Sometimes true; for example, the data set 1, 2, 2, 5 has a range of 4, so half the range is 2. But the data set 11, 12, 12, 15 still has a range of 4, so half the range is 2, which is outside the spread of data values. Critically, the range does not tell us anything about the values of the data themselves, only about how spread out they are.
   f Always true: the mode is the most frequent value, so has to be one of the data values.
   g Sometimes true; true for the data set 1, 2, 3 but false for the data set 1, 2, 3, 4.
   h Sometimes true; true for the data set 1, 2, 3 but false for the data set 3, 4, 5. The range tells us about the spread of the values, not the values themselves.

7 4, 5, 5, 7

8 a 1, 4, 5, 6, 10, 11, 12   b 5
   c 11
   d The number 10 below 9 is −1, but it is impossible to have −1 parking spaces, so for a range of 10, the missing value must be 1 + 10 = 11.

9 The median of 10 whole numbers will either be one of these numbers, or half-way between two of them, so will either be a whole number or end in '.5'.

10 a 0   b 10
    c Answers would be the same however many values there were.

11 a 0   b There isn't one.
    c Answers would be the same however many values there were.

12 a Five numbers, middle number = 7.5
    b Four numbers, sum of middle two numbers = 15

Reflect

13 In part **a**, the median is the 3rd value = 7.5, so you can write this first and write numbers around it. These could be all 7.5, or you could write any two values less than or equal to 7.5, and any two values greater than or equal to 7.5.
In part **b**, you start by writing 2nd and 3rd values that have 7.5

as 'middle value'. These could both be 7.5, they could be 7 and 8, or 6 and 9 – any two values that add to 15. Then you write one less than or equal to the 2nd value, and one greater than or equal to the 3rd value.
Same: You could write all values 7.5, but you can also write two values less than the median and two values greater than the median.
Different: For an odd number of values, the median value is the middle data value (as in part **a**). For an even number, you have to write two numbers that have the median value as a 'half-way' value.

1.2 Displaying data

1 a
Animal	Frequency
cats	21
dogs	24
rabbits	8

   b It is not immediately clear how many students a partial stick person represents.
   c
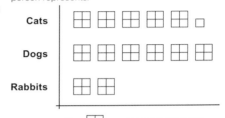

Key ⊞ represents 4 students

2 Any sort of pictogram that shows the data clearly.

3 a
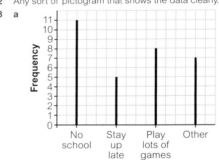

   b No school
   c The reasons given cannot be ordered.

4 The frequencies are as follows:
Number of robins	Frequency
0	5
1	4
2	7
3	3
4	1

Any chart which represents this data clearly would suffice. It might be appropriate to have a pictogram with robins on it to show the data, or something similar.

5 a
Number of spots	Tally	Frequency
11	I	1
12	II	2
13								7
14	II	2
15	I	1
16	I	1
17	I	1

b

Number of spots on ladybird

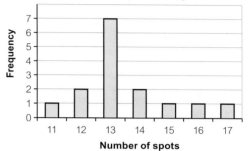

Number of spots on ladybird

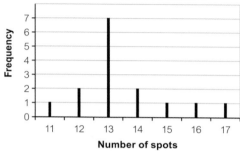

c 13

d George is correct. Justine chose the middle category rather than the middle data value.

6 a 3   b 17

Reflect

7 Bar-line graphs are easiest to draw because you only draw a line. Bar charts and pictograms are more colourful and eye-catching, e.g. for a newsletter report. Bar-line and bar charts may be easier to interpret than pictograms as you can read the value off the scale, instead of counting symbols and multiplying/dealing with half symbols.

1.3 Grouping data

1 a No, it isn't possible to work out the total number of students.

  b The smallest possible total number of students is 22 and the largest possible total number is 30.

2 There should be no gaps between the bars.

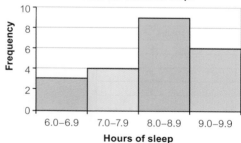

3 a 30–34

  b Yes, Shailee can be correct. The median will be half-way between the 14th and 15th values (when ordered). The 14th value is between 30 and 34 and the 15th is between 35 and 39, so if the two values were 33 and 35, then the median would be 34.

4 a 10 pages

  b

Number of pages	Frequency
6–7	6
8–9	4
10–11	5
12–13	2
14–15	1

c 6–7

d The mode is a better representation because the modal class does not contain the mode. It is also much lower than the mode.

5 a 30–39

  b Hashid is not necessarily right. The 30–39 class will break into two classes: 30–34 and 35–39. These will have 8 students between them, so one of the classes will have at least 4 students. If it breaks equally (4 and 4), then these could both be modal classes. But the modal class need not be one of them. For example, the 0–9 class could break into 1 student in the 0–4 class and 6 students in the 5–9 class, or the 20–29 class could break into 0 and 5 students, so it is possible that one of these classes is the modal class instead.

  c The modal class is a good way of giving some idea of which class is the most common. But it can depend very much on how the data is grouped, so it is not wise to use it on its own without looking at other averages.

Investigation

6 a i

Time (min)	Frequency
0–19	12
20–39	7
40–59	4
60–79	1
80–99	1

ii

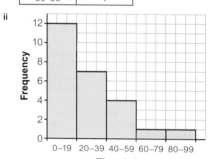

b i

Time (min)	Frequency
0–9	6
10–19	6
20–29	5
30–39	2
40–49	2
50–59	2
60–69	0
70–79	1
80–89	0
90–99	1

ii

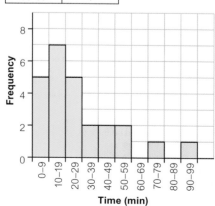

c The first shows the general trend in the data better.

d Students' own answers.

Reflect

7 Use grouped data when the set of data is large; for example, it would not be suitable to group data if there are only five values. It can make sense to have different class widths if the data is not evenly spread across the range; for example, you could have a group of 60–99 for the investigation.
How many items of data there are, e.g. 10 groups for 10 data items is pointless. How many equal class intervals there will be. What the boundaries of the class intervals will be – e.g. if the data is from 10 to 20 g, five class intervals are 10–12, 12.1–14, etc., whereas four class intervals are 10–12.5, etc. – avoid non-integer class boundaries.

1.4 Averages and comparing data

1 a Mean: 27.5 minutes
      Median: 20 minutes
      Modes: 18, 20 and 21 minutes
   b Median, because it isn't affected by extreme values. There are three modes, so it isn't a very good average to use.
   c 100 minutes; the mean is most affected.

2 a 2   b 8
   c i $1\frac{2}{3}$ and $8\frac{1}{3}$
      ii $1\frac{3}{7}$ and $8\frac{4}{7}$
   d Smallest mean is 10 divided by the number of values. Largest mean is 10 × (number of values − 1) divided by the number of values.

3 a Smallest mean: 6.4 (1, 1, 10, 10, 10)
   b i 7 (1, 1, 10, 10, 10, 10)
      ii 6.14 to 2 d.p. (1, 1, 1, 10, 10, 10, 10)
   c For odd numbers: Subtract 1 from the number and then divide by 2. Add this number of 1s to one more than this number of 10s. Divide by the number of numbers.
      For even numbers: Divide by 2. Add one less than this number of 1s to one more than this number of 10s.

4 a i 93.2 kg
      ii 22.7 kg
      iii 94.8 kg
   b i The Oxford rowers were heavier on average, because their mean is greater (94.8 kg vs 92.0 kg).
      ii The Oxford rowers were heavier on average, because their median is greater (93.2 kg vs 91.9 kg).
      iii The weights of the Oxford rowers varied more than weights of the Cambridge rowers, because their range is greater (22.7 kg vs 19.0 kg).
   c i 92.5 kg
      ii Reduced from 93.2 kg to 92.5 kg, because the cox is lighter than the rowers.

5 Probably recommend type B, because the mean number of wrong presses is lower (15 vs 23) and the ranges are not very different (12 vs 9).

Investigation

6 a 4
   b 5; it has increased by 1.
   c 12; it has been multiplied by 3.
   d i Divides by 2   ii Mean is 2, so correct.

7 a 5
   b 0.5 (dividing every value by 10)
   c 0.5 (including an extra 0.5 in the list, which equals the mean, does not change the mean)
   d 3.5 (adding 3 to every value)
   e 350 (multiplying every value by 100)
   f 349 (subtracting 1 from every value)

Reflect

8 You could use the median or mean for the TV screen size. The 'average American' is probably not about any particular value or quantity, and so the phrase probably means 'most Americans'. We can't sensibly use mean, median or mode to describe it.

1.5 Line graphs and more bar charts

1 a
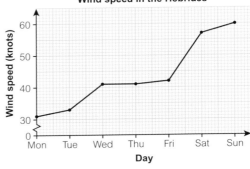

   b Students' own answers. For example: 'The wind speed is likely to vary according to the seasons, and may be quite different after a few months.'

2 a Saturday
   b Sparrows
   c She only saw two of the different types of birds on those days.

3 a 'Digging'
   b 'There is Another Sky'
   c The total height represents 100% of the letters in each poem.

4 a
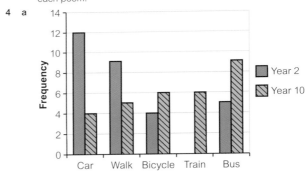

   b Car
   c Year 10 students are more independent, so they are much more likely to make their own way to school. This accounts for the decrease in car travel and increase in bicycle use. Also, they may well come from further away, hence the increase in train and bus travel. This, of course, depends on where pupils live, and will change from context to context.

5
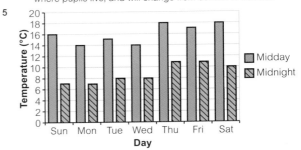

6

	Brown	Blue	Other	Total
Boys	8	6	4	18
Girls	10	3	0	13

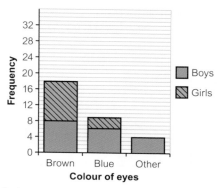

Reflect

7 a 5 bars

b To draw a bar chart he needs two bars for each group. He should put Car, Walk, Bicycle, ... along the horizontal axis and then draw a bar for Year 2 and a bar for Year 10 for each transport category.

1 Extend

1 a Because she can note down the answer very quickly when it is given.

b Clothes: groups have different sizes, making it difficult to work out the total.
Food: no grouping, so very hard to count total.
Cosmetics: inconsistent strike-through, so could be confusing or lead to errors.
Toys and games: groups have different sizes, making it difficult to work out the total.
Other: horizontal strike-through might lead to confusion over where next group begins; diagonal strike-through is a little clearer.

2 a Science fiction

b Realistic fiction

c More boys like it, but there are more boys in total, so it is hard to compare. The percentage of girls who like humour (12%) is greater than the percentage of boys who like humour (10%), so a greater proportion of girls prefer it.

d It is a misleading chart because there are different numbers of boys (40) and girls (25). It is better to give the percentage of boys and of girls who like each type of book, so that they can be compared fairly. Also, it is better to use a dual bar chart as this allows for easy comparison; it is not meaningful to split the type of book up as boys vs girls, so a compound bar chart is inappropriate. This is what a percentage bar chart looks like:

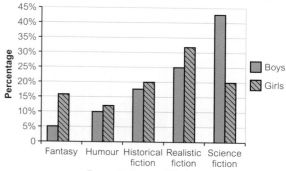

3 The data set contains at least two 8s; the middle two numbers are 5 and 6, 4 and 7, or 3 and 8.
The range is 6, so either the largest number is 3 + 6 = 9 or the smallest number is 8 − 6 = 2.
So the possibilities are:
Smallest = 2, largest = 8: 2, 3, 5, 6, 8, 8; or 2, 3, 4, 7, 8, 8; or 2, 3, 8, 8, 8, 8; or 2, 2, 3, 8, 8, 8.
Smallest = 3, largest = 9, so the largest three must be 8, 8, 9 or 8, 9, 9. Therefore, the middle two are 3 and 8, giving: 3, 3, 3, 8, 8, 9, however this is impossible as then the mode would be 3, not 8.
So the smallest is 2, the largest is 8 and there are four possibilities.

4 a The five numbers sum to 50, and the given numbers sum to 25, so the other two numbers must sum to 25. If you allow any numbers, positive or negative, then there is no largest possible range (for example, −1000 and 1025 would be allowed for the other two numbers). However, if you restrict to positive whole numbers, then 1 and 24 gives a range of 23, which is the largest possible, while 12 and 13 give a range of 7, which is the smallest possible.

b If the remaining two numbers are at most 9 and at least 16, then the median is 9. If the two numbers are 10 and 15 or two numbers between 10 and 15, then the median is 10. Therefore, the median is either 9 or 10. If you allow for fractional numbers, then one of the numbers could be between 9 and 10, say 9.5, and the other would be greater than 10, so the median would be between 9 and 10. Either way, the largest possible median is 10 and the smallest possible median is 9.

5 The mean number of legs that people have is slightly less than two, as not everyone has two legs, but no one has more than two legs. As most people have two legs, most people have more than the mean number of legs. If the median or mode was used instead, then most people would have the average number of legs.

6 a Multiple possible answers. For example: 3, 4, 5, 6, 6, 6, 7, 8, 9.

b Multiple possible answers. For example, the trivial set of data, that has only one value: 0. Also acceptable is a set of data with three values; for example: 1, 1, 2 or 2, 2, 4.

7 a Multiple possible answers. For example: 1, 2, 3, 4, 4, 5, 5, 6, 8, 9; or 2, 3, 3, 4, 5, 7, 7, 10; or 3, 4, 4, 5, 5, 11.

b A set of data with six values, for example: 1, 4, 4, 5, 5, 9.

Investigation

8 a Yes, for example: 1, 2, 5, 6, 6
Mean = 4, median = 5, mode = 6

b Yes, for example: 1, 2, 7, 100, 100
Median = 7, mean = 42, mode = 100

c All orders are possible.

d Yes, for example: 1, 2, 3, 3, 4, 5, 5, 5. Examples exist for all orders.

Investigation

9 a 7.5 cm only

b 10 cm only; in general, the median side length is always $\frac{1}{4}$ of the perimeter.

c 1 × 30 gives 15.5 cm; 2 × 15 gives 8.5 cm; 3 × 10 gives 6.5 cm; 5 × 6 gives 5.5 cm.

d 1 × 36 gives 18.5 cm; 2 × 18 gives 10 cm; 3 × 12 gives 7.5 cm; 4 × 9 gives 6.5 cm; 6 × 6 gives 6 cm. The smallest is 6 cm, the largest is 18.5 cm. In general, if area is A, then the largest median is $(A + 1) \div 2$, and the smallest median is when the side lengths are as close to each other as possible (which are the largest factor of A less than or equal to the square root of A, and the smallest factor of A greater than or equal to the square root of A), and the median is at least the square root of A, equal to it only if A is a perfect square.

Investigation

10 a If you allow any size angles, then there is no smallest possible median: the two smallest angles can be as small as you like (for example, both 0.1°) with the third angle being very close to 180°, and then the median is 0.1°. If you restrict the angles to whole numbers of degrees, then the smallest possible median is 1° if the angles of the triangle are 1°, 1° and 178°. For the largest possible median, if you allow any size of angle, there is no largest possible, but the median must be less than 90°. For example, you could have angles of 0.2°, 89.9° and 89.9°. If you restrict the angles to whole numbers of degrees, then you can have a median of 89°, in a triangle with angles of 1°, 89° and 90°, for example. If the median were 90° or larger, then two angles would have to be 90° or larger, and that is impossible.

b The mean is the sum of the angles divided by 3. But the angles of a triangle always sum to 180°, so the mean angle is always 60°.

Reflect

11 Students' own answers.

UNIT 2 Number skills

2.1 Mental maths

1. a 8000
   b Thousand
   c The digit 2 starts as two hundred and finishes as 200 thousand.
2. a 5   b 7   c 5   d 7
3. a e.g. $1 \times 24\,000 = 24\,000$, $2 \times 12\,000 = 24\,000$, $3 \times 8000 = 24\,000$, $4 \times 6000 = 24\,000$, $6 \times 4000 = 24\,000$
   b e.g. $1 \times 100\,000 = 100\,000$, $2 \times 50\,000 = 100\,000$, $4 \times 25\,000 = 100\,000$, $5 \times 20\,000 = 100\,000$, $10 \times 10\,000 = 100\,000$
4. a $12 + 8 + 3 \times 2$ b $8 - 6 + 4 \times 2$
5. 336
6. 5×50 with short books, or 3×80 with tall books. 250 short books or 240 tall books. A difference of 10 books.
7. a B and C
   b e.g. $1 + 2 \times 6 - 4$
8. £365
9. B 29   D 41   A 42   C 66
10. Ali: 630, Dan: 9.
11. 20
12. a −   b +   c ×
13. E.g. $14 = 5 + 3 \times (10 - 4) \div 2$
    $15.5 = (5 + 3 \times 10 - 4) \div 2$
    $24 = (5 + 3) \times (10 - 4) \div 2$
    $33 = 5 + (3 \times 10) - (4 \div 2)$
    $64 = (5 + 3) \times (10 - 4 \div 2)$
    $78 = (5 + 3) \times 10 - 4 \div 2$
    $18 = 5 + (3 \times 1 - 4) \div 2$
    $29 = 5 + 3 \times (10 - 4 \div 2)$
14. Ten million steps in two years would be five million steps in one year. 5 million $\div$ 10 000 = 500. There are only 365 days in a year, not 500, so 10 000 steps a day for two years will be less than ten million steps.
15. a $(1 + 2) \times 3 + 4 \times 5$ b $1 + 2 \times (3 + 4) \times 5$
    c $(1 + 2) \times (3 + 4) \times 5$
16. a $(3 + 4) \times (5 + 2)$ b $(4 + 5) \times (2 + 3)$
17. a $27 \times 10 \times 8 = 27 \times 8 \times 10 = (20 \times 8 + 7 \times 8) \times 10 = (160 + 56) \times 10 = 216 \times 10 = 2160$
    b To make it clear which part has to be done first.
18. $(1 + 2) \times 3 + 4 \times (5 + 6 + 7) = 81$
19. Luke would need to multiply by 10 000.

Reflect

20. E.g. The digits in numbers correspond to the number of 1s, 10s 100s = 10^2, etc.

2.2 Addition and subtraction

1. a Manchester United 70 000
      Arsenal 60 000
      Liverpool 50 000
   b Watford 400 000
      Stoke City 600 000
      Reading 200 000
   c Luis Fonsi 33 million
      Ed Sheeran 19 million
      PSY 16 million
2. 21 927
3. 122
4. 201
5. a
   ```
     6 5 2
   + 2 2 3
   -------
     8 7 5
   ```
   b
   ```
     2 7 5
   + 5 6 7
   -------
     8 4 2
   ```
   c
   ```
     6 2 9
   - 3 0 5
   -------
     3 2 4
   ```
6. £41 306
7. £143 982
8. $21 + 98$, $98 + 21$, $91 + 28$ or $28 + 91$
9. E.g. $193 + 827$

10. a, b Multiple solutions possible, e.g.
    ```
      5 9 8 6          5 9 8 4
        7 4 2            7 6 3
    +     3 1    or  +     1 2
    ---------        ---------
      6 7 5 9          6 7 5 9
    ```
11. 1839
12. Smallest 5000, largest 5499
13. a Use $387 + 439 = 826$, not 836 so his answer is incorrect.
    b Addition is the inverse of subtraction so addition can always be used to reverse a subtraction calculation.
14. Either $10\,049 - 85 = 9964$ or $10\,049 - 964 = 9085$.
15. 523 is 23 more than 500, 489 is only 11 less than 500. This will combine to give more than 1000.
16. a Inverse operations   b $15\,052 - 8524$
17. a $40\,000 + 40\,000 = 80\,000$
    b 79 471
    c $79\,471 - 43\,985 = 35\,486$ and $79\,471 - 35\,486 = 43\,985$
    d $35\,000 + 45\,000 = 80\,000$
18. $1599 - 902$ reveals Charlie started with 697.
    $697 + 63$ reveals Liam started with 760.
    $760 - 58$ reveals Anita began with 702.

Reflect

19. The words in a problem won't always tell you exactly what calculation you need to do. However, it should be possible to work out what calculations are required from the information given in the question.

2.3 Multiplication

1. Profit, £85
2. 950
3. 3768 pairs
4. $18 \times 15 + 29 \times 52 + 11 \times 75 = 2603$
5. 684
6. a 285 714   b 428 571   c 571 428   d 714 285
7. a 253 253   b 387 would end up with 387 387
   c 387 387
8. a 2025   b 2024   c 784
   d 783   e 1521   f 1520
   g The second answer is always one smaller than the first. 24×26 would be 624.
9. a Largest is $521 \times 43 = 22\,403$
   b Smallest is $135 \times 24 = 3240$
   c i 354×12 ii 125×34
      iii 314×52

Investigation

10. a i 21×34, by 198
       ii 32×45, by 198
       iii 43×56, by 198
    b The pair of numbers that are closer together is always 198 bigger than the pair that are further apart.
    c 45×76 and 54×67
    d The same happens, but now the bigger answer is 297 bigger.
    e Same but 396 bigger.
    f Same but 495 bigger, e.g. $12 \times 76 = 912$, $21 \times 67 = 1407$, $1407 - 912 = 495$.
11. a 24   b 120   c 5040
    d 40 320   e 362 880   f 9!
12. 36 km
13. £23
14. 13 436 928

Reflect

15. Estimating means working out $450 \times 100 = 45\,000$, so the answer needs to be much larger. 'Final digits' means working out $2 \times 7 = 14$, so the final answer needs to end with a '4'.
    Estimating:
    Advantage: Shows if the answer is of about the right size, or that it is not.
    Disadvantage: Doesn't show that the answer is wrong if, e.g. only the final digit is incorrect.
    Final digits:
    Advantage: Quick way of checking that an answer is not

correct (if final digit is wrong).

Disadvantage: Doesn't tell you anything about the accuracy of the non-final digits.

2.4 Division

1 865 × 7
  a 6589 × 11 **b** 653 × 18 **c** 986 × 27
2 a

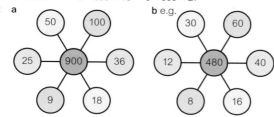

  b e.g.

3 26 toilets if the number is rounded up.
4 28 test tubes
5 a £47.55 **b** 10p
6 22, 52 or 82
7 55
8 65
9 a 146 914 ÷ 17 = 8642 **b** 21 625 ÷ 5 = 4325
  c 55 718 ÷ 13 = 4286 **d** 300 041 ÷ 7 = 42 863
10 a 165.4 cm
  b Mean decreases to 165, so decreases by 0.4 cm
11 £240.38 (nearest penny)

Investigation

12 Remainders will always be either 1 or 5. A remainder of 2 or 4 is not possible because this would mean the original number was even, which can't happen with a prime number. A remainder of 3 would mean the original number could be divided by 3, which can't happen with a prime number.

Reflect

13 Always. You can use multiplication to check the answer to a division calculation.

2.5 Money and time

1 Hours and minutes do not use a decimal system. 60 minutes make up one hour. 1 hour 15 minutes is 1.25 hours and 1 hour 30 minutes is 1.5 hours, so the correct answer is 3 hours 45 minutes.
2 10 days and 10 hours
3 a £3.50; £35
  b £15; £150
  c 40 minutes; 6 hours and 40 minutes
  d 33 minutes and 20 seconds;
    5 hours, 33 minutes and 20 seconds
  e **c** and **d** are harder because there are 60 seconds in a minute and 60 minutes in an hour but money is based on 100p in £1.
4 a Fashion Heights £8099.70; Legs 11 £7682.73; Walking Smart £6445.88
  b No. Fashion Heights paid the most but Legs 11 got the most clicks per week.
5 £57
6 128 packets (4 Mega + 4 Supa)
7 67 500
8 Greatest cost = £4.95, so her change is 5 × 1p coins. Least cost = 10p, so her change is £2, £2, 50p and two 20p coins.
9 Lily has £14.
10 8
11 As an individual payment, option **A** is better on the eighth time when it would give £1.28. As a total so far, option **A** would be better by the tenth time when the total is £10.23.
12 1840 minutes or 30 hours and 40 minutes
13 Sally has 7 × 60 = 420 minutes over two weeks. Her cousin has 2 × 4 × 50 = 400 minutes over two weeks. Sally has 20 minutes more maths every two weeks.
14 13 600

Reflect

15 For example: Agree, because money calculations are based in 100s and time calculations are based in 60s.

2.6 Negative numbers

1 a 6 **b** −6 **c** −6 **d** 6
  e −10 **f** −10 **g** −36 **h** −36
2 Students' own calculations that give an answer of −12, e.g. 6 × −2, 10 − 22, −20 + 8, −60 ÷ 5
3 a Edinburgh 11 °C, Belfast 6 °C, Leeds 13 °C
  b Edinburgh 2 °C, Belfast 7 °C, Cardiff 13 °C
  c Leeds, Edinburgh, Belfast, Cardiff
  d Brighton could have been −2 °C or −3 °C
4 a −24 **b** 24 **c** −16 **d** 16
  e −70 **f** −70 **g** −246 **h** −246
5 a −1 °C **b** 6 °C
6 a −4, −8 **b** 3, −15 **c** 19, −31
  d −3, −9 **e** −1, −11
7 1120 m
8 −5
9 a 1 − 432 = −431
  b 432 − 1 = 431
  c 31 − 24 = 7 (or 24 − 31 = −7)
10 −6
11

Arthur	5	6	11	7	−7	0
Leah	−15	−13	−3	−11	−39	−25

12 28 + 72
13 a 2 − 5 = −3
  b Students' own temperature question using calculation from **a**.
14 a i −20 **ii** −95 **iii** −5 **iv** −380
  b iv, ii, i, iii
  c e.g. 40 − 9 × 5

Reflect

15 The answer is negative. You can have negative temperature, but you can't have a negative number of apples (unless you owe someone some apples).

2.7 Factors, multiples and primes

1 6, 18, 26, 52, 117

Investigation

2

5	1	12	16	19	1	26	16
6	6	13	1	20	22	27	13
7	1	14	10	21	11	28	28
8	7	15	9	22	14	29	1
9	4	16	15	23	1	30	42
10	8	17	1	24	36		
11	1	18	21	25	6		

  i Deficient: 5, 7, 8, 9, 10, 11, 13, 14, 15, 16, 17, 19, 21, 22, 23, 25, 26, 27, 29
  ii Perfect: 6, 28
  iii Abundant: 12, 18, 20, 24, 30
3 a 6 in the middle, 12 opposite 18, and 54 opposite 60
  b Worked out that the HCF of 24 and 30 is 6, then compared factors of the other numbers to find the pairs that also have a HCF of 6.
4 Two turns on the large cog and three turns on the small cog.
5 a LCM of 4 and 5 is 20
    LCM of 4 and 6 is 12
    LCM of 4 and 10 is 20
    LCM of 5 and 10 is 10
    LCM of 5 and 6 is 30
    LCM of 6 and 10 is 30
  b 5 and 10 have an LCM of 10.
  c 4 and 5 and 4 and 10 both have an LCM of 20.
    6 and 5 and 6 and 10 both have an LCM of 30.
6 The LCM of 9 and 15 is 45.
7 8, between 89 and 97

8 a 3, 5, 33 and 55

b 1, 3, 5, 33, 55, 165

c 3, 5 and 11

d 166 = 165 + 1 and 165 ÷ 11 = 15, so 166 has a remainder of 1 when divided by 11.

Reflect

9 a If a number is a factor of another number, then the other number is a multiple of the factor.

b Every number has factors that are prime.

c A number divided by its factor will give a remainder of 0; a number +1 divided by one of its factors will give a remainder of 1; a number +2 divided by one of its factors will give a remainder of 2, etc.

2.8 Square numbers

1 a 1: 1

4: 1, 2, 4

9: 1, 3, 9

16: 1, 2, 4, 8, 16

25: 1, 5, 25

36: 1, 2, 3, 4, 6, 9, 12, 18, 36

b 4

2 a <   **b** >   **c** <

d >   **e** >   **f** >

3 $\sqrt{49}$, 3^2, $\sqrt{100}$, 6^2

4 $12^2 ÷ 6 = 2^2 × 6 = \sqrt{4} × 12 = 24$

5 a 10

b 27.5

c 5

6 a 4

b 400

c 40 000

d Multiplying a number by 10 multiplies its square by 100.

7 Yes: the seats can be arranged in a square of 30 by 30.

8 a 49 tiles

b 36 tiles and 16 tiles

9 a $11^2 = 121$, $101^2 = 10 201$, $1001^2 = 1 002 001$

b 100 020 001

c $22^2 = 484$, $202^2 = 40 804$, $2002^2 = 4 008 004$

10 a The last two digits are always 25.

b Starting numbers are 2, 6, 12, 20. This increases by 2 more each time (+4, +6, +8, ...), so next two numbers should start with 30 and then 42.

c $55^2 = 3025$ and $65^2 = 4225$.

11 144 and 169

12 2 and 13

13 a 100, 225, 400, 625, 900   **b** 196, 441 and 784

c 169 and 676

Investigation

14 a 9 cm² and 16 cm²

b 25 cm²

c She is not correct because to calculate $3^2 + 4^2$ you need to work out the powers first.

$3^2 + 4^2 = 25$ $(3 + 4)^2 = 7^2$
                                      $= 49$

d No, it is not true for any squares that are different sizes.

Reflect

15 All factors of a number come in factor pairs. However, the 'pair' of the square root of a square number is itself, so this 'pair' only contributes 1 to the number of factors. Added to the even number of other factors, this means that the total number of factors is odd.

2 Extend

1 −190

2 Nearer to 7 because 7^2 is nearer to 50 than 8^2.

3 2706

4 78.3 kg (to 1 d.p.)

5 Just 2 – the 1st and the 31st.

6 2 678 401

7 21 978

8 138 064

9 a 5700   **b** 9900   **c** 250 500   **d** 613 872

10 4:45 pm

11 30%

12 4

13 792

14 6 cards, from 15 to 20, totalling 105

Investigation

15 Yes: $12 = 3 + 3 + 3 + 3$ and $3 × 3 × 3 × 3 = 81$.
This is the largest solution possible.

Reflect

16 Students' own answers.

UNIT 3 Expressions, functions and formulae

3.1 Functions

1 **a** $-2, -1, 1$ **b** $5, -4, -13$

2 Debbie is correct. Her function works for all three values.

3 **a** $+4$ **b** $\times 20$

4 **a** For example,
$\times 1 +8, \times 2 + 6, \times 3 +4, \times 0 + 10, \times(-2) +14, \times\frac{1}{2} +9$

   b $\times 3 +4$; there are no other possibilities (geometrically: two points define a line).

   c 22   **d** The function is $\times(-1) +12$, so
$6 \times (-1) + 12 = 6$

5 **a** Add 2; $+2$

   b **i**

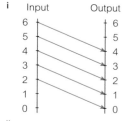

Input   Output

   ii

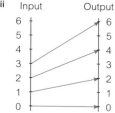

Input   Output

   iii

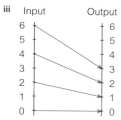

Input   Output

   c For subtraction: the diagram still has parallel lines, but they go down from left to right rather than up; it is the reflection of the addition diagram. For multiplication and division: the lines are no longer parallel – they 'spread out' (for $\times 2$) or 'get closer together' (for $\div 2$); the two diagrams are reflections of each other (because they are inverse functions).

6 It is calculating the mean of the five inputs.

7 $\times 0$

8 **a** 1st machine: 1, 4, 7; 2nd machine: 3, 6, 9

   b Yes; the two function machines would usually give different answers if the operations were in a different order.

   c **i** No. For example, $+ 2 + 5 = + 7 = + 5 + 2$
   ii No. For example, $- 4 - 8 = - 12 = - 8 - 4$
   iii No. For example, $- 2 + 3 = + 1 = + 3 - 2$

   d **i** No. For example, $\times 2 \times 10 = \times 20 = \times 10 \times 2$
   ii No. For example, $\div 4 \div 3 = \div 12 = \div 3 \div 4$
   iii No. For example, $\times 2 \div 5 = \times \frac{2}{5} = \div 5 \times 2$

Reflect

9 **a** Yes   **b** $\times 0$

3.2 Simplifying expressions 1

1 $4b + c - a$

2 Correct answers: $6b - 3a$ and $-3a + 6b$

   Incorrect answers:

   $3a + 6b$; student did $6 - 3$ for the a terms, or didn't like the idea of writing $-3a$.

   $3b$; student did $3 + 7 - 6 - 1 = 3$, and just put a b because that was the last thing.

$3a - 6b$; $3a$ because $6 - 3 = 3$, $- 6b$ because $7 - 1 = 6$ but the last b to appear has a minus in front of it.

$9a + 8b$; student ignored the minus signs.

$18a - 7b$; student multiplied the 3 and 6 to get 18, and the 7 and 1 to get 7.

$3a + 6b - 6a$; it is a partial simplification, but the a terms have not been simplified.

3 **a** $3z - 3z = 0$ **b** $2x - 2x = 0$
   c $-4y + 4y = 0$ **d** $-t + t = 0$

4 **a**

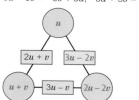

5a + 4b		
3a + 2b	2a + 2b	
2a	a + 2b	a

   b Infinitely many
   c Only possible completed pyramid is

3a + 5b		
2a + 2b	a + 3b	
a	a + 2b	b

5 **a**

8	1	6
3	5	7
4	9	2

   b

$c + a$	$c - a - b$	$c + b$
$c - a + b$	c	$c + a - b$
$c - b$	$c + a + b$	$c - a$

6 **a** **i** Yes   **ii** Yes   **iii** Yes
   b $3 - 5 = -5 + 3, 5 - 3 = -3 + 5$
   c $3 \times 2 - 5 \times 4 = -5 \times 4 + 3 \times 2$
   $5 \times 4 - 3 \times 2 = -3 \times 2 + 5 \times 4$
   d $3a - 5b = -5b + 3a, -3a + 5b = 5b - 3a$

7 **a**

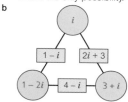

This is the only possibility.

   b

This is the only possibility.

   c e.g.

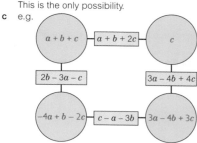

There are infinitely many possibilities.

Investigation

8 **a** Yes. Add all three boxes to get twice the total of the circles, then halve to get the total of the circles. Find the top circle by taking the circle total and subtracting the bottom box (= bottom two circles), and the other two circles likewise.

b The top and bottom boxes sum to the total of the four circles, as do the left and right boxes. So these two sums must be equal if there is to be a solution. If they are equal, then the top left circle can be anything and you can fill in the rest of the circles to make the sums work.

c Pentagon: this is like the triangle – the sum of all five boxes equals twice the sum of the circles. Add two non-adjacent boxes to find the sum of four circles, then subtract this from the total to get the fifth circle. You can do this for all five circles.

Hexagon: this is like the square – three alternate boxes sum to total of all six circles, as do the other three boxes. These two sums must be equal for there to be a solution. If they are equal, one circle can be anything, and then you can find the rest of the circles to make the sums work.

In general, if there are an odd number of sides, it is always possible, and there is just one solution found in a similar way to triangles and pentagons. If there are an even number of sides, then the two sets of alternating boxes have to have equal sums to give a solution, and if they do, you can complete one circle in any way and then fill in the rest.

Reflect

9 Order is important in subtraction, but not in addition, as for numbers.

Same number rules apply: i.e. $3 + 5 = 8$ whether they are just numbers or coefficients of like terms.

Inverse of $+ 3z$ is $- 3z$ and vice versa, the same as $+ 3$ is the inverse of $- 3$.

Different because you only get one term in the answer to a number addition/subtraction, but in algebra you may get one, two, three, etc. terms, with different unknowns.

3.3 Simplifying expressions 2

1 $7 \times 635 = 7(600 + 30 + 5)$
$= 7 \times 600 + 7 \times 30 + 7 \times 5$
$= 7a + 7b + 7c$ where $a = 600$, $b = 30$ and $c = 5$.

2 a For example, $4 \times 4y$, $2 \times 8y$; $32y \div 2$, $64y \div 4$
b For example, $2 \times 5b$, $10b \times 1$; $20b \div 2$, $50b \div 5$
c For example, $1 \times 12d$, $2d \times 6$; $60d \div 5$, $120d \div 10$
d For example, $5 \times 3x$, $15x \times 1$; $120x \div 8$, $15x \div 1$

3 a Yes   **b** No   **c** Yes
d i 1 and 12, 2 and 6, 3 and 4
   ii 1 and $12b$, 2 and $6b$, 3 and $4b$, 4 and $3b$, 6 and $2b$, 12 and b
e $8c$ has more factors because it has all the number factors, plus numbers with c, i.e. 1, 2, 4, 8, c, $2c$, $4c$, $8c$.

4 a Hasn't multiplied the 2 by 4.   **b** $4x + 11$

5 a $12x + 20$ **b** $18x - 19$

6 $8(2x + 5) + 3(4x - 5) = 16x + 40 + 12x - 15$
$= 28x + 25$

$4(7x + 6) + 1 = 28x + 24 + 1$
$= 28x + 25$

7 10; no

8 First box: 6, second box: 7; no

9 a $a + b + 3$ **b** $4(a + b + 3)$ **c** $4a + 4b + 12$

10 a Sum = $15c$, mean = $3c$
b Sum = $12x$, mean = $3x$
Note that the answers do not depend upon knowing the value of c or x.

11 a $3a$ **b** $4f$ (mid-way between $3f$ and $5f$)
c h
d There is no way to know; it depends on the values of a and b.

12 a Four ways:
$1(24x + 18)$, $2(12x + 9)$, $3(8x + 6)$, $6(4x + 3)$
b The HCF is 6; the numbers in front of the brackets are all the factors of 6.

Investigation

13 a Six ways   **b** No
c As before, none of the expressions are the same.
d No: they will always all be different. If the three numbers are a, b, c, then the coefficient of x will be one of ab, ac,

bc; these are all different. The only way of getting the same coefficient of x is to have $a(bx + c)$ and $b(ax + c)$ (or similar), and then the constants are different.
e There are now 24 ways to place them, and you might have expressions the same, for example if the numbers are 1, 2, 3, 6, then $1(2x + 6) = 2(1x + 3)$.

Reflect

14 Order of terms is important in division and not in multiplication, as for numbers.

$3 \times 5 = 15$ whether they are just numbers or coefficients of like terms, i.e. same number rules apply.

Inverse of $\times 3z$ is $\div 3z$.

Multiplying a bracket is the same as for a number because you multiply each term inside by each term outside.

Different because you can multiply and divide a term like $10x$ by a letter, a number or a term involving a letter and a number.

Multiplying a bracket is different than for a number because you end up with two terms (if there are two terms in the bracket), instead of a final number answer.

3.4 Writing expressions

1 a $x + y$
   b i $x + y - 3$ **ii** $x + y - 3$

2 a $b + 5$ **b** $4b + 10$

3 $2a + 2b$

4 $4a + 10$

5 $3s$ cm

6 a $70 + 60h$ **b** $40 + 2m$

7 a $3t$ pence   **b** $\frac{s}{3}$ pence
c $4a$ **d** $\frac{4b}{3}$ **e** $3c + d$
f $e + \frac{f}{3}$

8 a $x + 3x + 9x = 13x$
b The longest side has length $9x$. The other two sides, x and $3x$, only have a combined length of $4x$, which is not even long enough to get between the two ends of the longest side, so it is impossible to make a triangle.

9 a $3x + 2$ **b** $6y + 5$ **c** $4a$ **d** $5b + 4$

10 a $3a + 1$ **b** 4

11 a $\times 4$ then $+7$, or $\times 2$ then $+ 6x + 5$, for example.
b $\times 3$ then $+ 4x + 1$ is the most straightforward possibility.

Reflect

12 Function machine multiplies by 3 and then adds 2.
Expression in Q9 part **a** is $3x + 2$, which shows that for any input value x you multiply by 3 and then add 2. But $3x + 2$ is shorter. Algebra can save time and space, by avoiding writing lots of words. Also, algebra is an international language – you could understand $3x + 2$ in a textbook in any language.

3.5. Substituting into formulae

1 a £36   **b** £50   **c** £64   **d** £113

2 a i 50N   **ii** 700N   **iii** 300N
   b i 8N   **ii** 112N   **iii** 48N

3 a 150   **b** 320   **c** 160   **d** 105

4 a 5°C   **b** 15°C   **c** 25°C   **d** −5°C

5 a 17   **b** $4x - 3$ **c** 17
d They are the same; they will be the same as long as the same number is used in both.

6 a 3000   **b** 16   **c** 10000   **d** 6

7 a They equal 14, 15, 12, so the median is $2c + 8$
b The answer is different for different values of c. The median is $2c + 8$ when $c = 3$, it is $3c + 6$ when $c = 1$, and is $4c$ when $c = 5$. (There are other values of c which also work.)

8 a Bob is faster, as he runs further in the same time; speeds are: Alice 6 m/s, Bob 7 m/s.
b Charlie has the greater speed, as he takes less time to run the same distance; speeds are: Charlie 8 m/s, Dave 6 m/s.

9 a c increases, as you are subtracting a fixed amount from a larger amount.

b c decreases, as you are subtracting a larger amount from a fixed amount.

10 a r increases, as you are dividing a larger amount by the same fixed amount; thinking in terms of sharing, there are the same number of people to share between, but more to share.

b r decreases, as you are dividing a fixed amount by a larger amount; again thinking in terms of sharing, there are more people to share the same amount of stuff between.

11 a $6x + 4$ **b** $12a + 4$ **c** Yes

Investigation

12 $3n$ is larger when n is greater than 1.5, and $n + 3$ is larger when n is less than 1.5. They are equal when $n = 1.5$.

Reflect

13 a They can take any value – i.e. can vary.
b i True   **ii** True   **iii** False

3.6. Writing formulae

1 a 42   **b** $2n + 2$
2 a i 28   **ii** -7 **iii** -32 **iv** $5x + 3$
b $y = 5x + 3$
3 a 301   **b** $M = 3s + 1$
4 The student has not explained the meaning of their variables. They should begin with 'Let b = the number of egg boxes and e = the number of eggs'. The formula is also the wrong way round: it should read $e = 6b$, as the number of eggs is 6 times the number of egg boxes.
5 $P = 54C$
6 a 7 cm
b Substituting $x = 3$ into this formula gives $p = 2(3 + 1) = 8$, but the perimeter is 7 cm. So this formula is wrong.
c $p = 2x + 1$
7 a 33
b The boxes read: ×4 then +5
8 Let s = side length, p = perimeter. Then $p = 3s$. (Units could be included, so s = the side length in cm, p = the perimeter in cm, for example.)
9 e.g. $P = 4s$ where P = perimeter and s = side length.
10 Let l = length, w = width, A = area, p = perimeter.
a $A = lw$ **b** $p = 2(l + w)$ or $p = 2l + 2w$

Investigation

11 a 10; could systematically list all handshakes, could draw a network, could say that each person shakes hands with 4 other people so 20 handshakes, but each is counted twice.
b 15
c A possible formula is $H = \frac{n(n - 1)}{2}$.

Each of the n people shakes hands with everyone else (i.e. $n - 1$ people). This gives $n(n - 1)$. You then need to divide by two because each handshake has been counted twice.

Reflect

12 a Saves time
b Saves time and is quicker to write and remember, others can understand it without having to read lots of words.

3 Extend

1 $2a + 2b$

2 a $\times \frac{1}{4}$ then -2 **b** 40

3 a Always true; adding on 2 always results in a larger number.
b Sometimes true, e.g. true when $x = 1$ but false when $x = 0$ or $x = -1$. General answer: true whenever $x > 0$, false whenever $x \leq 0$. Doubling does not always make numbers larger.

4 a Before: $p = 4185$, after: $p = 5016$. Imagine you are offered 5 lots of £837 or 6 lots of £836; the latter is more money. Alternatively, you lose 5 by reducing 837 to 836, but then you add on another 836, which more than compensates. Alternatively, think about the areas of a 5 × 837 and 6 × 836 rectangle; overlap the rectangles to see what the difference is.

b If m and n of part **a** are swapped around (so $m = 837$, $n = 5$), then p will decrease. If m is 1 less than n, then increasing m by 1 and decreasing n by 1 will leave p unchanged (as m and n are simply swapped). In general, if m is less than $n - 1$, then p will increase; if $m = n - 1$, then p is unchanged, and if m is greater than $n - 1$ (equivalently for whole numbers: if m is at least n), then p will decrease.
c In this case, you have very similar behaviour, but now the dividing line between p increasing and decreasing occurs when $m = n - 2$.

5 a, b When $a > b$, increasing both a and b by 1 decreases the value of c, whereas if $a < b$, the value of c increases. If $a = b$, the value of c is unchanged. Thinking about dividing a cakes among b people, you are adding one extra cake and one extra person. If each person was getting more than one cake beforehand (so $a > b$), then this extra cake will not be enough for the new person if the division is fair, so everyone will end up with less cake. On the other hand, if each person was getting less than one cake beforehand (so $a < b$), then the extra cake is more than the extra person fairly deserves, so everyone will end up with more cake. Finally, if the number of cakes is equal to the number of people ($a = b$), then each person gets one cake. Adding one extra person and one extra cake does not change this.

6 a Students' own answers, for example 7, 8, 11.
b, c e.g. 6 ways, these are:
$a = 7, b = 8, c = 11$
$a = 7, b = 11, c = 8$
$a = 8, b = 7, c = 11$
$a = 8, b = 11, c = 7$
$a = 11, b = 7, c = 8$
$a = 11, b = 8, c = 7$
d In the given example, there are three different values, namely 67, 85 and 95.
e The largest is three different values; the smallest is two different values.

7 a Students' own answers, for example 7, 8, 11.
b Up to six different values. Exact answer depends on student's choice of numbers in part **a**.
c The largest is six different values; the smallest is five different values.

8 a The values are 13, 17, 23, 31, 41 which are all prime numbers.
b No, for example when $n = 10$, it is 121 (the first non-prime number in the sequence), or when $n = 11$, it is $143 = 11 \times 13$.
c The values are now 19, 23, 29, 37, 47 which are all prime numbers, but it is not prime when $n = 16$ ($289 = 17 \times 17$) or $n = 17$ ($323 = 17 \times 19$).
d No, because when $n = c$ or $n = c - 1$ the expression is divisible by c, so is not prime. This is true for all $c > 1$. When $c = 1$, choosing $n = 4$ means that $n^2 + n + c = 21 = 3 \times 7$, which is not prime.

Investigation

9 a ×2 then +3; +1.5 then ×2
b Only two pairs are needed.
c A general observation is that the multiplication step is always the same in both machines. Also, if the first machine is ×a then +b, the second machine will be +$\frac{b}{a}$ then ×a.
d ×0 then +5. The second machine cannot be made to give these outputs.
e ×0 then +4. The second machine cannot be made to give these outputs.
f ×0 then +3. The second machine cannot be made to give these outputs.
g If the output is always a, the rule is ×0 then +a. The second machine cannot give this output. The only exception is if the output is always 0, in which case the second machine can be +b then ×0 for any choice of b.

Reflect

10 An expression is just a collection of variables combined together in various ways. It doesn't have an equals sign. You can use it, for example, to give the length of the side of a shape, or the number of sweets that someone has.

A function gives a rule for turning one number into another. You can express it using algebra. For example, you could have a function which tells us to multiply a number by 3 and then add 2, and express this as the rule that x gives $3x + 2$.

A formula gives a rule for connecting one variable with another, and involves an equals sign. For example, you might have a formula for connecting a distance measured in miles with the same distance measured in km.

Symbols have an advantage of taking less effort to write, and also that it is much easier to manipulate symbols (for example multiplying them together, or forming more complicated expressions) than it is to describe the same thing in words.

UNIT 4 Decimals and measures

4.1 Decimals and rounding

1 a 0.72, 0.712, −0.712, −0.724, −0.73, e.g. −0.74
   b 12.92, 12.9, 12.874, −12.874, −12.9, −12.92, e.g. −13
   c 0.291, 0.29, 0.24, 0.203, 0.2, e.g. 0.19
   d 0.491, 0.49, 0.45, 0.43, 0.405, e.g. 0.4

2 a i   0.311, 0.315, 0.352, 0.37, 0.376
      ii 18.4, 18.411, 18.42, 18.429, 18.49
      iii 0.107, 0.13, 0.17, 0.7, 0.73
      iv 0.502, 0.514, 0.52, 0.55, 0.562
   b Students' own answers, for example:
      i   0.32   ii 18.415
      iii 0.15   iv 0.518

3 0.098 cm, 0.1 cm, 0.0955 cm

4 A and E

5 Rounding each, 5 × 12 = 60 so the answer cannot be 85.3.

6 3 ÷ 0.5 = 6

7 Total is 1p more than collected. Either someone donates
   an extra 1p, or one charity needs to receive 1p less
   than the other two.

8 Sally is correct. Keith's 4 coaches will only take 200 students,
   leaving 20 behind.

9 a 18 ÷ 3 = 6 is easier to work out than 17 ÷ 3.
   b i   27 ÷ 3 = 9   ii 36 ÷ 4 = 9
      iii 60 ÷ 12 = 5   iv 75 ÷ 5 = 15

10 Any three from: 20 040.5, 20 040.6, 20 040.7, 20 040.8, 20 040.9,
   20 041.0, 20 041.1, 20 041.2, 20 041.3, 20 041.4

11 Students' own answers, for example: 998.78, 998.8,
   998.81, 998.85, 998.87

12 60 × £8.33 is £499.80. The school will be 20p short. Better to
   charge each student a little more.

Reflect

13 Sometimes you will end up with fewer 'things' than you need if
   you round down. For example, you cannot fit all the people on
   the coach in **Q8** if you round down.

4.2 Length, mass and capacity

1 a 0.047   b 47
   c 0.047   d 4.7

2 a 7000 mm   b 55 000 mm
   c 109 000 mm   d 830 mm

3 a 12 m   b 1.4 m   c 2.75 m   d 0.439 m

4 The washing-up bowl

5 a 1.19 m, 120 cm, 124 cm, 1.31 m
   b 1.09 km, 1100 m, 1.2 km, 1300 m
   c 1155 mm, 1.16 m, 1209 mm, 1.23 m
   d 1105 mm, 111 cm, 1.13 m, 1210 mm, 1.23 m, 128 cm

6 2760 m

7 0.0058 km

8 a Any wing span between 13 cm and 14 cm.
   b Any mass between 20 g and 22 g.

9 176 cm

10 28 cm

11 51 cm

12 2.7 mg

Investigation

13 a A and D, B and C
   b 1000 ÷ 100 ÷ 10; 10 ÷ 1000 × 100; 100 ÷ 1000 × 10
   c i   Yes, she is correct because you multiply by 10 to
          change millimetres to centimetres, then multiply by 100
          to change centimetres to metres.
      ii ÷1000

Reflect

14 The metric system is described as a 'base 10' system because
   all the units are based on powers of 10.

4.3 Scales and measures

1 a 10 cm   b 9.5 cm   c 9.7 cm
2 a 200 ml   b 175 ml   c 180 ml
3 a 250 ml   b 250 ml   c 260 ml

4 a 20 km   b 24 km   c 12 km
5 a £200.50   b 200 500 g
   c 200 500 mm   d 12 030 minutes
6 a
   +----+----+----+----+----+
   0 m   0.02 m 0.04 m 0.06 m 0.08 m 0.1 m
   b
   +----+----+----+----+----+
   0 mm 20 mm 40 mm 60 mm 80 mm 100 mm

7 a For example: 200 ml and 250 ml can be found.
   b For example: 105 ml and 455 ml cannot be found, because
      divisions of 5 ml are too small to be measured with the
      scale on this jug.

8 a 7.5 lb   b 3.4 kg

Reflect

9 Students' own answers, for example: Pounds and pence is
   easiest to interpret when shown on a calculator; hours and
   minutes is hardest to interpret when shown on a calculator.

4.4 Working with decimals mentally

1 a 0.2905   b 290.5   c 29.05
   d Students' own answers, for example:
      0.083 × 35, 0.0083 × 350, 0.000 83 × 3500,
      8.3 × 0.35, 83 × 0.035, 830 × 0.0035
   e 2.905 has been multiplied by 10 too many times.
      It should be 2905.

2 a Estimate 12 × 0.7 = £8.40
   b Calculator says £8.74

3 a 640, 6400, 64 000   b 6.4

4 a 27.72   b 2.772

5 a 8   b 0.8   c 0.08   d 0.008
   e 0.0008   f 25   g 2.5   h 0.25
   i 0.025   j 0.0025

6 0.3 is $\frac{3}{10}$ and 0.03 is $\frac{3}{100}$, so $\frac{3}{10} \times \frac{3}{100} = \frac{9}{1000}$, which is 0.009

7 a 422.62 ÷ 4.52 = 93.5   b 422.62 ÷ 93.5 = 4.52

8 a 17.3   b 173   c 0.173
   d 8.6   e 86   f 0.86

9 3.45 ÷ 2.5, 34.5 ÷ 2.5, 3.45 ÷ 0.025

10 a 2.89   b 0.0289

11 a 12   b 1200   c 600
   d 60   e 30   f 300

12 a 0.24 × 1200 ÷ 6.4 = 45
   b 0.12 × 1200 ÷ 1.6 = 90
   c 12 × 12 ÷ 320 = 0.45
   d 0.012 × 1.2 ÷ 1.6 = 0.009

Reflect

13 Students' own answers, for example:
   Numbers that are the same as in the original calculation.
   The new calculation is a rearrangement of the
   original calculation.
   A number in the new calculation is e.g. 10 times bigger than a
   number in the original calculation.

4.5 Working with decimals

1 a 2.8   b 6.6   c 3.66   d 91.5
2 £9.61
3 a £300   b £296.75
4 a
   +----+----+----+----+----+
   0   5.88   12p

   b
      5 9 1
      6.00
    − 5.88
      0.12

   c Anna's method to find 12p seems easier than Ed's method.
5 12.5 seconds
6 Median is 3.4, range is 3.41 − 3.04 = 0.37

7

0.2	0.13	0.18
0.15	0.17	0.19
0.16	0.21	0.14

8 £23.75

9 2.5×0.4

10 15600 g

11 127.5 g tuna, 82.5 g tomatoes, 0.3 g paprika

12 a i 3.824 **ii** 3.86 **iii** 4.01
  b Part **ii** is easiest because it has just hundredths to keep track of and there is no carrying.
  c Part **i** has thousandths as well, and part **iii** needs carrying.

13 John's method seems quicker.

Reflect

14 Students' own answers. Something like **Q13**, where subtracting £2.99 is easier done mentally.

4.6 Perimeter

1 a 18 cm **b** 2000 cm **c** 28 cm

2 a Any three rectangles that have perimeters of 20.6 cm, for example: 3 cm by 7.3 cm, 6 cm by 4.3 cm, 7.5 cm by 2.8 cm.
  b 5.15 cm

3 a 16.5 m **b** 20.5 m **c** 5.45 m **d** 3.16 m

Investigation

4 11 and 1, 10 and 2, 9 and 3, 8 and 4, 7 and 5, 6 and 6
Consider each integer in turn, until values repeat.

5 a $2a + 2b$ **b** $2a + 4b$ **c** $3a + 3b$ **d** $3a + 2b$

6 a $14 + 4x$ **b** $54 + 4x$ **c** $3x + 21$

7 a 24 **b i** 24 **ii** 24
  c The parts added in match the parts removed.

8 The ds in the formula for the perimeter cancel, so the perimeter is still 40 cm.

9 10 cm

10 a $P = 2l + 2w$ **b** $P = 4l + 2w$
  c $P = 6l + 2w$ **d** $P = 20l + 2w$

Reflect

11 You can substitute in different values for different measures on the shape. You can use the formula to help identify patterns.

4.7 Area

1 a i 34 cm and 60 cm²
    ii 34 cm and 70 cm²
    iii 34 cm and 52 cm²
  b Meera is not correct – parts **i**, **ii** and **iii** had the same perimeter but different areas.

2 a i 22 m and 24 m²
    ii 24.8 m and 24 m²
    iii 28 m and 24 m²
  b Jack is not correct – parts **i**, **ii**, and **iii** had the same area but different perimeters.

3 a 10.8 m **b** 7.3 m² (1 d.p.)
  c 3.6 m² (1 d.p.) **d** 0.1 m² (1 d.p.)

4 Students' own answers, for example:
  a Length = 3.5 cm, width = 1 cm, perimeter = 9 cm; 9 is an odd number.
  b Length = 4 cm, width = 3 cm, area = 12 cm²; length = 8 cm, width = 6 cm, area = 48 cm²; 48 cm² is not double 12 cm².
  c Length = 4 cm, width = 4 cm, perimeter = 16 cm, area = 16 cm²; ignoring the units, perimeter = area.

5 a Students' own answers, showing the perimeter of each shape is 20 m.
  b Design **B**: area is 21 m²

6 a 52 cm²
  b 52 cm²
  c Students' own answers.

7 a 42 cm² **b** 5.32 cm²
  c 1675 cm² **d** 617.01 cm² (2 d.p.)

8 a 15540 mm² **b** 31080 mm²
  c 62370 mm² **d** 124740 mm²
  e 249480 mm²
  f 498960 mm² and 997920 mm²

Investigation

9 a, b Students' own answers **c** 4
  d If the measurements are halved, then the area is divided by 4.

10 17 m²

11 350 cm²

12 Border 36 cm², area inside is 64 cm²

13 Perimeter should be in cm, and area in cm²

Reflect

14 The same: both ways to describe and measure a shape. Different: perimeter measures a length and its unit is in linear units (cm, m, km, etc.); area measures space covered and its unit is in square units.

4.8 More units of measure

1 a 1800 g **b** 3 litres **c** 18 litres

2 Yes. 430 × 1500 kg = 645000 kg = 645 tonnes; 137 × 40 = 5480 tonnes; 645 + 5480 = 6125 tonnes.

3 Yes. Peter's rucksack has a capacity of 66.3 litres.

4 Area is 9600 cm² or 0.96 m², perimeter is 400 cm or 4 m.

5 Area is 1350000 m² or 1.35 km², perimeter is 4800 m or 4.8 km.

Investigation

6 From cm² to m² you need to divide by 100², so divide by 10000 not just 100.

7 a Callum needs to convert them into the same unit.
  b Lucas is wrong; it would be better to convert the single miles units into metres, rather than the four metric units into miles.
  c 600 m, 800 m, 1800 m, 3200 m, 4800 m, so the total is 11200 m.

8 2070 m or 2.07 km

9 Yes. 17 acres = 6.885 hectares; 6.885 × 6000 = 41310; so a sale price of 40000 euros is below the average price.

10 a 2.24 cm² **b** 9.204 m² **c** 2.34 m² **d** 0.68 m²

Reflect

11 Litres are a unit of volume whereas centimetres and feet are both units of length. You can compare two lengths, but you cannot compare a length to a volume.
Litres can be compared to cm³.

Extend

1 32 cm

2 3.1624

3 0.6

4 No; 14 × 24 = 336 cm², 4 × 54 = 216 cm²

5 Jake cycles further. He cycles 15 + 15 = 30 miles, 30 × 1.6 = 48 km; Esther cycles 36 + 10 = 46 km.

6 24 cm

7 140

8 36 cm

9 7632000 m²

10 150 cm²

11 3136.32 m²

12 4.544 litres

13 The tiles are measured in metric units. Wei needs to calculate the area in metric units. 12 feet is very close to 9 tiles (i.e. 3.60 m) but 15 feet is 4.5 m, which needs 11.25 tiles, so Wei will need to think about the 'bits' of tiles he cuts off. He could just buy 108 (so 9 by 12).

Investigation

14 a 64 cm² **b** 625 cm² **c** They are both squares.
  d i 130 cm **ii** 32 cm **e i** 202 cm **ii** 40 cm
  f Rectangles with largest perimeter are 1 cm wide. Rectangles with smallest perimeter are squares.

Reflect

15 Students' own answers.

UNIT 5 Fractions and percentages

5.1 Comparing fractions

1 No, $\frac{5}{8}$ is shaded (the square at bottom left is equivalent to two triangles).

2 a $\frac{1}{2}$

   b Four more triangles so that 12 out of 16 triangles are shaded.

3 $\frac{4}{5}$ is larger as it covers 16 squares whereas $\frac{3}{4}$ only covers 15 squares.

4 No, she isn't correct, because $\frac{1}{15}$ means '1 divided by 15', so it is smaller than $\frac{1}{14}$ (1 divided by 14).

5 Bikram can see three pieces, and two are shaded so he thinks $\frac{2}{3}$. Theo is correct because the two shaded pieces are bigger than the unshaded piece. The unshaded piece will fit four times into the whole, so the fraction ought to be out of 4. The unshaded fraction is then $\frac{1}{4}$ and the shaded part $\frac{3}{4}$.

6 $\frac{1}{154}, \frac{1}{54}, \frac{1}{24}$

7 One more square needs to be coloured in.

8 $1\frac{1}{5}, 1\frac{1}{3}, 1\frac{1}{2}$

9 $\frac{23}{22}$ is closer

10 $\frac{49}{100}$ is closer

11 Any denominator between 40 and 48 is correct.

Investigation

12 Students' own answers.

Reflect

13 Smaller, e.g. $\frac{1}{10} < \frac{1}{8}$.

5.2 Simplifying fractions

1 Choi has simplified the fraction, but $\frac{9}{15}$ can be simplified further to give the simplest form, which is $\frac{3}{5}$.

2 a $\frac{2}{5}$ b $\frac{1}{2}$ c $\frac{4}{7}$ d $\frac{5}{8}$

3 $\frac{40}{120}$, which is $\frac{1}{3}$.

4 $\frac{11}{5}$

5 a $1\frac{2}{11}$ b $1\frac{2}{13}$ c $1\frac{2}{15}$ d $1\frac{2}{17}$

6 $\frac{23}{5}$

7 $\frac{18}{15}$, as all the rest are equivalent to $\frac{4}{5}$.

8 $\frac{12}{15}$ and $\frac{8}{10}$ are the same – so nearest to each other.

9 $\frac{48}{84}$ and $\frac{60}{105}$

10 a $1\frac{1}{6}$ b $1\frac{2}{7}$ c $1\frac{1}{2}$ d $1\frac{1}{6}$

11 $\frac{49}{15}$

12 $\frac{39}{50}$

13 a $\frac{65}{80}$ b $\frac{50}{57}$ c $\frac{243}{256}$

14 a $\frac{1}{6}$ b $\frac{17}{30}$ c $\frac{23}{30}$

Reflect

15 a $\frac{2}{10}$; the denominator is smallest.

   b $\frac{7}{9}, \frac{1}{5}, \frac{7}{12}, \frac{3}{4}$; yes.

5.3 Working with fractions

1 For example: $\frac{1}{9}$ and $\frac{2}{9}$.

2 a $\frac{15}{17}$ b $\frac{15}{37}$ c $\frac{15}{41}$

3 a James $\frac{3}{8}$, John $\frac{3}{8}$, Tim $\frac{1}{4}$

   b $\frac{5}{8}$

4 a $\frac{22}{25}$ b $\frac{9}{25}$ c $\frac{25}{25}$

5 $\frac{3}{11} + \frac{7}{11}$

6 $\frac{6}{80}$ better

7 a $\frac{7}{25}$ b 2

8 a 20   b 27   c 16

9 $\frac{2}{5}$ of 45

10 £10

11 1

12 a $4\frac{1}{4}$ b $3\frac{1}{8}$ c $3\frac{1}{12}$ d $1\frac{5}{18}$

13 21

14 1

15 40 km

16 5.1 km

17 12 miles

18 £36

19 54

20 a Two numbers smaller than 6, 6, two numbers greater than or equal to 6.
   b One number smaller than 6, two 6s, two numbers greater than or equal to 6.
   c Three 6s, two numbers greater than or equal to 6.
   d $\frac{1}{6}, \frac{2}{6}, \frac{3}{6}$

21 $\frac{6}{71}$

Investigation

22 $\frac{19}{95}$ and $\frac{26}{65}$ appear to work. There are probably more.

Reflect

23 a $\frac{1}{5} + \frac{2}{5} = \frac{3}{5}$, so $\frac{3}{5} - \frac{2}{5} = \frac{1}{5}$

   b $\frac{2}{7} + \frac{3}{7} = \frac{5}{7}$, so $\frac{5}{7} - \frac{2}{7} = \frac{3}{7}$

   c $\frac{3}{11} + \frac{6}{11} = \frac{9}{11}$, so $\frac{9}{11} - \frac{3}{11} = \frac{6}{11}$

5.4 Fractions and decimals

1 a $\frac{13}{20}$ b 0.65

2 a $\frac{4}{5}$ b 0.8

3 a $\frac{1}{14}$ b $\frac{5}{7}$

4 a $\frac{2}{3}$ b 24   c 6

5 a 0.06   b 0.06   c 0.07   d 0.09

6 a $\frac{1}{2}$ b $\frac{1}{20}$ c $\frac{1}{200}$

   d $\frac{1}{5}$ e $\frac{12}{100} = \frac{3}{25}$ f $\frac{112}{1000} = \frac{14}{125}$

7 **a** $\frac{151}{100}$ or $1\frac{51}{100}$ **b** $\frac{501}{200}$ or $2\frac{101}{200}$ **c** $\frac{8403}{1000}$ or $8\frac{403}{1000}$

8 **a** 0.085, $\frac{1}{10}$ **b** 0.23, $\frac{6}{25}$

   c $\frac{17}{50}$, 0.39 **d** $\frac{22}{200}$, 0.12

9 0.06

10 $\frac{768}{1000} = \frac{96}{125}$

11 0.28

12 $\frac{7}{24}$

13 $\frac{1}{40\,000}$

14 0.125

15 $\frac{17}{32}$

16 **a** $\frac{2}{5}$ **b** $\frac{2}{50}$ **c** $\frac{2}{500}$

17 0.05 is $\frac{1}{2}$ divided by 10, which is $\frac{1}{20}$.

Reflect

18 Yes. For example: $0.7 = \frac{7}{10}$, $0.23 = \frac{23}{100}$, $0.561 = \frac{561}{1000}$

5.5 Understanding percentages

1 **a** $\frac{39}{50}$ **b** $\frac{21}{100}$ **c** $\frac{1}{100}$

2 620%; 6.2 × 100 = 620

3 **a** 75% and 70%; $\frac{3}{4}$ is larger

   b 45%, 70% and 55%; $\frac{35}{50}$ is largest

   c 85%, 56%, 90% and 80%; $\frac{81}{90}$ is largest

4 **a** 0.2, 20% **b** 0.6, 60% **c** 1.3, 130%
   d 1.08, 108% **e** 1.4, 140% **f** 0.45, 45%

5 **a** 50% **b** 50%

6 **a** $\frac{3}{10}$ **b** 30% **c** 0.4

7 **a** $\frac{9}{20}$ **b** 0.25

Reflect

8 **a** 82%, 88%

   b For example: $\frac{41}{50}, \frac{44}{50}$

   c Comparing out of 50 and out of 25 is fairly easy both
   ways. The equivalent fraction out of 50 seems easier.
   If the mark was out of 45 instead, then the percentage is
   probably easier.

5.6 Percentages of amounts

1 **a** 57.5% of students have a bicycle.
   b 33.75% of people went abroad this year.
   c 94.8% of people watch football on TV.
   d 57.6% of students have a mobile phone.

2 **a** 70% **b** 15%

3 £415.43

4 **a** 12 cm
   b 10%
   c 130%

5 4.2 kg is 105%, 4.5 kg is 112.5%

6 £210

7 £12

8 £15

9 £15

10 2 m

11 **a** $\frac{200}{250} = \frac{4}{5}$ **b** 180%

12 $\frac{66}{50}$ = 132%

13 125%

14 1.6, 160%

15 204%

16 **a** There are 20 days, so 40 possible registers and $\frac{1}{40}$
   is more than 1%.

   b 97.5%.

17 46

18 £1.24

19 13 weeks

20 Brand A

21 **a** 30% **b** 0.1 **c** $\frac{1}{2}$

Reflect

22 The first two make sense. 100% effort means 'doing your best',
and it is impossible to do more than your best.

5 Extend

1 **a** $\frac{7}{48}$ **b** $\frac{9}{77}$

2 120

3 4

4 $\frac{69}{300}$

5 8

6 133.1%

7 0.698% (3 d.p.)

8 $\frac{1}{28}$

9 **a** 44.4% (1 d.p.)

   b **i** $\frac{1}{9}$ **ii** 11.1%

Investigation

10 **a** 0.09090909..., 0.18181818..., 0.27272727...
   b The repeated pairs of digits are the multiples of 9.
   c 0.72727272...
   d 1.18181818...

11 **a** Students' own answers.

   b **i** $\frac{7}{9} \times 360 = 280$ **ii** $\frac{4}{7} \times 280 = 160$

12 **a** £15, £5 **b** £10, £5

   c Taking $\frac{1}{2}$ then $\frac{1}{3}$ is the same as taking $\frac{1}{3}$ then $\frac{1}{2}$

   d $\frac{1}{6}$

   e $\frac{1}{2}$ of $\frac{1}{3}$ is $\frac{1}{6}$

13 **a** 90.9 m **b** 82.6 m

14 60%

Reflect

15 You could make them into equivalent fractions $\frac{145}{696}$ and $\frac{144}{696}$, or
decimals 0.2083 and 0.2069, or even percentages 20.83%
and 20.69%. All these give the same conclusion; that $\frac{5}{24}$ is
slightly larger.

UNIT 6 Probability

6.1 The language of probability

1 **a** Even chance **b** Unlikely
   c Likely **d** Unlikely

2 **a** Unlikely **b** Likely **c** Impossible

3 For example:
   a Roll a 13 **b** Roll an even number
   c Roll a 2 **d** Roll any number from 1 to 12

4 Wednesday

5 For example: impossible = 0; very unlikely = $\frac{1}{6}$; unlikely = $\frac{1}{3} = \frac{2}{6}$; even chance = $\frac{1}{2} = \frac{3}{6}$; likely = $\frac{2}{3} = \frac{4}{6}$; very likely = $\frac{5}{6}$; certain = 1.

6 0% = impossible; 40% = unlikely; 50% = even chance; 90% = very likely; 100% = certain

7 Although the size is different, A and R both take up the same fraction of the spinner so will have the same probability.

8 Blue is twice as likely as green or yellow because there are twice as many blue counters (6) as there are green counters or yellow counters (3 each).

9 **a** Unlikely **b** Certain

Reflect

10 Isla is more precise because she gave an exact value; Lucy's statement of 'likely' means that the probability could be anything between 0.5 and 1.

6.2 Calculating probability

1 **a** (sky, sky), (sky, beach), (beach, beach), (beach, sky)
   b $\frac{1}{4}$

2 Although there are three choices the areas are clearly *not* equal, so the probabilities will not be equal.

3 The possible outcomes may not be equally likely.

4
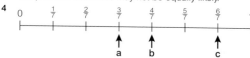

5 **a** 50% **b** 20% **c** 40%

Investigation

6 18 red, 17 white, 10 blue and 5 pink

7 **a** 0.5 **b** 0.4 **c** 0.6 **d** 0.75

8 For example:

9 **a** $\frac{1}{5}$ **b** Increases to $\frac{6}{10}$ **c** 20

10 **a** $\frac{2}{26} = \frac{1}{13}$ **b** $\frac{4}{13}$ **c** $\frac{5}{21}$

11 **a** 6
   b 9
   c Comparing $\frac{3}{6}$ with 25%, more likely to have dark hair if they wear glasses.

12 Golf ball = $\frac{1}{9}$, tennis ball = $\frac{2}{9}$, basketball $\frac{6}{9}$ (or $\frac{2}{3}$)

Reflect

13 Writing decimals or percentages makes sense when the number of objects is a factor of 10 or 100 (e.g. **Q9** is out of 5). Fractions make sense when this is not the case (e.g. **Q10** is choosing from 26 objects).

6.3 More probability calculations

1 0.72

2 **a** $\frac{11}{29}$ **b** $\frac{7}{29}$ **c** $\frac{20}{29}$

3 **a** $\frac{7}{8}$ **b** $\frac{6}{8}$ **c** 1

4 2 As, 3 Bs, 3 Cs

Investigation

5 **a** There are 12 outcomes: 1H 2H 3H 4H 5H 6H and 1T 2T 3T 4T 5T 6T
   b Heads *and* 5 or 6 = $\frac{2}{12} = \frac{1}{6}$

6 **a** $\frac{3}{4}$ **b** $\frac{5}{8}$ **c** $\frac{3}{8}$

7 **a** $\frac{4}{9}$ **b** $\frac{5}{9}$
   c The probability reduces from $\frac{2}{9}$ to $\frac{1}{8}$.

8 **a** 9 **b** $\frac{12}{30} = \frac{2}{5}$ **c** $\frac{3}{10}$

Reflect

9 Add up the probabilities for red and green *or* find the probability of yellow and then subtract from one.

6.4 Experimental probability

1 November weather is not the same as August weather.

2 **a** 0.888
   b No, because you don't know the seasonal variation.

3 **a** 30
   b $\frac{20}{30} = \frac{2}{3}$

4 **a** **i** $\frac{17}{50}$ or 0.34 or 34%
       ii $\frac{23}{50}$ or 0.46 or 46%
   b Some customers may have ordered two pairs of glasses *and* tinted glasses. These would have been counted twice.

5 **a** **i** $\frac{8}{40}$ or $\frac{1}{5}$ or 0.2 or 20%
       ii $\frac{15}{40}$ or $\frac{3}{8}$
       iii $\frac{2}{40}$ or $\frac{1}{20}$ or 0.05 or 5%
       iv $\frac{4}{40}$ or $\frac{1}{10}$ or 0.1 or 10%
       v $\frac{38}{40}$ or $\frac{19}{20}$
   b About 10 times
   c Perhaps not, because more people shop on Saturday than on Monday.
   d No; fewer people will enter the lift because not all customers will visit the top floor.

6 Carrying out more rolls is likely to give more reliable results. We should trust Daisy's results more than Rosie's.

7 A drawing pin is not easy to predict – it isn't symmetrical like a dice or a coin. The two outcomes may not be equally likely – he can test that by his experiment.

8 **a** **i** $\frac{3}{4}$ **ii** $\frac{11}{20}$
   b Because she is likely to improve as she trains.

9 The matches are not just random. Next week's game might be against the best team, and they might have played weaker teams so far. His team are not guaranteed to win.

Reflect

10 You should look at experimental data. You should also remember that even with two choices this does not mean they are equally likely.

6.5 Expected outcomes

1 About 4 290 000

2 The game is likely to lose money. For every 216 players, the game would take £43.20 and pay out £50 in prize money.

3 20 wins expected in 100 games.
   Total value of prizes = 20 × 40p = £8.
   Need to take £10 + total value of prizes = £10 + £8 = £18.
   100 people play, so each go must cost at least
   £18 ÷ 100 = 18p.

4 6

5 $\frac{6}{20} = \frac{3}{10} = 0.3$, which is greater than 0.22, so there is evidence
to suggest that the production process might not be working
properly. However, as 0.3 is fairly close to 0.22, and the sample
is fairly small, it is possible that the machine *is* working properly.

6   50

7   10

8   **a**   20   **b**   10   **c**   30

9   **a**   50

    b   5

    c   Yes – this is a lot fewer than the $300 \times \frac{1}{6} = 50$ times
that are expected.

10 4 out of 10 and 9 out of 20 are not surprising enough and not
different enough from $\frac{1}{2}$. Jenny should not conclude it is biased
based on those results. 20 out of 50 is more surprising and she
could use that as evidence.

11 Neither! He should expect 10 As and 10 Xs.

Reflect

12 No; this is a reasonable difference due to the dice landing
randomly. He is correct to expect 12 out of 24, but actually
obtaining 10 is very close and not a surprise.

6 Extend

1   Red 90°, green 120°, blue 150°

2   **a**   **i** $\frac{7}{20}$ **ii** $\frac{3}{4}$ **iii** $\frac{3}{5}$

    b   The counters with one black and one white side
are counted twice.

3   **a** $\frac{1}{2}$ **b** $\frac{1}{3}$

4   **a**   200   **b**   1   **c**   No

5   **a**   2   **b**   None

6 $\frac{1}{13}$

7   15

8   **a**   5%   **b**   20   **c**   45

9   4

10 $\frac{48}{100}$

11 **a** $\frac{5}{9}$ **b** $\frac{4}{9}$ **c** $\frac{6}{9}$

12 $\frac{1}{6}$

13 $\frac{1}{3}$

14 0.4

15 $\frac{1}{62}$

Investigation

16 Students to look into historical weather for Christmas and
Easter. Answer may depend on how late/early Easter is.

Reflect

17 We would expect 100 for each number. The number 2 looks
suspiciously low, and the 5 looks suspiciously high.

UNIT 7 Ratio and proportion

7.1 Direct proportion

1 £1260

2 Jonathon travels 9 miles on 1 litre, Sandra only travels 8 miles on 1 litre. Jonathon's car is more economical.

3 To make the recipe for 14 people, Sophie needs 700 g of flour, 1225 ml of milk and 7 eggs.
   She does not have enough milk.

4 £1.35

5 Large, as it is the cheapest per packet of crisps.

6 a Offer C
   b Students' own answers, for example '4 for £13.80'.

7 500 seconds

8 a 1200 minutes or 20 hours.
   b 20 people are likely to get in each other's way.

9 a 48   b 160   c 25

10 a Need to be clear that $\frac{1}{2}$ of a $\frac{1}{2}$ is a quarter, so halving and halving again first cuts into two halves, and then cuts a half into two halves, so making quarters. To divide by 8, you need to do one more halving, so halve, halve again and halve a third time.
   b To divide by 16, you need to halve, halve again, halve again, and then halve again (four times).
   c 29

11 a Both are doubled.
   b Both are divided by 3.

12 20

13 Her sister's method is better.

Reflect

14 a Answers will depend on the methods that students have used for each question.
   b Use halving or doubling when the amount is double the other amount.

7.2 Writing ratios

1 9:7

2 a 16:13
   b Team A on average scored more points per match than team B.

3 a 1:4
   b One sheep gives 50:101; one duck gives 50:199

4 a 2:1:2   b 2:1:1   c 1:2:3

5 7:8:5

6 a 1:3:9   b 2:4:11
   c 2:11:13   d 20:27:14

7 4:5:6

8 1:2:3

9 a 12:8:6 (or 6:4:3)
   b Same as part **a**
   c 6:4:4 (or 3:2:2)

10 a 13:7   b 7:1
   c 9:11   d 9:21:24:46

Investigation

11 a 1 and 23, 2 and 22, 3 and 21, 4 and 20
      6 and 18, 8 and 16, 12 and 12
   b 1:23, 1:11, 1:7, 1:5, 1:3, 1:2, 1:1

Reflect

12 Tim 35:14, Janet 35:15 so her paint has slightly more white and will look slightly paler.

7.3 Using ratios

1 £910

2 a 0.15 litres or 150 ml
   b 0.3 litres or 300 ml
   c 0.15 + 0.3 = 0.45

3 1.14 kg (Check: 1.14 + 0.06 = 1.2)

4 a 28 g   b 80 g

5 £500

6 a 2:1   b no

7 a 4:3   b 5:8   c 5:3   d 10:3
   e 4:1   f 1:6   g 315:1   h 1:1

8 a 5:3   b 7:5   c 16:9

9 a 10:5:1   b 0.75 litres

Investigation

10 1:1, 1:2, 1:3, 1:4, 1:5, 1:7, 1:9, 1:11, 1:14, 1:19, 1:23, 1:29, 1:39, 1:59, 1:119

11 3:6:8

12 245 g

13 Coach is 2 staff, 48 students. Each minibus is 1 staff, 14 students. Total 4 staff and 76 students which is 1:19 which is better than 1:20.

14 James has £67.50, Osaka has £30 and Karim has £15.

15 30 pieces, because there is 1.5 times as much butter as for 20 pieces but more than 1.5 times as much sugar and flour.

16 Chaya has 2 parts of the ratio more than Amy. 5 sweets more would mean one part of the ratio is worth 2.5 sweets. This is not possible because Amy can't have 7.5 sweets.

17 101:200

Reflect

18 Looks like the 4 part could increase by half to make 6, but this would turn Amy's part into 4.5 and Chaya's part into 7.5 but these are not whole numbers.

7.4 Ratios, proportions and fractions

1 1:7

2 3:2

3 7:3

4 5:1

5 $\frac{1}{2}$ and $\frac{1}{2}$ would be 1:1. A 1:2 ratio is $\frac{1}{3}$ to $\frac{2}{3}$.

6 a 12:8:5
   b James $\frac{12}{25}$, Jaya $\frac{8}{25}$, Fernando $\frac{1}{5}$

7 Egg, $\frac{1}{8} > \frac{1}{9}$

8 a No. In 2012 just under half (49.2%) of the visitors went to Chester.
   b No. In 2011 about $\frac{1}{6}$ of the visitors went to Whipsnade.

9 a 5:1:4
   b $\frac{2}{5}$

10 $\frac{1}{7}$

11 a 2:3   b 24   c 60

12 a 3:7   b 18   c 60

13 a British Museum 29:28, Tate Modern 489:530, National Gallery 265:271
   b In 2011, 36% of the total visitors to the top three attractions went to the British Museum.
      In 2012, the proportion had reduced to 34%.

14 1:4

15 $\frac{2}{9}$

16 3:2

17 5:8

Reflect

18 A ratio compares a part with a part. A proportion compares a part and a whole.

7.5 Proportions and percentages

1 a 30%   b 40%

2 a 73%   b Stunt 1

3 a Team A 50%, Team B 55%
   b Team B

4 Jennie's lemonade contains 40% lemon, Claire's lemonade contains 45% lemon.
   Claire's lemonade is stronger.

Investigation

5 10%, 15%, 20%, 25%, 30%, 35%, 40% and 45% are all possible.

6 **a** 3:2   **b** 600 ml
    c **i** 3.75 litres   **ii** 150 ml

7 **a** **i** $\frac{3}{5}$ **ii** $\frac{2}{5}$ **iii** $\frac{4}{5}$
    b **i** 60%   **ii** 40%   **iii** 80%
    c **i** 3:2   **ii** 2:3   **iii** 4:1

8 **a** 7:13   **b** 32.5 minutes

9 6:9:5

10 **a** Omar 90% **b** Zane 96% **c** Adele 76% **d** Jaya 99%
    Only Zane and Jaya meet Amber's criteria.

11 **a** 7:10:3   **b** 6

12 **a** Cans 135°, glass 90°, boxes 45°, newspapers 90°
    b 3:2:1:2   **c** 8 boxes
    d They recycled more boxes in August.

Reflect

13 You can use ratio to compare the quantities of two different
categories, such as the ratio of orange juice to apple juice in a
mixed-juice drink. You can use proportion to find the quantity
of one category out of the total, such as the proportion of
matches lost out of the total matches played.

7 Extend

1 5:3

2 **a** 18 C   **b** 18 C   **c** 22 C

3 7:6

Investigation

4 1 × 24 rectangle: 12:25
    2 × 12 rectangle: 3:7
    3 × 8 rectangle: 4:11
    4 × 6 rectangle: 3:10

5 4.8 seconds

6 196 bags

7 70 g oats, 1.175 litres of milk

8 124 chickens

9 **a** 250 g apple, 300 g melon, 450 g pineapple
    b Percentage, as 1 kg = 1000 g and 1000 = 10 × 100,
so multiply the percentages by 10 to get the mass of
each ingredient.

10 802 members

11 **a** 2:1 this year and 13:7 next year
    b 12:13

12 8:105

13 6:1

14 4:3

Reflect

15 E.g. profit as a proportion of total income

UNIT 8 Lines and angles

8.1 Measuring and drawing angles

1 Students' own accurate drawings, for example:

2 Angle f

3 a Chocolate b Book

4 Not necessarily; you could get an acute angle.

5 There are four angles: DEC (122°), DCE (29°), DEA (58°), EDA (61°).

6 a 6°   b 11°   c 17°   d 22°

7 Three appropriate angles, for example:

a   b   c

8 He has read the wrong side of the angle, but 40°, 70° and 30° do not make 180° in total. The middle angle must be correct, so the correct angles are 40°, 110° and 30°.

9 Three

10 One

11 a Either obtuse and acute angle, or two right angles
   b Three acute angles; one right angle and two acute angles; one obtuse angle and two acute angles
   c Four acute angles; one right angle and three acute angles; one obtuse and three acute angles

12 a Possible

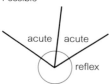

   b Not possible
   c Possible

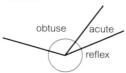

   d Possible

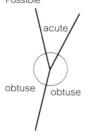

   e Not possible

13 Answers will depend on students' handwriting, for example:
   a EFHLT   b AKXY   c AKXY

14 a S   b S   c N

15 24

16 Acute: ∠DAE, ∠AED, ∠EDA, ∠CDE, ∠ECD, ∠DAC, ∠ACD, ∠BDA, ∠ABD, ∠CDB, ∠DBC
   Right angle: ∠CDA, ∠BCD, ∠DAB
   Obtuse: ∠DEC

Reflect

17 a One obtuse angle is bigger than a right angle, so impossible.
   b Obtuse angles are bigger than 90°, so two of them together give an angle greater than 180°, so impossible.

c Obtuse angles are less than 180°, so two of them together give an angle less than 360°. Another angle is required to make up the 360° around a point.

8.2 Lines, angles and triangles

1 a 10 cm
   b Angles are 90°, 37° and 53°

Investigation

2 a 6.4 cm   b 12.8 m

3 Right-angled isosceles

4 Both are correct; a triangle can have two parts to its name.

5 a For example:

   b No. 90° + 90° = 180°. But the *three* angles in a triangle need to add up to 180°, and none of them can be 0°, so a scalene triangle cannot have two right angles.

6 a For example:

   b For example:

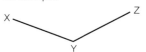

7 a isosceles triangle
   b equilateral triangle
   c isosceles triangle
   d right-angled scalene triangle
   e right-angled isosceles triangle

8 a ABC is 40°   b GHI is 60°

9 a Students' own sketches, for example:

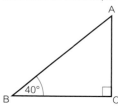

   b Students' own sketches, for example:

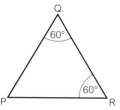

Investigation

10 Three: 20°, 20°,140°; 40°, 40°,100°; 80°, 80°, 20°.

Reflect

11 a Scalene and right-angled; isosceles and right-angled
   b No; a triangle can only be one of scalene, isosceles or equilateral.

8.3 Drawing triangles accurately

1 a 62 mm   b 57 mm   c 85 mm

2 For example:

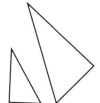

3 For exemple:

4 Regular pentagon drawn with sides of length 5 cm, for example.

5 Height should be about 5.2 cm

6 Two triangles with sides 4 cm, 4 cm, 3 cm and 4 cm, 3 cm, 3 cm

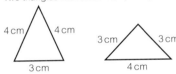

7 Difference between longest and shortest sides is 3 cm.

8 All three sides are the same, and the three angles are the same – the triangles should be reflections of each other (or can imagine turning one over to get the other).

9 Hypotenuse should be about 7.1 cm

10 Students' own drawings, for example:

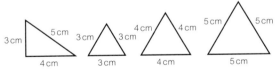

11 Students' own drawings, for example:

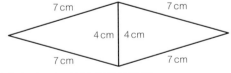

12 Perimeter should be close to 22 cm

13 Perimeter should be close to 26 cm

14

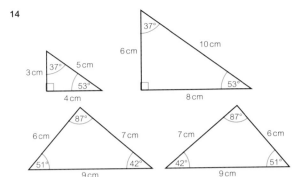

Investigation

15 Isosceles: 1 cm, 1 cm, 10 cm; 2 cm, 2 cm, 8 cm; 3 cm, 3 cm, 6 cm; 2 cm, 5 cm, 5 cm
Equilateral: 4 cm, 4 cm, 4 cm
Scalene: 1 cm, 2 cm, 9 cm; 1 cm, 3 cm, 8 cm; 1 cm, 4 cm, 7 cm; 1 cm, 5 cm, 6 cm; 2 cm, 3 cm, 7 cm; 2 cm, 4 cm, 6 cm
Right-angled: 3 cm, 4 cm, 5 cm

Reflect

16 Liam is correct, but Sam is not. If two triangles have the same lengths of sides, then the angles will be the same in the two triangles.

8.4 Calculating angles

1 The reflex can be from 181° to 268°, the obtuse from 91° to 178°, and the acute the remainder of 360°.

2 30°

3 168°

4 A pie chart drawn showing angles of 36°, 72°, 108° and 144°, for example:

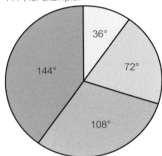

5 $a = 75°$ (angles on a straight line add to 180°);
$b = 60°$ (vertically opposite angles are equal);
$c = 120°$ (angles around a point add to 360° or angles on a straight line add to 180°)

6 $a = 46°$, $b = 116°$, $c = 64°$

7 30°

8 15°

9 132°

10 72°

11 20°

12 a 12°   **b** 2°   **c** 1°
    d 0.1°, but it would be impossible to draw an angle this small. Perhaps 0.5° (720 angles) would be possible.

13 a 30   **b** 120 cm

14 a   **i** Yes   **ii** Yes
      iii No   **iv** No
   b Angles are 30°, 60°, 60°, 60°, 60°, 90°. For example:

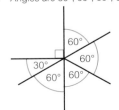

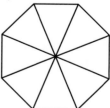

UNIT 9 Sequences and graphs

9.1 Sequences

1 a Infinite **b** Finite **c** Infinite
   d Finite (or infinite if decimal temperatures are considered)
   e Infinite **f** No

2 Students' own answers, for example,
   a 1, 3, 5, 7, 9 (+2); 1, 3, 9, 27, 81 (×3)
   b 1, 5, 9, 13, 17 (+4); 1, 5, 25, 125, 625 (×5)
   c 3, 6, 12, 24, 48 (×2); 3, 6, 9, 12, 15 (+3)
   d 8, 4, 0, −4, −8 (−4); 8, 4, 2, 1, $\frac{1}{2}$ (÷2)

3 a Sequences a, b and c
   b No; the sequence could be ascending or descending depending on the value of the second term, for example 8, 6, 4, ... or 8, 10, 12, ...

4 a 16 **b** seventh square

5 a i £260 ii £220
   b If the deal continued indefinitely, the cost would eventually drop to £0.

6 a $1\frac{2}{3}$, 2, $2\frac{1}{3}$ **b** 1, $\frac{1}{4}$, $-\frac{1}{2}$
   c $\frac{1}{5}$, $\frac{1}{6}$, $\frac{1}{7}$ **d** 9, 13, 15
   e 9, 14, 24 **f** −4, −6, −8
   g 9.5, 9.2, 8.6 **h** 0.8, 1.1, 1.4

7 a d, e, h **b** b, f, g **c** 0

8 11

9 a $\frac{9}{30}$, $\frac{11}{36}$, $\frac{13}{42}$ **b** $\frac{24}{480}$, $\frac{27}{960}$, $\frac{30}{1920}$
   c $\frac{243}{1024}$, $\frac{729}{4096}$, $\frac{2187}{16384}$

10 a 18, 25 **b** 53, 60
    c 35.5, 42.5; term-to-term rule is 'add 3.5'
    d 4, 7.5, 11, 14.5, 18, 21.5, 25, 28.5, 32, 35.5

11 Only first four are positive, so more negative numbers.

Investigation

12 a i 20, 10, 5, 6, 3, 4, 2, 1
       ii 19, 20, ... (follows above)
       iii 18, 9, 10, ... (as in the first one)
    b 33

13 a 103 **b** 127 **c** 122

14 Students' own answers, for example 'First term, 9. Term-to-term rule: double and subtract 2.'

Reflect

15 All go on forever, but some go on forever towards positive infinity; some towards negative infinity; some may tend to a particular number, e.g. zero.

9.2 Pattern sequences

1 a i 4, 8, 12 ii 40
   b i 4, 8, 12 ii 40
   c i 5, 10, 15 ii 50
   d i 6, 12, 18 ii 60
   e i 7, 14, 21 ii 70

2 a i
   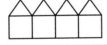

   ii

Term number	1	2	3	4	5
Number of lines	6	11	16	21	26

   iii 1st term = 6, term-to-term rule = +5
   b i

   ii

Term number	1	2	3	4	5	6
Number of dots	1	6	15	28	45	66

   iii 1st term = 1, term-to-term rule = add every other odd number, starting at 5

3 4, 8, 12. 22 won't be in the sequence as they are all a multiple of 4, and 22 isn't.

Investigation

4 13 rabbits

5 Sequence is 6, 12, 18, nearest to 100 is the 17th being 102 (16th is 96 which is further from 100).

6 a 34 **b** 56 **c** 90
   d i 42 blue ii 90 white

7 Students' own answers

Reflect

8 The number of sides in the shape is the first term, and the term-to-term rule is to add the number of sides.
   In an octagon: first term = 8, term-to-term rule = +8.

9.3 Coordinates and midpoints

1 a
   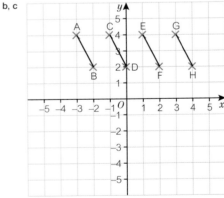

   b Octagon

2 a (8, 4), (10, 5), (12, 6)
   b (0, 9), (−4, 11), (−8, 13)
   c (−1, −6), (−3, −8), (−5, −10)
   d (5, −2), (11, −7), (17, −12)

3 a (**14**, 8), (10, **12**) **b** (0, **3**), (**−3**, 6)
   c (**1**, 3), (**3**, 1)

4 a i (**−3**, 4), (−1, 4), (**1**, **4**), (3, 4)
      ii (−2, 2), (**0**, **2**), (2, 2), (**4**, 2)
   b, c

   d Coordinates of midpoints: (−2.5, 3), (−0.5, 3), (1.5, 3), (3.5, 3). The midpoint is the average of the two x-coordinates and the average of the two y-coordinates.

5 (19, 5)

6 a (2, 8) **b** (8, 4) **c** (4, 7)
   d (5, 1) **e** (−3, −1) **f** (8.5, −4.5)

7 a (−1.5, 1.5) **b** (9, 17)

8 a (5, 5)
   b i (5, 2) ii (7, 5) iii (8, 3.5)
      iv (4, 3.5) v (6, 3.5)

9 Students' own answers. For example:
   a A (2, 4) **b** B (−4, −1) **c** C (1, −4)

d Midpoint AB = (−1, 1.5), midpoint BC = (−1.5, −2.5), midpoint CA = (1.5, 0)

10 −4

11 −5

12 a (9, 8)　　**b** (10, 8)　　**c** (14, 12)　　**d** (14, −4)

13 a Find the mean of the x-coordinates of A and C
($\frac{1}{2}$ of (4+8) = 6) and mean for y-coordinates
($\frac{1}{2}$ of (4+12) = 8), so X is (6, 8).

b The other diagonal in a rectangle will meet in the same place, Y = (6, 8).

14 (−2, 2)

Reflect

15 Take the mean of the x-coordinates and the mean of the y-coordinates to give you the x- and y- coordinates of the midpoint. $\left(\frac{1}{2}(3+5), \frac{1}{2}(8+16)\right) = (4, 12)$

9.4 Extending sequences

1 a 1, 1, 2, 3, 5, 8, 13, 21, 34, 55, 89, 144.
b 10th number is 55 and 5th is 5. 55 ÷ 5 to give 11.
12th number is 144 and 6th is 8. 144 ÷ 8 to give 18.

2 a £460　　**b** £880
c Third year £1720, fourth year £3400. No, this is not an arithmetic sequence, as it does not go up in equal steps.

3 a 15, 12, 9, 6, 3
b −50, −55, −60, −65, −70
c 0.05, 4.05, 8.05, 12.05, 16.05
d 9.5, 9.7, 9.9, 10.1, 10.3
e −12, −11.7, −11.4, −11.1, −10.8
f **i** Arithmetic (increasing)　**ii** Arithmetic (decreasing)

4 a 3000
b Arithmetic sequence, because it goes up in equal steps of 100.

5 a **i** Geometric
ii First term = 5, term-to-term rule = ×5
iii 3125, 15625
b **i** Geometric
ii First term = 128, term-to-term rule = ÷2
iii 8, 4
c **i** Arithmetic
ii First term = 0.5, term-to-term rule = −0.2
iii −0.3, −0.5
d **i** Geometric
ii First term = 0.1, term-to-term rule = ×2
iii 3.2, 6.4
e **i** Geometric
ii First term = 1, term-to-term rule = ÷2
iii $\frac{1}{16}, \frac{1}{32}$

Investigation

6 a 1, 3, 5　　**b** 1, 4, 9
c Square numbers　　**d** Neither

7 a

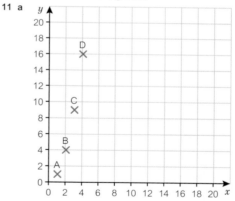

Population growth

b No. Students' own explanations. For example: 'When there are more people, there will be more births.'
c Yes. The new data shows it is not necessarily an arithmetic sequence.

8 a

Side length of a square	1	2	3	4	5
Perimeter of a square	4	8	12	16	20

b

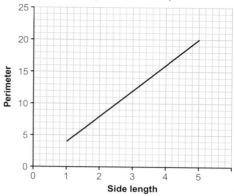

Relationship between side length and perimeter of a square

c Arithmetic

9 a, b

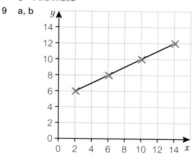

c 2, 4, 6, 8, 10, 12, 14
d Arithmetic sequences

10 Because it forms a straight line.

11 a

b Because they don't form a straight line.
c Without the graph – the points don't have a constant difference in their y-coordinates.

Reflect

12 Students' own answers.

9.5 Straight-line graphs

1 a Points P, R and S　　**b** Points Q and T
2 $y = 1$ and $y = −3$ form the top and bottom, $x = −3$ and $x = 2$ form the left and right sides.
3 A, $y = x$　　B, $y = 4$　　C, $x = −2$
D, $y = −x$　　E, $y = −2$　　F, $x = 4$

4 a

x	0	2	4	6
y	−3	1	5	9

c

x	0	5	10
y	6	1	−4

b, d

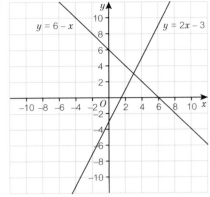

e (3, 3)

5 90°

6 a i $x = 3$ **ii** $y = -2$

  b No. Horizontal lines through the point have to be $y = y$-coordinate of point and vertical lines through the point have to be $x = x$-coordinate of point.

7 a i 96 km **ii** 37.5 miles

  b 400 km

8 a

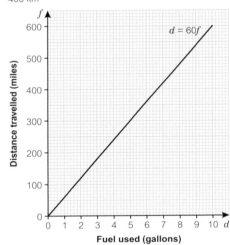

  b i 2.5 gallons **ii** 210 miles

Investigation

9 a i

x	0	1	2	3	4
y	0	1	2	3	4

    ii

x	0	1	2	3	4
y	0	2	4	6	8

    iii

x	0	1	2	3	4
y	0	3	6	9	12

  b i 1 **ii** 2 **iii** 3

  c i When the x-value increases by 1, the y-value increases by 4.

    ii

x	0	1	2	3	4
y	0	4	8	12	16

d i

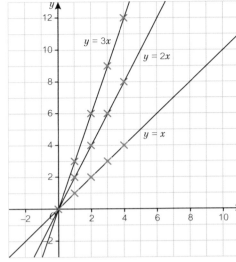

    ii $y = 3x$

  e i Graph A

Reflect

10 Students' own answers, for example:
Linear: $y = 2x - 3$; $y = 6 - x$
Non-linear: $x = -2$

9.6 Position-to-term rules

1 a No. 35 is not a multiple of 10.

  b 6th term **c** 11th term

2 a 5 **b** 10 **c** 23 **d** 200

3 a 7, 10, 13, 16, 19 **b** 7, 9, 11, 13, 15

  c 2, 6, 10, 14, 18 **d** 13, 14, 15, 16, 17

  e 2, 7, 12, 17, 22 **f** 2, 1, 0, −1, −2

  g The common difference is the same as the number before n in the nth term.

4 a

  b Multiply the number of dots in the top section by 2, then subtract 1.

  c $p = 2y - 1$

5 a

Position	1	2	3	4	5	6
Term	5	7	9	11	13	15

  b i 4, 6, 8, 10, 12, 14

    ii −3, −1, 1, 3, 5, 7

    iii 12, 14, 16, 18, 20, 22

  c The common difference is 2 in all of the sequences.

6 Students' own answers, for example,

  a $9n + 15$ **b** $n + \frac{1}{2}$

7 a Infinite **b** The 1st term, −17.5

8 $2n + 3$ is larger for the first 4 terms and smaller from the 5th onwards.

9 Because the first term is larger (8 compared to 5) and $5n$ goes up in 5s and $3n$ goes up in 3s, so the $5n$ starts ahead and always stays ahead.

Investigation

10 a $2n$

  b Term in part **b** is term in part **a** add 1.

  c $2n + 1$

  d Term in part **d** is term in part **a** subtract 2.

  e $2n - 2$

  f i $2n + 3$ **ii** $2n + 10$ **iii** $2n - 5$

Reflect

11 The first term and term-to-term rule, the general term or the position-to-term rule.

Extend

1 **a** **i** 5, 7   **ii** $2n - 1$
       b **i** 9, 27
              ii 1st term = 1, term-to-term rule = ×3

2 **a** 21   **b** 14th

3 10 days whole paper, 9 days $\frac{1}{2}$, 8 days $\frac{1}{4}$, 7 days $\frac{1}{8}$, 6 days $\frac{1}{16}$, 5 days $\frac{1}{32}$

4 **a** 8, 13   **b** 6.75, 10.5, 14.25
       c 6, 9, 12, 15

5 During the 9th day the frog would reach the surface.

6 **a** $\frac{5n-2}{7n-2}$ **b** $\frac{30-3n}{30-2n}$

       c $\frac{2n+6}{5n+5}$ **d** $\frac{4n+11}{11n+9}$

7 **a** 1st   **b** 7th
       c 7th   **d** 4th

8 **a** $6n$ **b** 5 hours   **c** 6 hours

9 **a** $y = 31$ **b** $x = 19$

10 The lines are at right angles – they are clearly horizontal and vertical, and all the same length.

Investigation

11 Students' own answers, e.g.
       a 203 years (less than 1g left)
       b Yes; eventually the final atom will have decayed.

Reflect

12 Students' own answers.

UNIT 10 Transformations

10.1 Congruency and enlargements

1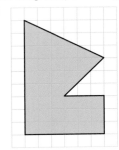

2 a 2   **b** 3   **c** 1.5

d

Square	Perimeter (cm)	Area (cm²)
A	8	4
B	16	16
C	24	36

e

Squares	Ratio of side lengths	Ratio of perimeters	Ratio of areas
A:B	1:2	1:2	1:4
A:C	1:3	1:3	1:9
B:C	2:3	2:3	4:9

  f The ratio of the side lengths and the ratio of the perimeters is the same as the scale factor. The ratio of the areas is the square of the scale factor.

3 a 1:400   **b** 160 m

4 a No, they are both rectangles, but one could be 5 cm × 10 cm and the other 5 cm × 20 cm, for example.

  b No, it might be different sides which are 5 cm long.

  c No, they must now be congruent.

5 Alison is right. Becky has calculated that the width of the rectangle has increased by adding 12, so the height should too.

Investigation

6 a 3

  b 18:12 = 3:2 for both triangles; they are the same.

  c We can multiply or divide both sides of a ratio by the same number without changing the ratio, so the ratio of corresponding sides is always the same.

  d Yes

7 a 2.5   **b** 30

Reflect

8 a Corresponding angles are the same, corresponding lengths are the same. They may be in different positions, or at different orientations (rotated), or one might be a reflection of the other, or some combination of these.

  b Corresponding angles are the same, and the ratio of corresponding side lengths is the same. Corresponding lengths are (usually) different (only the same if the scale factor is 1); they may be in different positions, or at different orientations (rotated), or one might be a reflection of the other, or some combination of these.

10.2 Symmetry

1 a Kite or isosceles trapezium

  b Rhombus or rectangle

  c This is impossible.

  d Square

2 A, C, D

3 a 3   **b** 4   **c** 1

4 a 600 m   **b** 20 000 m²

  c Horizontal line of symmetry:
    i 200 m × 50 m   **ii** 500 m
    iii 10 000 m²
    Vertical line of symmetry:
    i 100 m × 100 m   **ii** 400 m
    iii 10 000 m²

  d One of the dimensions is halved, the other is the same; the perimeters are more than half of the original perimeter; the area is exactly half of the original area.

  e For a square, there are four lines of symmetry; when cutting down a diagonal, the resulting shape is a right-angled triangle with no side half of the original field width or length. But if cutting down the horizontal or vertical line of symmetry, one side length is halved. For all lines of symmetry, the perimeter is more than half of the original perimeter, and the area is exactly half of the original area.

5 The student has confused the meaning of 'line of symmetry' with one of its properties. A line of symmetry is a straight line which divides the shape into two parts, and when one of them is reflected in the line, it gives the other. In the first case, the reflection of the lower half does not give the upper half; in the second case, the line is not straight.

6 a

Shape	Order of rotational symmetry	Number of lines of symmetry
Equilateral triangle	3	3
Square	4	4
Regular pentagon	5	5
Regular hexagon	6	6
Regular octagon	8	8

  b The order of rotational symmetry is the same as the number of lines of symmetry. If a polygon has n sides, then the order of rotational symmetry is n. If n is odd, then there are n lines of symmetry, each of which joins a vertex to the midpoint of the opposite side. If n is even, there are $\frac{n}{2}$ lines of symmetry joining two opposite vertices and $\frac{n}{2}$ lines of symmetry joining midpoints of opposite sides. So in either case, the number of lines of symmetry is the same as the order of rotation.

7 Students' own answers, for example:

  a   **b**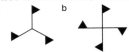

8 Both groups of students could be considered correct.

9 a Yes; for example:

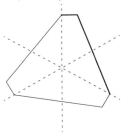

  b Order 2, for example:

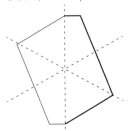

For order 4, there would have to be 4 copies of the part which is rotated, which means that the number of sides would be a multiple of 4. But 6 is not a multiple of 4, so there cannot be a hexagon with rotational symmetry of order 4.

10 **a, b** Yes for all three: here are some examples. The first two have exactly 3 lines of symmetry, the third has exactly 1 line of symmetry, and the last one has exactly 2 lines of symmetry.

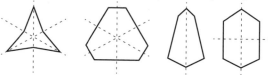

11 **a** The three planes of symmetry are rectangles.

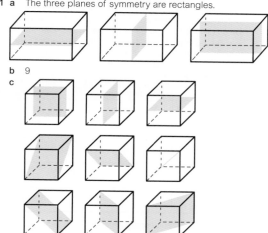

b 9

c

d For the horizontal and vertical planes of symmetry, the faces made are squares; for the diagonal lines of symmetry, the faces made are rectangles.

12 **a** For example, a triangular prism, or a pyramid.
b For example, a hexagonal prism.

13 An octahedron has this property.

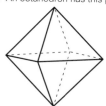

Investigation

14 **a** Any multiple of 3
b Order 4: Any multiple of 4
Order 5: Any multiple of 5
Order 100: Any multiple of 100
c Any multiple of 3
d Order 4: Any multiple of 4
Order 5: Any multiple of 5
Order 100: Any multiple of 100

Reflect

15 **a** A shape which has one line of symmetry does not need to have rotational symmetry (e.g. a kite), but once a shape has more than one line of symmetry passing through a single point, it will have rotational symmetry.
b A shape which has rotational symmetry does not need to have lines of symmetry, as shown in Q8.

10.3 Reflection

1 **a** $y = -1$ **b** $x = 1$ **c** $x = -1$ **d** $x = 0$

2 **a, b**

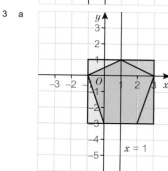

3 **a**

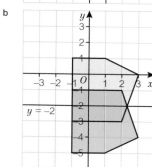

b

c

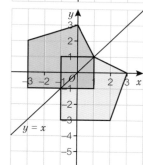

4 Shape B is the reflection of shape A in the line $x = 0.9$
Shape C is the reflection of shape A in the line $x = 0.2$
Shape D is the reflection of shape A in the line $x = -0.3$
Shape E is the reflection of shape A in the line $y = 1.1$
Shape F is the reflection of shape A in the line $y = 0.1$
Shape G is the reflection of shape A in the line $y = -0.5$

5 **a** **i** $(-3, 4), (-4, 1), (0, 3), (-1, 0), (-2, 2)$
ii The y-coordinate stays the same, the x-coordinate is multiplied by -1.
iii The image is $(-a, b)$.
iv Points on the reflection line $x = 0$ (the y-axis)
b **i** $(3, -4), (4, -1), (0, -3), (1, 0), (2, -2)$
ii The x-coordinate stays the same, the y-coordinate is multiplied by -1.
iii The image is $(a, -b)$.
iv Points on the reflection line $y = 0$ (the x-axis)

c The image of (a, b) is $(2 - a, b)$.
d The image of (a, b) is $(a, 4 - b)$.
e **i** The image is $(2c - a, b)$.
   ii Points on the line of reflection
   iii The image is $(a, 2d - b)$.
   iv Points on the line of reflection

6 **a** Square with vertices at $(-2, 1)$, $(-2, 3)$, $(-4, 3)$, $(-4, 1)$.
 b Square with vertices at $(0, 1)$, $(0, 3)$, $(-2, 3)$, $(-2, 1)$, which is 2 to the right of the first reflection.
 c Square 4 to the right of the first reflection, vertices at $(2, 1)$, $(2, 3)$, $(0, 3)$, $(0, 1)$. Moving the image 2 units to the right.
 d The same as the original square. $x = 3$ is a line of symmetry of the square.
 e $c = 2$

7 **a** Reflections in $x = 4$ and $y = 5$
 b 2
 c These are the two lines of symmetry of the rectangle.

8 **a** $(4, 3)$, $(1, 4)$, $(0, 2)$, $(1, 1)$
 b The coordinates are swapped; the image is (b, a).
 c $(-4, -3)$, $(-1, -4)$, $(0, -2)$, $(-1, -1)$. The coordinates are swapped and multiplied by -1; the image is $(-b, -a)$.

9 $x = 3$, $y = 4$, $y = x + 1$, $y = -x + 7$

Investigation
10 a

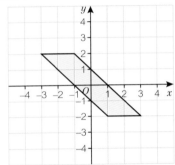

 b $y = 0$
 c, d Any shape which has rotational symmetry of order 2 (or a multiple of 2) about the origin.

Reflect
11 a Vertical and horizontal lines remain vertical and horizontal respectively when reflected in $x = c$ or $y = c$.
 b Vertical lines become horizontal and horizontal lines become vertical when reflected in $y = x$.

10.4 Rotation
1 **a** Rotation of 90° clockwise about $(-4, 2)$
 b Rotation of 180° about $(0.5, 2)$
 c Rotation of 180° about $(-2.5, 1)$

2 **a** Rotation of 90° anticlockwise about $(4, 3)$
 b Rotation of 180° about $(-2, 3)$
 c Rotation of 90° anticlockwise about $(1, 0)$
 d Rotation of 90° anticlockwise about $(-2, 0)$
 e Rotation of 90° clockwise about $(2, -4)$

3 **a** $(0, 1)$, $(-2, 1)$, $(-2, 0)$
 b $(3, 0)$, $(3, 2)$, $(2, 2)$
 c $(1, -2)$, $(1, -4)$, $(2, -4)$
 d 2; 2
 e Rotation does not change the distance from the centre of rotation; think about the tracing paper approach – everything remains the same distance from the fixed point.

4 **a** $(0, -1)$, $(-1.2, -0.5)$, $(0.5, 0.7)$
 b $(1.5, 0.5)$, $(1, -0.7)$, $(-0.2, 1)$
 c $(-0.6, 0.4)$, $(-0.1, 1.6)$, $(1.1, -0.1)$

5 **a** Rotations about the centre of the square $(4, 5)$ by 180°, 90° clockwise, 90° anticlockwise (and rotation by 0°).
 b 4; this is the number of rotations (if we include 0°) or 1 more than the number of rotations (if we don't) which take the square to itself.

Investigation
6 **a**

Centre	Image of (3, 2)	Image of (5, 2)	Image of (5, 3)
i (0, 0)	$(-3, -2)$	$(-5, -2)$	$(-5, -3)$
ii (1, 0)	$(-1, -2)$	$(-3, -2)$	$(-3, -3)$
iii (2, 0)	$(1, -2)$	$(-1, -2)$	$(-1, -3)$
iv (3, 0)	$(3, -2)$	$(1, -2)$	$(1, -3)$
v (0, 1)	$(-3, 0)$	$(-5, 0)$	$(-5, -1)$
vi (0, 2)	$(-3, 2)$	$(-5, 2)$	$(-5, 1)$

 b They are always -2, -2, -3.
 c $(2a - 5, -2)$, $(2a - 5, -3)$
 d They are always -3, -5, -5.
 e $(-5, 2b - 2)$, $(-5, 2b - 3)$
 f Yes
 g **i** $(2a - 3, 0)$, $(2a - 5, 0)$, $(2a - 5, -1)$
   ii $(2a - 3, 2)$, $(2a - 5, 2)$, $(2a - 5, 1)$
   iii $(2a - 3, 4)$, $(2a - 5, 4)$, $(2a - 5, 3)$
   iv $(2a - 3, 2b - 2)$, $(2a - 5, 2b - 2)$, $(2a - 5, 2b - 3)$

Reflect
7 One unit upwards means the image moves two units upwards. One unit to the right means the image moves two units to the right.

10.5 Translations and combined transformations
1 **a** Translation 3 left and 2 up
 b Translation 4 left and 6 up
 c **a:** 5 left + 2 right = 3 left
   3 up + 1 down = 2 up
   b: 3 left + 4 left = 7 left
   4 up − 2 down = 4 up + 2 up = 6 up

2 **a** True
 b False. There is no centre of rotation that takes A onto C.
 c False. There is no line of reflection that takes A onto D.

3 **a** **i**

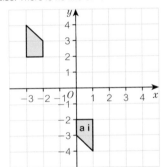

   ii Rotation of 180° about $(-1, 0)$
 b **i**

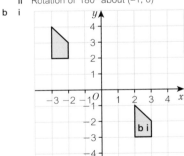

   ii Translation 5 squares left and 5 squares up

Investigation
4 **a**

	A	B	C	D
Kite 1	(1, 2)	(2, 4)	(6, 2)	(2, 0)
Kite 2	(1, −2)	(2, −4)	(6, −2)	(2, 0)
Kite 3	(−1, −2)	(−2, −4)	(−6, −2)	(−2, 0)
Kite 4	(−1, 2)	(−2, 4)	(−6, 2)	(−2, 0)

b Reflection in the y-axis

c Same as rotating by 180° about (0, 0)

5 **a** Rotation of 180° about the point (3, 5).

b Rotation of 180° about the point (a, b).

c Translation 2 right

d Translation 6 right

e Translation $2b$ right

f For example, a reflection in $x = 0$ followed by a reflection in $x = -1$ is the same as a translation 2 left (or −2 right).

g Translation 2 left, which is the opposite of part **c**.

6 **a**

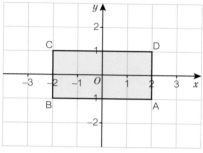

b

c R

d

		Second transformation			
		I	**R**	**X**	**Y**
First transformation	**I**	I	R	X	Y
	R	R	I	Y	X
	X	X	Y	I	R
	Y	Y	X	R	I

e For example: every row and every column contains one of each letter, like a Sudoku puzzle; the diagonal is all "I"; the X's and Y's "stick together" and the I's and R's "stick together"; any pair of the transformations gives one of the same four transformations; the table is symmetrical along both diagonals (it doesn't matter which order you do these transformations).

f Changing the order of transformations will often give a different combined transformation.

Reflect

7 Students' own answers, for example the object and image in these transformations are always congruent shapes.

10 Extend

1 **a** Infinitely many

b $x = a$ and $y = b$ for every integer a and b

c Order 2

d Every point with integer coordinates

2 **a** **i** 60°

ii It must have rotational symmetry of order 3 (and only of order 3).

b As in part **a**, 4 lines of symmetry would mean rotational symmetry of order 4. This would mean that the number of sides of the polygon would have to have a multiple of 4. But a hexagon has 6 sides, so this is impossible.

3 **a** **i** It points from (0, 0) to (−1, 0).

ii It points from (0, 0) to (1, 0).

iii It points from (2, 0) to (3, 0).

iv It points from (4, 0) to (3, 0).

b R then S then R then S

c R then S then R then S then R

d There is no point doing R then R or S then S, because the combined effect is nothing.

R then S then … R then S makes it point from (even number, 0) to (even number + 1, 0).

R then S then … R then S then R makes it point from (minus even number, 0) to (minus (even number + 1), 0).

S then R then … S then R makes it point from (minus even number, 0) to (minus (even number −1), 0).

S then R then … S then R then S makes it point from (even number, 0) to (even number − 1, 0).

(5, 0) to (6, 0) is pointing from (odd number, 0) to (odd number + 1, 0), and none of the combinations of R and S result in this. So it is impossible.

4 **a** $(2a, 2b)$

b **i** $(1, 0) \rightarrow (2a - 1, 2b)$; $(2, 0) \rightarrow (2a - 2, 2b)$; $(3, 0) \rightarrow (2a - 3, 2b)$

ii $(x, 0) \rightarrow (2a - x, 2b)$

c **i** $(0, 1) \rightarrow (2a, 2b - 1)$; $(0, 2) \rightarrow (2a, 2b - 2)$; $(0, 3) \rightarrow (2a, 2b - 3)$

ii $(0, y) \rightarrow (2a, 2b - y)$

d $(2a - x, 2b - y)$

5 Translation 3 left and 2 up

Investigation

6 **a** Students' own answers, for example

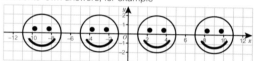

b Students' own answers, for example

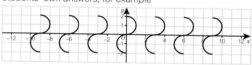

c Students' own answers, for example

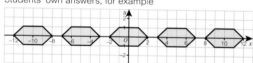

d It has the same lines of symmetry and rotational symmetry of order 2 about the same points.

Reflect

7 Examples include tiled floors or walls, brickwork, curtain patterns, and so on.

Index